PSYCHIC GIFTS
IN THE
CHRISTIAN LIFE

TOOLS TO CONNECT

PSYCHIC GIFTS
IN THE
CHRISTIAN LIFE

TOOLS TO CONNECT

Tiffany Snow D.D.

Spirit Journey Books
San Diego, California

Published by
Spirit Journey Books
P.O. Box 61
San Marcos, CA 92079

www.SpiritJourneyBooks.com

Toll-Free 1(800) 535-5474

For more information regarding Tiffany Snow's workshops, seminars and books, please visit:

www.TiffanySnow.com
or: emailTiffanySnow@aol.com

Edited by
Adrienne Adams

Cover Design by
Tiffany Snow
Sierra Neal
Cat Stevenson

Library of Congress Catalog Number:
2003091910

International Standard Book Number
ISBN 0-9729623-0-1

1. Spirituality. 2. New Age. 3. Religion.

DEDICATION

Abba, Father,
Thank You for holding me
In the palm of Your hand,
So gentle, and loving.
Thank You for Your patience,
Even when I knew no purpose,
You had a mission for me.
Thank You
For letting me be there,
To see wondrous things
When You touch people.
Thank You
For Loving Me.

TIFFANY SNOW has been called a Modern-Day Mystic, along the spiritual paths of Teresa of Avila or Kathryn Kulhman. She is a Gifted Healer, Medical Intuitive, Minister, Public Speaker and Spiritual Communicator. Tiffany Snow simply calls herself, "A Worker for The Big Guy." Quite a difference from her previous life of producing records and writing songs in Nashville, Tennessee!

But, it took some persuasion. So, a lightning strike and incredible near-death-experience gave her a "push." Tiffany says, "The best thing that happened in my life, was almost losing it..."

Now, her "stage" is conducting workshops and motivating others as she offers a buffet of personal tools, techniques, and experiences, including ancient Biblical ones, to help accelerate each person's own spiritual development.

You won't find Tiffany Snow in white billowy dresses, separating and elevating herself above others and belting out a religious agenda – instead, you will find her wearing green or blue nurse "scrubs," while working and moving among people of all faiths, beliefs and non-belief systems, as she helps and inspires through words and demonstrations to all.

Tiffany Snow is a woman on a mission, "led by the Spirit," encouraging others with her stories, and actively sharing The Gifts. She is able to help people "fill their God-Spot" and see "Supernatural Gifts manifest in their own lives as they access the Divine Connection."

She draws people to her like moths to a flame. They come to feel her warmth, be healed by her hands, and bask in the glow of her simple communion with God. All the while, she teaches. She gently reminds people that she is not special or in any way different from them, and all can have the gifts she has. She tells them, "I am a child of God. Just like you! We are the same."

In New Mexico she was welcomed and accepted in a Pueblo Indian reservation to work side-by-side with their local medicine woman; in the hollows of Kentucky she was "adopted" by locals to heal their farms - all inclusive of people, horses, dogs and cats. In the "Bible Belt" of Tennessee, she was quietly brought into hospitals and churches to heal the sick and infirm. In Hawaii, she gave astonishing and validated information on Hawaiian history and archeology, as she also did in Tennessee and New Mexico. She has helped on missing person cases, and with the FBI on 9/11. As an ordained minister, for decades she has "released" ghosts, "bound" entities, and offered Deliverance (Exorcism). Tiffany Snow, D.D., is leading an interesting life!

Tiffany was born in Vista, California. As an only child, she grew up in a motor-home traveling the back roads of the American Dream. She is a "local girl makes good" to many hometowns. Tiffany started writing, playing musical instruments and painting as a child. She went on to produce instrumental and country albums, toured extensively, and received standing-ovations at the Grand 'Ole Opry. Her advice on successful marketing is included in "The Musician's Guide to Making and Selling Your Own CDs" (Jana Stanfield, *Writer's Digest Books*).

In her youth, Tiffany had successfully accessed many of the Supernatural Gifts that were held by the Biblical men and women of old. But, through time and pressure from family, well-meaning friends and misunderstood religious beliefs, Tiffany learned to ignore and deny the gifts. Now, many would agree that she has found them again. Coming full circle, Tiffany now lives back in Southern California with her family and the sea, where she continues to work as a "Hands-On-Healer" at three clinics, and is a CE provider and teacher for the CA-Board of Nursing, a full member of OSL (International Order of St. Luke the Physician), and IANDS (The International Association for Near-Death Studies, Inc.).

"It's all about learning to yield, and loving the Giver, instead of just the gifts; then he will give you both in Unconditional Love. We All Have Gifts!"

CONTENTS

INTRODUCTION

Dr. Tiffany Snow's book is an invitation to take a journey, to embark upon a voyage of self-exploration, leading to a self-discovery that can unleash the special powers of healing with which we are all endowed. By rending the veil that hides our "God-Spot," we can become aware of our role, our vocation in the task of co-creation, of "making all things new."

But as she clearly illustrates in describing her own journey, no self-discovery is risk-free. As you, dear reader, enter what may be for you, uncharted waters, that in the words of the poet Dante "have never been crossed (by you) before," reflect upon the blissful rewards of such an undertaking.

By implementing the strategies outlined by Dr. Snow, exemplified and amplified by her own self-revelation and experience, you too can become a part of a people "set apart." That is to say, you can become a manifestation of the Spirit in the world by becoming an intermediary of the Spirit's supernatural powers. This is achieved through activating the gifts already given us and brought to awareness by our own journey of self-discovery.

While written from a Christian perspective, this book is a guide that can be used by people of all belief and non-belief systems. The emphasis is on the nature of our human nature and the struggle each of us goes through to make effective our particular virtues and strengths in the literal meaning of the word.

Leonardo da Vinci wrote, "Long is the life that is well spent. And just as a day that is well spent gifts us with contented sleep, so does a life productively engaged reward us with contentment at life's end."

Tiffany Snow's book is a guide to just this sort of daily living, a guide pointing the way to activating our virtues, our gifts, and making them well spent. This is a wake-up call to begin the voyage of self-discovery. For this reason it is more than a "How-To" book. It is an invitation, a clarion call, to "why not you?"

Rev. Francis J. Marcolongo
S.T.L., S.S.L., Ph.D., MFT
Escondido, California

AUTHOR'S NOTE

This book is about *Connecting to God.* This book Bridges the Gap between Spirituality and Religion, "New Age" and Christianity; by showing that God has historically used Supernatural Intervention to connect with Him, and continues to today. This a self-help book, because its message is that *we ourselves* can choose to yield to the "God-Spot" and *see Divine Power manifest daily in our lives.*

Do you have good intuition about people? Do you wish you had listened to your "gut-instinct" about that investment deal? Do you want to make it "louder" and easier to hear? *You can!* That tiny voice inside is *just one line of connection* to God. If you truly want your life choices placed on a stronger footing, and a sense of certainty and confidence in *everything* you do, you need to develop more Tools to Connect.

From a sumptuous buffet laid before you, you will be able to choose from many tools to learn *how to use and develop these gifts* to hear, see, and sense the Source of Unconditional Love. Games will help sharpen your ability to yield, becoming more intuitive and sensitive. This book will help develop your Natural-Born Gifts and show you how to ask for the Supernatural Gifts as well, on physical, emotional, and spiritual levels.

Through the intervention of the Spirit, we humans can change the world with a message that never changes at all – the awareness that God loves them, and that we should love each other. By truly understanding this and letting him work through us and have full reign in our lives, we gain a sensitivity and peace that we have never experienced before. *And we will see miracles unfold before our very eyes.*

For you, everyday can be an adventure! We all have natural gifts of many kinds. Some of us have gifts of the Spirit too. Yes, you are not alone! It is time to "put the light on the lamp-stand…and let your light shine before men, that they may see your good deeds and praise your Father in heaven." (Mt. 5:15,16) Whenever we find the Holy Spirit in evidence, *we find the Divine Supernatural*, the manifestation of *God's unlimited power!*

As you read the story about "John," please use your intuition and read between the lines for the real meanings behind the "characters" and "the gifts." Here's a hint: "the pages of the letters" is the Bible. The answers you will find at the end of the story.

I

Young John shuffled his feet under the table and fingered the pages of the letters again. His dad has been out of town for so long now; and all he has are these pieces of paper. The letters reminded him of the good times they had shared together, and also told him how to behave until he got back. They also talked about how he should help take care of his brothers and sisters. John sure did miss his dad. The boy looked around his desk. He didn't even have a picture of him. "There is no camera here that would do me justice!" his father would tease. "Just look in the mirror, you are the spitting image of me anyway; why do you need a picture?" John smiled. How he wished to be able to feel his father was really there in his life.

Once a week, on Sunday, he would go visit Aunt Martha who would encourage John to bring his letters with him. She would gently put them in order and read some parts of them out loud, following each line carefully with her finger, and commenting on each one. "Your daddy loves you, don't forget that. He doesn't like being away from you right now, Johnny, but it just can't be helped. But, everything will be alright, I'll take care of you. Just listen to me and things will work out fine."

One day, John heard a distinct knock on the front door, and was surprised to find a large cardboard box on the step, with no one around. It was addressed to him - and it was from his dad! He excitedly unwrapped it and started pulling out such colorful and wonderful gifts – a cell phone; a pair of binoculars; a magnifying glass and even a special headset that magnified sound! And look at this! Dad had even thrown in his own knitted sweater – his very favorite! John buried his face in it and breathed in the familiar aroma. It was like dad was really there in the room! It was exactly what he had been hoping for all this time! He hurried and put the sweater on, gathered up all the gifts, and rushed over to Aunt Martha's house, bursting with joy from ear to ear as he leapt up the steps.

"Johnny..." Aunt Martha frowned, meeting him at the door, "What do you have there?" John started showing her all the gifts, excitedly picking up each one, telling her what it was good for, and quickly assuring her he would share with his brothers and sisters too. "Look at this one, a cell phone!" John exclaimed. "Now dad and I can even talk to each other! Can you believe it! He loves me so much! It will be just like he's here!"

"No!" Aunt Martha tightened up her lips and sternly stared at John. "NO! You don't know if any of these things are really from your father – and a cell phone! Why, it could be some stranger at the other end of the line, telling you to do some terrible thing or wanting to hurt you! And you are so gullible, Johnny, you wouldn't even know it! These things are not gifts! They're evil! These things will harm you - and they will harm your brothers and sisters too. You don't want to be responsible for that, now do you?" she stammered on.

II

"Johnny, I will not allow them in my house. You take these so-called 'gifts' of yours and leave here right now! You throw them away, and never speak of them again. These letters we have from your father are enough! I mean it Johnny, you are not welcome here anymore until you get rid of them!

"But Aunt Martha," John begged, "I just <u>know</u> these things are from my dad…!"

"Believe me, Johnny," Aunt Martha interrupted. "I know better; I am much older and better educated than you – your father would not send you such things. I know you are young and naive so I will overlook your ignorance this time, but do not let it happen again, ok? Umm, Johnny, you will be coming back, won't you? Remember, you still need me to read over the letters for you, so I can explain them and you can understand them correctly; and also, I have many chores that need to be done around here."

John left his Aunt's house rubbing the tears from his eyes, and feeling confused and angry. "Why was Aunt Martha so upset about me getting such wonderful gifts? Doesn't she want only the best for me, why can't she just be happy for me? I know they are from my father, they have to be, and I'd know the smell of my own dad anywhere! Well, I think I would…" So John began to doubt, and he took off the sweater and placed it gently back in the box, giving it one last sniff. "These have to be from dad, something inside me just knows." He threw himself onto the bed to cry.

"Wait a minute!" John sat up. "In the letters, didn't dad talk about using some of these things with other people he has stayed in contact with? Yes! I remember he did! Why didn't Aunt Martha remember that too? As she says, she knows dad's letters better than anyone!"

All of a sudden, the cell phone rang from inside the big cardboard box. "Oh no!" John whispered. "But what if Aunt Martha is right? What if it <u>is</u> a stranger on the other end? What I don't really understand what the letters mean?" The phone continued ringing. "But, wouldn't I know my own father's voice? And even if it was a bad connection, I would know by the words that he said that it was really he. Besides, I wouldn't do something wrong just because someone told me to. I am <u>not</u> gullible and naive!" John reached down to answer the phone. His hand stopped just shy of picking up the receiver.

It rang two more times. "I'll have to be quiet around Aunt Martha about all this," John thought to himself. "But maybe if I throw one or two things away, then I wouldn't really be lying when she asks me about it. And of course, I won't be able to tell anyone about it, not even my brothers and sisters." The phone continued ringing.

John reached out his hand. He hesitated for a moment, cleared his throat, and put it to his ear. "Hello?" he softly said.

"Hello John, this is Dad!" The warm, familiar voice made John's heart jump – it had been so long, but he knew that voice anywhere! It <u>was</u> his father!

His father began: "I've been trying to get through to you for so long, son...I was afraid you didn't get the package; or that you didn't like the gifts. I'm so glad you answered the phone! I have been saving these special things for just the right time in your life; I know you so well, I was able to pick out just the right ones for you. Now we will be able to stay in touch a lot better! With these presents, and a little practice in using them, you will be able to reach me whenever you want to! Call me anytime, I would love hearing from you! You can relay messages for your brothers and sisters also! So, son, stay out of trouble and call me whenever you have a question, whenever you need help, or when you just want to say Hi! I love you!"

John called his father every day after that – on some days even two or three times! John also found just the right area to be in to get the best reception. He also read all the manuals and learned how to use with skill the binoculars and magnifying glass and the headset. He also found others who owned these same items, and who shared their experiences with him. They also helped him to use his gifts with even clearer reception and ability. And, John would put on his father's sweater every time he used the gifts, because it gave him a feeling of being surrounded by his father's unsurpassed and never-ending love.

It was a wonderful time! But, it was also a secret from Aunt Martha. Too bad, John is sure she would have enjoyed talking with dad more too. And John was determined to share with his brothers and sisters this wonderful connection with their dad. Until they learned how to use the gifts themselves, John would go ahead and be the "middle man" for them. Now, he thought, who is the ignorant one? Everyday he can connect with his dad and they have become so much closer! And John smiled and closed his eyes, so thankful he had opened the box, and learned how to use the gifts...

***

How did you do? Did you see that Almighty God was John's father? Did you understand that Aunt Martha's negativity typified some misinformed but often well-meaning religious systems? Had you guessed what the uses for the "gifts" were before the end of the story? The cell phone is our gift of *prayer, intuition,* and *knowing* (clear sensing - clairsentience). The binoculars and magnifying glass are our gifts of *prophecy* and *clear seeing* (clairvoyance). The headset is *clear hearing* (clairaudience). And the father's sweater is our God-given *conscious,* to know right from wrong and ability to test things out.

IV

What about the admonition to use our gifts to help our brothers and sisters? God is the type of Father who wants his kids to get along, and to share the good things he gives them. That is one of the main reason he gives gifts, so we can help each other. But the main reason is to strengthen our connection with him.

Think of this book as the instruction manual that came with John's gifts. You are about to learn many new things. You are on the threshold to an enhanced life – a leap toward God-and-Self-Awareness and Validity, on an expanding spiritual plane unique to His Will, your will, and the *choices* you make regarding each one!

From a sumptuous buffet laid before you, you will be able to see many gifts, and how they work before you decide to ask Dad to put them on your Christmas wish list. As parents ourselves, if we ask our kids what they want for Christmas, we don't want to see a fake smile and hear, "anything you want to get me, Mom." We want them to be specific and reply with enthusiasm, "I would really like the 'Hot Player' game system, Mom! I think its cool!" It lets our children have fulfilled expectations, and pure joy at receiving the gifts from our place of love for them. It allows their free-will to make the choices. And God is big on the issue of Free Will!

From numerous personal accounts, I will be sharing several stories of *how to use and develop* these gifts in real life, and some strange-but-true occurrences that can happen while doing this that will "knock your socks off!"

One final thought - I believe everything happens for a reason. Perhaps you sought out and picked up this book intentionally, or perhaps you felt it was simply by chance. I don't believe in chance, or in mere coincidence. I believe you picked up this book because you have gotten to the point in your life where you are ready to continue onward in your Spirit Journey. You are earnestly seeking a higher understanding, a better connection with the Utmost Supernatural Being, and with each other. "Divine Coincidence" has stepped in: *Supernatural Intervention.*

Life is a continuing education process. There is an old saying that goes, "When the student is ready, the teacher will come." God is our Greatest Teacher! It doesn't matter that he is invisible. There are so many ways to "see" him at work in your life. *Make the connection! Stay in contact!* The cardboard box is on the front step. He is ringing the phone…ringing…ringing….why don't you answer his call?

May the Lord guide you in your quest to become closer to him! *Love Each Other!*

Many Blessings,
A Fellow Worker - Tiffany Snow

VI

CHAPTER 1

Are We "Sinning" by Ignoring the Gifts?
The Holy Spirit – Supernatural Power of God

Empty. Alone. Feeling like we don't belong. Feeling like we don't fit in anywhere, ever. Searching every face we see for familiarity, for answers, for love. Finding only confusion, depression and humiliation; we avert our eyes from faces, and start looking down at our own feet. Soon we close our eyes, and refuse to look at anyone, anymore, for evermore. Walled off inside the corners of our own heart, we sit down in emotional and spiritual darkness. Scared. Angry. Depressed. *We are the fatherless child.*

But wait. *Who is that...?* Who is that stranger who smiled at us as he walked by? Just for an instant our heart fluttered. Familiarity...familiar...*family!*

Smiled at! Accepted! Approved! The possibilities! Communication! Having a friend! Being laughed with and hugged! *Loved!!!*

Love is the magic password that we use to open the door to God. And when we open that door and are welcomed through, it is often *two by two.* Love your neighbor and totally accept his or her spot on life's road map. Sharing love with another is what makes the puzzle 'click.' It is when we surrender ourselves 100% that we experience joy, peace and contentment. We are all God's children! Welcome. Welcome to Love! *Your Father has been waiting for you!*

"For I know the plans I have for you, says the Lord. They are plans for good and not for evil, to give you a future and a hope." (Jer. 29:11)

From Fatherless Child to Millionaire Kid

So many of us are blessed with Divine Gifts! *You are not alone!* Yet, most of the time we keep quiet about them, largely because we have been taught by our religious upbringing or social system that they are "bad." So, we are taught from an early age to hide, ignore or destroy our gifts. We learn to fear even discussing such matters; and we are sometimes taught to even *hate* that part of ourselves which connects with the gift!

But, let's take this into consideration: if God is perfect in all his works, doesn't he know what he is doing by *giving humans* gifts to begin with? Doesn't he do *all* things with a higher purpose in view? "For you created my inmost being; you knit me together in my mother's womb. I praise you because I am fearfully and wonderfully made; your works are wonderful, I know that full well." (Ps. 139:13-

14) So, perhaps *God knew what he was doing when he gave you the gift! He has big plans for you!*

Christians Are Blessed With Gifts!

The Holy Spirit's work demonstrated that *Christianity is Supernatural.* It identified a people that worked with the blessing of the Divine. Jesus promised his followers that the Holy Spirit would never leave them, that it would be poured out upon his people, and would be sent in his name. (Jo. 14:26) "But you will receive power when the Holy Spirit comes on you…" (Acts 1:7)

"There are different kinds of gifts, *but the same Spirit.* There are different kinds of service, but the same Lord. There are different kinds of working, but the same God works all of them in all men. Now to each one the manifestation of the Spirit is given for the common good. To each one there is given through the Spirit the message of wisdom, to another the message of knowledge by means of the same Spirit, to another faith by the same Spirit, to another gifts of healing by that one Spirit, to another miraculous powers, to another prophecy, to another distinguishing between spirits, to another speaking in tongues. *All these are the work of one and the same Spirit, and he gives them to each one, just as he determines."* (1 Co. 12:4-11)

Gifts come in a variety of packages; and *they do not have to be considered Supernatural or Divine to be very worthy gifts.* We all have gifts that we are responsible for - to bring praise to our Father, and to share with our brothers and sisters. If you are a painter, that is a gift - are you giving some of your artwork to adorn the homes of others who have none? If you have good health, that is a gift - are you using it to vacuum, clean restrooms, or mow yards for those who can't do it on their own? If you bake, do you bake for others or teach them how? If you have advanced or specialized education, do you share your learning skills? If you read, there are many libraries, children's groups and elderly who would greatly appreciate your efforts. *If you still have breath in your lungs*, you can be an encouragement for those who seem to be breathless in their struggles with daily life. *All these things are Gifts from God!*

"Each one should use whatever gift he has received to serve others, faithfully administering God's grace in its various forms." (1 Pe. 4:10)

As you can see by now, each of us has a responsibility toward each other, each with our own unique gifts. Also, for those who have been given *specialized or supernatural gifts* by the grace of God, are you using them to their full potential? *The Lord asks more from those who have been given more.* The responsibilities increase with the richness of the blessings. Let God richly increase your blessings with abundance and fruitfulness. The efforts you show in sharing your gifts will multiply and come back to you, like "bread upon the waters." Enjoy the giving – that's one of the joys of having gifts!

If you have *supernatural gifts*, do you keep them hidden away, and only let them out when no one is around? Are you afraid to show the specialness that is in you? Are you hesitant to step forward to share? Where there is love, *it throws fear outside.* God loves you! It's time for you to show by your actions that you love God! *It is time to become the true potential that you already are.* Gifts are given to you for the purpose of giving to others. Share the love, feel the ripple effect in your life! It will come back to you as a *multitude* of blessings as you glorify our Father.

God is less prejudiced than most people are. He made the plants of the earth a full variety. Some have lacy, feathery green leaves; some have dark, leathery ones. Which one is more correct? Which one is closer to God's design? Look at the animals; is the horse more loved by God than the whale? He made them all. He made human beings in his likeness. Some have dark hair, yet others have light; some have light skin, yet others have dark. Which one does he prefer? God prefers the differences, that's what! "I praise you because I am fearfully and wonderfully made; your works are wonderful, I know that full well." (Ps.139:14)

If the Almighty wanted you to be somebody else, he would have made you somebody else. He made you to be *you.* And, if the Almighty wanted you to have a specialized gift that brings you closer to him and can help other people, *accept the gift graciously.*

In our need to feel like we belong, many people try to copy other people's styles, decisions or religious customs. But, there are so many different roads – who knows where they all lead? Start by looking at the destination - then trace his route *back* to you. This is the straightest road, and the surest route. You have already circled the destination spot on the map – *God.* Now, see the spot where you are, and *select the tool that best connects the two* with a straight line. The shortest distance between the two is the best route. This book will encourage your Free Will to do just that. This book will also encourage you to not desire anyone else's gift; you need not copy anyone.

Just like relationships in our daily life, love and friendship succeeds only with taking the time to develop good communication. Most people who talk to God have only a monologue, a simple one-way discussion. They do not listen when it's God's turn to speak! Or, perhaps it is only that they *do not know how.* This book will help you to listen, see and feel the very Spirit of God! This will help you develop *Great Love between You and Him!*

"He who belongs to God hears what God says…" (Jo. 8:47)

Science and "Signs and Wonders"

Einstein once stated, *"All matter is slowed down energy."* If God is Pure Spirit at its highest form, can't he manipulate matter? Isn't that exactly what he did when he used his Spirit to form the earth out of the void? "In the beginning God created the heavens and the earth…and the Spirit of God was hovering over the waters." (Ge. 1:1, 2) "When you send your Spirit, they are created, and you renew the face of the earth." (Ps. 104:30)

What happens if you take a magnifying glass outside and hold it above a piece of paper? The natural energy is concentrated to a spot that burst into flames. This is an example of *directed energy.* Isn't that what happens today when he directs his attention to answering prayers? Doesn't it make sense that the Holy Spirit often functions as the *Directed Energy of God?*

"For he is the living God and he endures forever; his kingdom will not be destroyed, his dominion will never end. He rescues and he saves; he performs *signs and wonders* in the heavens and on the earth." (Da. 6:26,27)

Many of the needs and yearnings of our heart need *physical manipulation of matter* to make things work out. This might come in the form of miraculous healings of the body; financial needs being met; new people being brought into our lives or beneficial situations opening up right before our eyes. These are only *some* examples of manifestations of Supernatural Gifts and Prayer. If it brings you or someone else closer to God and is the highest good for all concerned, it will be done - even though you might be surprised by how or when!

Modern science has shown that *everything in the universe is composed of energy,* and that the apparent difference between gases, liquids, solids, sound and light is merely the *frequency in their vibrational levels.* We live in a cosmic soup of vibrating energy! Everything that *surrounds* us, is *IN* us, and *IS* us, is *FROM* our direct link to The Original Source, the One, our Almighty Father. We are made in the image of God. (Ge. 1:26) "The Spirit of God has made me; the breath of the Almighty gives me life." (Job 33:4)

Similarly, most of the world's religions state in their belief system that all things created originate in the vibrational energy of the AUM, *or "Amen;"* the Word. "In the beginning was the Word, and the Word was with God, and the Word was God. He was with God in the beginning. Through him all things were made; without him nothing was made that has been made." (John 1:1,3)

So, we see that we are *all* made out of the *same thing* - vibrating energy particles - by the *same Spirit*. And yet people remain so prejudiced against each other. Why is it that most of the world's bloodshed, upheavals and wars throughout all periods of time, and in all parts of the earth, are fought about religious differences in the name of God? Is this the concept of "God is Love?" (1 John 4:8) No! True love respects the differences in other people. *True Love also freely shares the good things we have found with others.*

Salvation by grace is a *good thing.* Listening with greater sensitivity to God is a *good thing.* God is Love, he created all things – and we are all made in his likeness, as his children, all of us brothers and sisters with One Father. He has the ability to share with us openly, through the "God-Spot" radio that he has built into us. His is a "vibration frequency" that we are surrounded with. Think of accepting the Holy Spirit as being given the coordinates on a radio dial – coming from chaos and static to pure stereo tone!

As we acknowledge our place in God's will and *yield* to his purpose for us, we will find ourselves playing in his mighty symphony orchestra surrounded by many other top-notch musicians. We are there by grace – *not* because we are the best instrument there is, but because we have the *heart to be open to learning.* He has even set aside a personal instructor (Holy Spirit) for us, and expects us to do our homework! We also have to learn how to read the music and know it thoroughly (God's Word), and be finely attuned to the Conductor's leading (Jesus Christ). Are we ready to bring the song of praise to his ears?

The Glowing Face of Moses

Once a person comes in contact with God, he is a changed person. The things that used to be important go through a major shifting; and we find relationships and experiences, and not things, are the number one priority in our life. Often, people will look at us and ask, "Have you lost weight?" or, "Did you change your hair color?" They sense *something is different* about us, but they just can't put their finger on it. We now have a "radiance" and "inner shine." When Moses came before the presence of God, everyone could tell. Something was different about him. His face glowed! In fact, he started wearing a veil over his face because the people were afraid to come near him. When he went back before the Lord, he would let down the veil. (Ex. 34:29-35)

Empirical Evidence and Traditional Knowledge

The evangelist Tommy Tenney wrote in his book *The God Chasers*: "The Bible is where God has been, revelation is where he is now." The Almighty didn't just get up and quit after the Bible was written, deciding never to contact humans again. The scriptures say, "God is unchangeable." So, what is he up to today? Talk to ten average people, and see how many have had "Something" out-of-the-ordinary occur to them that they consider unusual, supernatural, or Divine. It might take some conversational digging for them to open up, since often they feel alone in their experiences and have hidden it deep in the fertile soil of the God-Spot, where it waits as a precious seed, full of possibilities.

Often we find ourselves never watering this seed or giving it the slightest hint of sunshine because we fall into the trap of measuring our personal *empirical* (first-person) experiences up to the *traditional* (second-person) ones. Yet, if ours aren't on the board, we may doubt the validity of the tradition, but never our own experience. *We are just afraid of being thought different or odd, or stupid, if we don't embrace all of the tradition.* So, we keep quiet, and try to forget or hide away the most wonderful one-to-one Divine Supernatural moment we have ever had. But, time after time, the person who has a 20 second experience with God will keep his belief that GOD IS, better than a scholar who has spent several years studying someone else's experiences!

Lets take an example. If you had the radio on late one night and suddenly a voice was using your name and talking personally to you through the airwaves by warning or encouraging you, what would you do? You would definitely remember it – but you may not ever tell anyone about it because, what would people think? You may be thinking, "that is not how God contacts people. I've never heard anyone talk of this method before. I'd better not say anything, they'll think I'm crazy." Or, they are afraid of what "Aunt Martha" will say. Or, they may feel they can't trust their ability to interpret the message – or that they will not "recognize Father's voice on the other end of the phone." Fear is what shuts out love. Yet, stranger things than voices on the radio have happened, as documented in the Bible. For example, what if it were actually an animal that started speaking to you? That has happened as a God-Connection too! (2 Pe. 2:15,16)

"There is no fear in love. But perfect love throws all fear outside, because fear has to do with punishment. The one who fears is not made perfect in love." (1 Jo. 4:18)

Why wouldn't the Creator of electricity and sound waves use our crude inventions to help him communicate with us in a way with which we are familiar? Why not? But, for us to ever admit to anyone that something Untraditional has happened in our lives can be akin to committing a form of social suicide! *Especially* in a church or place of worship! But, once *you* have empirical evidence, nothing will shake you now from knowing that Something exists beyond yourself. Because, you experienced it yourself, and no matter what anyone else says, it cannot be taken away from you. Often there is nothing to compare it to that would let your *brain acknowledge what your mind and spirit already knows and believes.*

There are many ways people have personal experiences, sometimes in a dream or vision, and sometimes by seeing angels. These methods are easier to talk about, because they are fairly common to acknowledge in these days. And, they are traditional experiences from ancient times, just brought up to date. But, depending on the religious tradition you are reading about, practicing or taught to believe, you may choose not to share those experiences either, as some religions say: "God taught us all we needed to know in times of old and nothing else needs to be said." What does your gut-instinct tell you about that? Is your answer based on an outer religious idea or an internal spiritual one?

The Difference Between Spiritual and Religious

The fact is this; there is often a big difference between being religious and being spiritual. *And, there is often a big difference in being religious and being Christian!* Religion is literally man's method, tradition or custom of worship. In the beginning, as you may remember in the Garden of Eden, there was no formal way of talking to God. You opened your mouth to speak, and *he spoke back directly – face to face!* (Ge. 3:8-10) Unfortunately, we are not in that favored position anymore. But, that *was* his original intended purpose. How wonderful to know that *we were created to share a conversation* with our Creator!

Although he is now unseen by human eyes, *he desires* that close connection even today, and through the sacrifice of his only-begotten son, we can come before him once again in a favored position, by grace. It makes no difference that we cannot see him with our visible eyes. We cannot see gravity either, or the wind, or x-rays or radio waves! But, we can see the undeniable proof that these things exist! Why should we allow various customs of man to cloud our communication with Our Maker? And if the ritual or custom in your church does not bring you closer to God, but makes you feel more apart and distant, why do you practice it?

There are many, many religions. Most of them are intolerant of each other. *Who are we to say which ones God approves of or not?* Only God can do that. We live according to what we know. Are you regularly increasing your spiritual knowledge? Perhaps you know more than another about how God wants to be worshipped. Perhaps you know less! Let the Lord guide each one on his spirit journey; the accurate information will be presented in time, and each person *will make his own choices with what he has learned and chooses to ignore or apply in his life.* But, if we are trying to say, 'I Love God,' how can we say 'I hate my brother for worshipping God differently than I do'? It misses the entire point of being a Godly person!

Some people are fond of saying all paths lead to God. But think of this – *we don't need to follow a path if we clearly see the destination from where we stand!* We keep our eyes fixed on the prize, and just keep walking. We *will* be on a path, but it will only be a means to get to our destination. We may not even take some of the turns that it does; we will have our eyes fixed on the Pathfinder and have faith that God will guide our feet successfully and true toward him.

What Religion is God?

In the great majority of cases, about 98% of the time your religion is cast by where in the world you were born. If someone is born in Egypt to Muslim parents, that person will very likely be a Muslim. If born to Buddhist parents in Burma, a Buddhist. To a Hindu parent in India, a Hindu - if to a Christian parent in the United States, a Christian. In all of these cases, the person may be fully committed to his faith, or merely affiliated with it. All of them have very different belief systems and customs to help facilitate the person's faith. In some of the religions, such as Christianity and Judaism, belief systems and customs are much further broken down into hundreds of branches and myriad versions of dogma. Yet, all profess to have the corner on God; with their method of worship culturally deemed the best.

So, how does a God-Seeker go about finding the right religion? *How about from the top down?* We may never make the journey if we trace out every path and follow it until we find ourselves lost. We will probably get scared of the complexity, run out of time, and consider it useless. Then we "throw the baby out with the bathwater." Sometimes we forget about the destination of God when we get twisted, dizzy and disheartened by the path, and others we meet alongside the road who seem beat up by it. *But* if we look at it simply... *what religion is God?* Starting at the top should help us get the idea of what the end of the journey should look like, especially if we are unsure of the particular path we may find ourselves on at this time. Can we really see God in the hazy reflection of the mirror of the world's religions? What kind of basic outline do we see sketched in the United States, where most people consider themselves followers of Jesus Christ?

Christianity in America

In America, where 84% of people surveyed consider themselves Christian, four out of 10 Christians do not attend church or read the Bible in a typical week.

Just 13% cite the *Bible* as the source of the principles or standards on which they base their moral and ethical decisions. The most common sources of guidance are *feelings* (25%) and what they learned from their *parents* (14%).

Barna Research Group (BRG), an organization that conducts a nationwide study every year of the country's religious practices and perspectives, concluded in their State of the Church Report 2001 that Americans consider themselves to be faithful and religious people - but seem to be mired in *"spiritual deadness and complacency."* Mr. Barna, the director of the study added: "There are magnificent exceptions throughout the country, but overall, Christian ministry is stuck in a deep rut...Like the churches of Laodicea and Sardis, described in the Bible as distasteful to God because of their complacency and spiritual deadness, too many Christians and churches in America have *traded in spiritual passion for empty rituals, clever methods and mindless practices." (italics mine)*

If the "single most common source of guidance is feelings," as Christians, why not choose to develop those feelings in *combination* with God's will for us? Wouldn't this be in our best possible interest? God has always used Divine Gifts to get his message across, as can readily be seen in the Old and New Testament. It was his original purpose for us to have *deep feelings for him,* showing him love freely and willingly. Divine love is the best feeling to be guided by!

The Original Purpose

"The God who made the world and everything in it is the Lord of heaven and earth and *does not live in temples built by hands.*" And he is not served by human hands, as if he needed anything, because he himself gives all men life and breath and everything else. *From one man he made every nation of men,* that they should inhabit the whole earth... "God did this so that men would seek him and perhaps reach out for him and find him, though *he is not far from each one of us."* (Ac. 17:24-28)

The original purpose, in the Garden of Eden, was to *receive love, spread love* and take care of everything around us. Now, we realize that we all have before us the same choices that Adam and Eve had. We can choose our destiny through free will. Are we going to kill our brother, like Cain did to Abel, because we are jealous, or because he thinks and worships differently than we do? Are we going to be silent and hide when God comes to us, Like Adam and Eve did? When he calls out "where are you," will we answer? (Ge. 3:8,9)

First, we must acknowledge the desire to worship God in every culture – *we were all made with a God-Spot to fill.* Accept that God has many children, and they are welcome up onto his lap too. If something is wrong with the perceptions and actions of some of his kids, have faith that he will be a good Father and reprimand them when the time and situation is right. *We* don't have to worry about it! *Just keep an eye upon your own self.* "Let you who is without sin cast the first stone." Do not be more worried about *people's opinions* than you are about doing *God's Will.*

To find yourself, find the God-Spots. Seek out God, learn everything about him you can. Find the tools that fit your hands and abilities the best, and practice using them. Plot out your course on the map, and plow straight ahead to your destination. *You have chosen not to be a fatherless child anymore.* You are the beloved prodigy of the One who created all the land, gold and precious gems in all the earth. You are the *millionaire's kid,* and you have *rich brothers and sisters too!*

Our Father wants to give us Good Gifts. Jesus said: "Which of you, if his son asks for bread, will give him a stone? Or if he asks for a fish, will give him a snake? If you, then, though you are evil, know how to give good gifts to your children, how much more will your Father in heaven give good gifts to those who ask him!" (Mt. 7:9-11) "But we have this treasure in jars of clay to show that this all-surpassing power is from God and not from us." (2 Co. 4:7)

"By Their Fruits You Will Recognize Them"

We should evaluate the words we hear and the actions we see by the final outcome they produce. The old adage of "cause and effect" applies here. God made us thinking, reasonable human beings, able to decide for ourselves our free moral agency. He is really big on Free Will. He wants us to come to him out of love, not consequences or any other reason. We weren't created as robots, we are not just acting out a preordained stage-play. We have the ability to choose what is right, and what is wrong. This means not all things are right, and some things *are* wrong.

Fate does not exist. God can choose to see the final outcome of all things. But he does not always choose to do so. Just like we, in our imperfectness, can see possible outcomes for ourselves if we drink too heavily, or drive too fast. God did not make Hitler, nor did he make Satan. These beings chose of their own Free Will their wrong course, and will suffer the consequences of their behavior. How can we accuse God of evil? If we believed in predestination, that is what we would be doing. We do not need to be sick to appreciate how it feels to be well. Neither do we need evil to appreciate good. How many of us pray for more unhappiness in our lives, so that we will appreciate happiness when it comes? No one!

Jesus said, "Why do you call me good? No one is good – except God alone." (Mk. 10:18)

Jesus also said: "Watch out for false prophets. They come to you in sheep's clothing, but inside they are ferocious wolves. By their fruit you will recognize them. Do people pick grapes from thornbushes, or figs from thistles? Likewise every good tree bears good fruit, but a bad tree bears bad fruit. A good tree cannot bear bad fruit, and a bad tree cannot bear good fruit. Every tree that does not bear good fruit is cut down and thrown into the fire. Thus, by their fruit you will recognize them." (Mt. 7:16-20)

We all remember the tragedies we have witnessed in the name of religion, in the name of worship of god. Jim Jones at Jonestown, Guyana - poison and suicide in the name of god. Not good fruit. The events at Waco, Texas. More of the same. Saddam Hussein – another rotten tree who used religion as an excuse for intolerance to terrorize and kill. All bad fruits. The list goes on and on. All in the name of god, but *not* in the name of the God of Love.

Although the initial "tree" might have grown up strong and straight toward the sun, something happened along the way, and the tree produced deadly, rotten fruit. 'By their fruits you will recognize them.' Given time, the unknown becomes known. If something is unfamiliar to us, test it out by the Spirit of God by bringing it to him in prayer, this gives us discernment and sensitivity to what is Holy, and what is not. Be sure that yours is *not a hasty decision based on fear of the unknown.* Are we being prejudiced because we don't understand it? Or does it seriously raise red flags, warning bells and whistles immediately? Most people don't care to wait for the tree to produce fruit of any kind. They are impatient and hasty, and pronounce all unknown trees rotten.

Unfortunately, that is why at church, we might get raised eyebrows and the conversation may die when we bring up a thought that wasn't already a "named tree" in the congregation's garden. What we are talking about might be considered a tree of a "strange variety" not previously known; so unfortunately, these trees are usually pronounced rotten before they have a chance to even bud.

Yet, many of these unknown trees produce *fine fruit,* and are a blessing to the garden, orchard and owner who takes the time to watch them grow. How many times have you known or heard of someone who had a near-death experience, and all of a sudden that person changes 180 degrees? He might have been a foul-mouthed, anti-god, selfish, never-like-anybody-or-anything workaholic last year; but since that heart attack, drowning, car accident, etc., he is the most wonderful, caring, joyous and fun-loving Godly person you could ever meet!

Some people might have a unique or unorthodox experience that directly connected them with God. What is wrong with that? Who are we to judge what method God uses to call his children? The point is the *validity of the final result.* Many, many occasions occur in people's lives that are unique opportunities to experience the Divine. Most people will not recognize them when they happen. Often, if they see a "tree" that has different "blossoms" than they are accustomed to seeing, they ignore it and state that the tree simply does not exist; or they will hurry to cut it down and root it out so that nothing of it remains. They do not care about what kind of "fruit" it could have borne. It was a risk they were not willing to take, and they wanted it gone.

11

Do you have the patience to see things through? Or are you quick to name everything unknown as evil? Do you have the faith needed to see "Divine Coincidences" in your life? Do you choose to bring out into the sunlight and openly question various experiences, and have faith-based opinions about topics that some people may consider "untraditional" or "shadowy?"

That shadow might just be the Person of God walking in among the garden, with the cool of the evening sun shining right behind him, calling to you. "Then the man and his wife *heard the sound of the Lord God as he was walking* in the garden in the cool of the day…" (Ge. 3:8) Adam and Eve ran and hid. What will you do?

Will you be like Adam and Eve? Or will you see what new tree God might be planting, maybe even for you? "…his (the godly man's) delight is in the law of the Lord, and on His law he meditates day and night. He is like a tree planted by streams of water, which *yields its fruit in season,* and whose leaf does not wither. Whatever he does prospers." (Ps. 1:2,3)

How God Spoke to People in the Past

Before judging others we should take into consideration the many ways God has chosen to manifest himself to his people *in the past.* And the scriptures say a most interesting thing about God. He is perfect and unchangeable. So, who are we to say how God interacts with his children today? Yet, many people vehemently choose to put a "restraining order" on the one they call Father.

Those who *choose to believe* in what's behind the veil wait for the seed to be planted, expectantly watch every tree as it grows, and wait for the fruit to drop. Then, they praise God for the goodness of the fine fruit, and eagerly gobble it up and share it with others. The rotten fruit they quickly discard, throwing the entire tree into the brush pile, and they think about it no more. And these people benefit extraordinarily well, with the God-given health, joy and happiness that comes from patience and lack of prejudice.

To the one *who doesn't believe,* no sign is good enough; to the one *who believes* no sign is needed. There is a *shared legacy of spirit* that connects all of us to God. It is this family wisdom and interconnectedness of being created in his image, by his will, and with his purpose that allows our God-Spots to be filled. And we *can* choose to let God personally connect with us successfully by various methods. We are all God's children, and his Spirit and our birthright intertwines us to all things, as all things were created by him, from the same basic materials, as we have seen. (Ge. 2:7) Lets look at some interesting ways that God has communicated to us in Biblical times:

12

The Cast of Lots

God has used many unusual ways to get our attention. What would be the opinion of your family and friends if you used dice to decide all life's weighty questions for you? The "roll of the dice" would decide what job you would take, what woman to marry, and even where to live. How about if you were a judge faced with deciding the death penalty, and after you heard all the arguments, you simply decided by tossing the dice, and declared the results were the infallible word of God? "Casting lots" was a common practice for hundreds of years in Bible times. "The lot is cast into the lap, but its every decision *is from the Lord."* (Pro. 16:33)

Today, people would roll their eyes and call for disbarment of a judge who operated that way! Family and friends would request psychological evaluation, and it would certainly take a long time before the person would be taken seriously in church again! But, at one time this was a tool used and ordained by God to actually communicate to his people.

Lots were cast even to decide who would be chosen to become an *apostle of Jesus.* First, a prayer was said: "'Lord, you know everyone's heart. Show us which of these two you have chosen to take over this apostolic ministry, which Judas left to go where he belongs.' Then they cast lots, and the lot fell to Matthias; so he was added to the eleven apostles." (Acts 1:21-26)

Dreams and Interpretations

In the days of old, God also used dreams to communicate with his people. "As the sun was setting, Abram (later known as Abraham) fell into a deep sleep, and a thick and dreadful darkness came over him. Then the Lord said to him..." Know for certain that your descendants...will inherit this land..." (Ge. 15:12-21) "God came to Abimelech in a dream..." (Ge. 20:3) "The angel of the Lord appeared to Joseph in a dream...take the young child (Jesus) and flee..." (Mt. 2:13)

Does God still use dreams today? Notice what the apostle Peter stated to the crowd gathered in Jerusalem. The people of God were being ridiculed for the *strange and unorthodox events* that were occurring to the Christians during the out-pouring of God's Holy Spirit at Pentecost. "In the last days, God says, I will pour out my Spirit on *all people.* Your sons and daughters will prophesy, your young men will see visions, your old men will *dream dreams...*" (Acts 2:14-17)

If God does use dreams today, how about visions and prophesy? Yes, he does. But, which ones and from whom? That is for you to decide. As with all of these things, the value and validity of them will *come from the fruit it produces.* Sometimes, we might find a person's own emotions can manifest so clearly that he feels it is the voice of God, *when really it is his own ideas or fears*. And just when we think we have it all figured out, we get a phone call from our own no-nonsense, practical mother who just had a dream about a plane crash and makes us promise not to travel. Then we watch the news and the plane has gone down. Some people have heeded these warning dreams and lives have been saved. There are also people who will see it all as coincidence, and nothing to do with the Supernatural at all. What do you think?

Native Americans often go on extended fasts to enhance their "vision quests" to connect with the Great Spirit. Is that any different? How about the self-imposed isolation, poverty and meditation chosen by the followers of many Eastern religions today, as did the ancient prophets of the Bible? Many people throughout the world joyfully seek visions and dreams for validation and guidance from God in their personal lives. There are also several Christian religions that feel revelation from God is an on-going process, and did not stop when the Bible was completed. The Catholic Church and the infallibility of the Pope as the spokesman for God is one tree that Catholicism chooses to recognize in its orchard. There are other religions that believe God guides directly each congregation or person individually, through the intermediary of Christ and his sacrifice at Calvary. *Look closely at the fruits!*

God's Message Written on the Wall

"Suddenly the fingers of a human hand appeared and wrote on the plaster of the wall, near the lamp stand in the royal palace. The king watched the hand as it wrote. His face turned pale and he was so frightened that his knees knocked together and his legs gave way." (Da. 5:1-30) Daniel, a humble servant of God "was found to have a keen mind and knowledge and understanding, and also the ability to interpret dreams, explain riddles and solve difficult problems." He was called on to interpret what *God had written on the wall,* and although he was offered great rewards for doing so, he said to the king, "You may keep your gifts for yourself and give your rewards to someone else. Nevertheless, I will read the writing for the king and tell him what it means."

We learn many things here about God. For one, that nothing restrains him and he will communicate with man *however he wants to*. Another, that sometimes it is in his plan to utilize a follower of God to be the *interpreter to the unbeliever*. Also, that in the past the ability to "interpret dreams and explain riddles" were gifts *approved of and utilized* by God; and that those who work to give God's message to others should not be in it solely for the *material gain*. This is where we get our modern-day saying: "I see the handwriting on the wall," meaning that proof has been given, by unusual means, of events about to come true.

14

Moses' Burning Bush

"Now Moses was tending the flock of Jethro his father-in-law, the priest of Midian and he led the flock to the far side of the desert and came to Horeb, the mountain of God. There the angel of the Lord appeared to him in flames of fire from within a bush. Moses saw that though the *bush was on fire* it did not burn up. So Moses thought, "I will go over and see this strange sight – why the bush does not burn up." When the Lord saw that he had gone over to look, God *called to him* from within the bush, "Moses! Moses!" And Moses said, "Here I am." (Ex. 3:1-4)

Sometimes God needs to do something drastic to get our attention. God may also use unexpected sources today when communicating with us. When he calls out for us, are we going to listen and respond? Or are we going to say, "I don't know if this from you, God, because you have never communicated like this before, so I'm going to ignore it!" *Remember that* you *have the tools to test out if it is from our Father or not.* Don't be afraid of new things! It might just be the latest "cell phone" to contact us!

God as a Pillar of Cloud, a Pillar of Fire

The Israelites were experiencing God's salvation from slavery and oppression in Egypt, having just seen plagues, destruction and miracles happen before their very eyes. They were now heading out towards the Red Sea, God using Moses as his spokesperson of choice, since the people were afraid to have God talk to them directly, saying, "You speak to us Moses, and have not God speak to us, for fear we may die!" Yet, the Lord wanted all to know that he was actively involved with their lives, and was there to hear their pleas, their praise and to protect them. What was he going to do? Spirit is invisible to imperfect, live mortal man. And as God told Moses, "you cannot see my face, for no one may see me and live." (Ex. 33:20)

God is like the wind – invisible by itself, but you can see it exists by the activity it produces. The trees bend, the sails billow, the dust gusts up. We also can't see gravity, but we know its laws and the dangers we face when we ignore them. It is the same with God. So, "By day the Lord went ahead of them in a pillar of cloud to guide them on their way and by night in a pillar of fire to give them light, so that they could travel by day or night. Neither the *pillar of cloud* by day nor the *pillar or fire* by night left its place in front of the people." (Ex. 13:21,22) What love! What ingenuity! He appeared as cloud and as fire! Yet, they still would not believe, and they complained and rebelled instead!

The form our faith may take is less important than the love it imparts, and God is the personification of Love. "How many are your works, O Lord! In wisdom you made them all; the earth is full of your creatures...when you take away their breath, they die and return to the dust. When you send your Spirit, they are created, and you renew the face of the earth. May the glory of the Lord endure forever; may the Lord rejoice in his works." (Ps 104:24-31)

Balaam's Donkey Speaks

"When the donkey saw the angel of the Lord standing in the road with a drawn sword in his hand, she turned off the road into a field. Balaam beat her to get her back on the road...then the Lord *opened the donkey's mouth*, and she said to Balaam, "What have I done to you to make you beat me these three times?" Then the Lord opened Balaam's eyes, and he saw the angel of the Lord standing in the road with his sword drawn. So he bowed low and fell facedown...then the angel of God said...'I have come to oppose you because your path is a reckless one before me. The donkey saw me and turned away from me these three times. If she had not turned away, I would certainly have killed you by now, but I would have spared her.'" (Nu. 22:21-33)

Guess what! This story shows that God can choose to use animals to communicate with us – and that animals can see spirits *without* the special human need of "having their eyes opened." I have witnessed this many times, that animals are able to *see* the "higher vibrations" just as some animals (in dogs it is well documented) have the ability to *hear* higher vibrational sounds.

Seers ("See-ers") and Fire From Heaven

"The Lord said to Gad, David's seer, "Go and tell David, 'this is what the Lord says: I am giving you three options...' so David built an altar to the Lord...he called on the Lord, and the Lord answered him with fire from heaven on the altar of burnt offering." (1 Ch. 21:9,26)

King David was given instruction by a *middle-man who was sensitive to hearing the word of God.* The seer was used, in this instance, by God to stop a terrible plague and to stop destruction of life and property.

"Saul said to his servant, if we go, what can we give the man? The food in our sacks is gone. We have no gift to take to the man of God. What do we have?" The servant answered him again. "Look," he said, "I have a quarter of a shekel of silver. I will give it to the man of God so that he will tell us what way to take." (Formerly in Israel, if a man went to inquire of God, he would say, "Come, let us go to the seer," because the prophet of today used to be called a seer.)" (1 Sa. 9:8,9)

We see here that it is proper to offer an exchange for services to one who has been gifted by God to help him cover his needs and thereby allowing him to continue to focus on fully utilizing the gift. Time and time again we see in the scriptures that God uses those who are sensitive to his voice to bring others to faith and Divine direction, and they are rewarded for it. "The worker is worth his wages." (Lk. 10:7)

So Many Miracles, So Many Methods Chosen By God

By just opening The Great Book anywhere and starting to read, you will shortly find a supernatural event that God used to impart information to his people. It does not matter where you start reading, Old or New Testament. Give it a try! The Bible is full of miracles and out-of-the-ordinary things. He is that kind of Guy! He can make a grand entrance, shout in an audible thunderous voice (Jo. 12:29), or softly in a whisper (Mt. 10:27). He can make unusual grain (manna) fall from heaven (Nu. 11:7) and two fishes become baskets full enough to feed over five thousand men (Mt. 14:19-21). There are *so many ways that he connects with us!* He is truly the Supernatural God, the Lord of Miracles. Kathryn Kulhman, a leading evangelist and healer said it best: "I believe in miracles, because I believe in God!"

Gather Yourselves Together

People like to be accepted. We all want to be respected and loved. It truly takes a brave and steady heart to let God be God, and to allow his manifestation in our lives. Often we risk rejection whenever we gather ourselves together and declare our Godly Connection openly, as some may have already cut down the tree that we have watched grow and produce fruit. It takes tolerance and love to allow differences between us. *Yet people can agree to disagree.* As always, the final outcome will solve and answer all the questions. We need just keep an eye on ourselves.

"God also testified to it (salvation) by signs, wonders and various miracles, and gifts of the Holy Spirit *distributed according to his will."* (Heb. 2:4)

Our heavenly Father likes his kids to get along with each other - play nicely, don't fight over the toys. Don't yell at each other and don't push to be first in everything. Sit down quietly at the table and share. Do your chores. The Lord feels very strongly about how we treat each other. He created people to need and want each other in their lives. He likes us to come together for work and for relaxation. He ordained that men and women come together to produce children. History shows that God allows people to speak in his place, including using different folks as his writing assistants in producing the Bible, when he could have just written it directly into our hearts or by an angelic hand.

The writer of Hebrews admonishes us, "Do not forsake the gathering of yourselves together, as some have the custom, but let us encourage one another..." (Heb. 10:25) Much scripture talks about the role of the church and the responsibilities the leaders have to use it to point to the Divine. It is meant to be a refuge (Ps. 84:1,4); to aid in resolving conflicts (Mt 18:18); to show love for the entire community (Rev.2:5); to aid widows and orphans (1 Tim.5:9-16); to pray as a team effort (Acts 12:5) and to preach the love of God and salvation (2 Tim. 4: 1,2). It is meant to encourage and to give praise. It is meant to be a glorious Thanksgiving feast where all are invited to sit down to the sumptuous table lay before them and taste that God is *good.*

Church is not a building, but people. "And in him you too are being built together to become a dwelling in which God lives by his Spirit." (Eph. 2:19-22)

But, please look at the fruits when you choose a church home. Jesus was condemned by the *religious leaders* of his day – they did not recognize this most precious Tree of Life planted by the Heavenly Father. In one instance, Jesus was accused by the Pharisees and teachers of the law that his disciples were breaking the religious traditions of their fathers. Jesus replied, "And why do you break the command of God for the sake of your tradition? You nullify the word of God for the sake of your tradition. You hypocrites! Isaiah was right when he prophesied about you: "These people honor me with their lips, but their hearts are far from me. They worship me in vain; their teachings are but *rules taught by men.*" (Mt. 15:1-13)

They had a *form* of godly devotion, but were proving false to its power. (2 Tim. 3:5) Jesus went on to address his followers who were *upset* that he had been so bold with the leaders: "Then the disciples came to him and asked, "Do you know that the Pharisees were offended when they heard this?" He replied, "Every plant that my heavenly Father has not planted will be pulled up by the roots." Hmmm, another reference to the 'by their fruits' illustration. Time reveals everything; for what intention will you use your gifts? If it is for ego and vanity, you will be humbled. If you don't use them at all, you could be sinning. Why not use them as he decreed? To facilitate a better connection between *him and you* – and for the benefit of his *other* children that need help!

The God-Spot will remain empty until then. No amount of material possessions will fill the hole. No amount of exotic vacations will truly satisfy. No amount of sexual partners or intoxicants. *With those things you will always feel empty, no matter how much you try to push them into the God-Spot.* Why not choose it to be full and overflowing with Divine Love? You will feel a satisfaction that surpasses any materialistic joy, and it will last much longer than anything that can rust, fall apart or be stolen! The choice is yours.

CHAPTER 2

Struck By Lightning! My Near-Death Experience
Christ Face-to-Face; My Life Unfolds

Not everyone needs to be struck by lightning, or have a miracle happen, to understand God's will for his life. But, that is the method that God used to fix up one of his most broken kids: me.

It was summertime in Tennessee. A time of good green pasture for the horses, ripe tomatoes on the vine, and long drives in the country. Life seemed wonderfully slow for me that gracious summer; as slow as the drone of the honeybees in the apple trees, as slow as the preparations for the upcoming county fair.

For the first time in many years, all four of my children had come together for vacation time, and I knew that it would probably be the last tick of the clock before their lives would get too busy to experience this again. I was making every opportunity to show them a full and adventurous summer. Life had never been so materially good! I was thankful to share the riches of my new life as a new wife. We would swim in the pool, watch movies and ride the go-cart. We would drive the jaguar in the country and go camping and have picnics. We would ride the horses.

I could overlook the growing detachment of my husband and the late night phone calls. I could also ignore the mysterious apathy and disdain my oldest daughter had for me. I could overlook the bill collectors' constant threats and the new expensive toys being brought home that we couldn't afford. I thought I could make it through anything - hadn't I just survived *my fourth* near-death episode? Even the doctors were amazed. The venomous spider bite had tried to shut down my breathing and my heart, but the doctors knew what drugs to pump through me and I had made it through – and this had happened just the previous week!

My husband and I had been married only a year and a half. The marriage counseling would work. He would stop comparing me unfavorably to his "special friend" of seventeen years, telling me just two weeks ago; and for me to "just deal with it." He would stop needing her. He would remember he loved only me. I hoped time would blow away the ominous gray clouds gathering in my personal life. I kept telling myself *time would help, and I would adjust again, somehow.*

I hoped that if I closed my eyes and wished hard enough, everything bad would just disappear. Hadn't I gone through this enough times? Why did this keep repeating itself? Why did I continue to make bad choices about the mate in my life? One thing I had learned - that I would feel that I didn't deserve this and that

God had abandoned me. Then I would usually try to fix things myself. When I would fail, I would then call upon him, and he would bail me out and slowly mend all the broken parts. But this time, I felt there was no way my life could be fixed. *I was broken beyond repair.* I felt I had no mission, that my life had no purpose.

I was so tired of starting over. For the first time in my life I felt I had some material advantage, and I did not want that to change – the children enjoyed it so much, and so did I. I chose not to pray about it – I felt I would sacrifice my happiness for the material gain of the children. I had messed up my life too much, too many times. There was nothing left for me. I decided I would do what my husband said, and just "deal with it." I would resign myself to ignoring the problems around me, and just struggle from day to day, with a fake smile and heavy heart. Love between people seemed only a façade for control. I felt already dead; my heart knew no joy. I was without hope, and helplessly broken.

Although I refused to see the storm swirling under my own roof, I couldn't ignore the rain and thunderclouds gathering outside over the valley. Strong winds were blowing up the hill over the pasture. The rain was pelting the garden and sounded like marbles dropping on the metal-roofed sheds. I had to go check on the horses. I had to make sure they were safe. That's when *I ran out of time.* And I would never look at time, and many other things, the same way again.

God, Lightning and Healing Hands

"Stars!" I shouted through the thunder to the appaloosa pacing behind the chain link fence where we kept the tractor and farm implements. "Stars! You are always the one getting into trouble! In the middle of a storm trying to fresh grass!" As I let the chain down off the shed with one hand, I steadied myself against a wooden structure pole with the other. The horse bolted up the pasture, as the finger of God bolted down. Standing in the pouring rain with my arms outstretched, I was killed by a bolt of lighting.

The last thing I remember about the strike itself was doing an uncontrollable electrical dance as my muscles spasmed and contorted this way and that. I felt no pain. In that split second, I remembered that electrical shocks often stop the heart; so I pivoted around and pushed my chest against the corner of the truck parked there, thinking to start it again. Before I could even put any weight against it, my eyesight narrowed and I felt my body slowly slide down the bumper onto the wet earth; and all went black…

I found myself standing on nothing, way up in the universe, and there were distant colorful planets all around me. I could see misty pinpoints of stars through my right arm, and when I moved my arm back and forth it made the stars look wiggly, like a reflection on agitated water. I felt dizzy. I had a sense of being able

20

to see not only in front of me, but all around me at the same time. Floating just a few feet from me, I saw a man with a spirit body just like mine (no wings), though he was short and had slanted eyes. He spoke to me with a voice that I heard inside my own head, saying: "Don't be afraid, it's ok."

On the other side of me, another spirit person, this one much taller and with chiseled facial features (again no wings), nodded approvingly at me. All the while, we were moving with great speed toward a great ellipsed ball of spinning light; it was brilliantly white in the middle and yellowish on the outside edges. The closer we got to it, the more I felt overwhelming Love; it seemed so warm and comforting, it encompassed my very being...like the security of a favorite grandfather's arms wrapped around a child as he crawls up onto his lap.

We stopped. The bright light was still far from me. I wanted to go on, I felt like a magnet, irresistibly drawn. The desire to "blend" had grown stronger the closer we got. I knew it was the very Presence of God himself.

Why had we stopped? As I stood there confused, yearning toward the Great Almighty beyond my reach, a glowing luminousness appeared in front of me. A Divine Presence was here!

A gentle voice called out from this realm of golden sparkles massed brilliantly in front of me - "What Have You Learned?" he asked, in a nondiscriminatory and non-accusing way. The voice was so soft and tender, yet the presence of Divine Authority was there; I knew that it was the voice of God's own son, the empowered Jesus Christ.

Then - all of a sudden, life events unfolded before my very eyes. Key moments where I showed anger, and where I showed love, appeared like a movie. I could feel the *anger* and hurt of the other person whenever I had been mean; and I also felt the anger as it rippled on through to others. I had never before faced the horrid deepness of my own sins. Then, where I showed *love* to people, I felt that too. How very much further that rippled out from person to person, as a warm pulse triggering cause and effect in all things that were wonderful and blessed...I had never before experienced such joy!

Then the presence of Jesus said, "The Flesh Is The Test Of The Spirit...Love Each Other." Words of wisdom imparted to me! I felt overwhelmed with love, and so privileged.

I wanted to stay! I wanted to join myself with God's swirling life force, His Essence, His Heaven, was just beyond the presence of Jesus! But, I wasn't allowed to go any farther. I wanted to go to God! I wanted to feel more Love! "Why can't I be with You now Father? Please, Abba, Please!"

I listened as hard as I could listen, waiting for His Words. Then, just on the outside of my understanding, I faintly heard voices singing the most beautiful melody I had ever heard in my whole life. I felt a "knowing" that these were the blessed voices of angels and those joined with God, and came from His Swirling Presence.

I knew it was praise for The Father, but I just couldn't make out what the words were saying. I felt so sad…I knew I was supposed to go back to the earth. I knew I had to make a "better movie." I wanted to stay. But, there and then, I vowed to be a vessel to do only His Will, if he could use me. I absolutely gave myself to him. His Will, not my own, would govern the rest of my life. If he could use this broken piece of clay from the earth, it was all his. I totally dedicated myself and surrendered all desires. Instantly, I felt a child-like sense of wonderment as a warm flood of bliss and peace overpowered me, and a warm tingling sensation filled me to my very toes. What was happening to me?

Again the spirit on my right side talked inside my head, and while I floated there before the Christ Consciousness, the very Presence of Jesus, the spirit told me something that I didn't at all understand: "Welcome to the world of healers," he said. This was a shock - I had no idea what that meant. At this point the Christ Consciousness of Jesus sparkled and faded away and the stars and space behind his glowing features were visible once again. Such effervescent beauty and colors twinkled around me, like being in the midst of a sparkling aurora borealis! So many shapes of heavenly bodies transfixed in the cosmos, all unique and necessary, all untold distances away. Yet they felt so close that it seemed I could reach out and pluck them out of the sky, and carry them home cupped in my hands.

Then the slant-eyed spirit went on and answered the many questions I was having about this experience. He then pointed out different stars, planets, distant colorful swirling lights of all kinds, and gave me names for all of them. Then he gave me answers to thousands of questions that I never had questions for! Reams of information seemed to be exploding in my brain, like an empty library suddenly being realized! Details flooded my being about many wonderful and sacred things. I wondered: were these things newly learned, or just remembered?

Most of this information I am still trying to integrate and understand. It is almost like trying to learn another language without being given the basic alphabet for it. So, at this point, these are deeper things I have told no one, and keep only to myself. Often, when in prayer to the Father I will ask him to further my understanding on these matters, yet I get the distinct feeling that true understanding will only be revealed on a "need to know" basis. However, for some reason a seed was planted within me. I do know some of this information came through as I was writing this book. There are things in here that I never knew that I knew!

I must remember that everything he does is for the Highest Good, always happens in the Perfect Time for it, and that it is His Will, not ever mine or anyone else's, that matters. His is Perfect, Love Personified! I am just a sinful (but forgiven), impatient person! But, for some reason a groundwork has been laid within me. I know that if he wants me to share this information later on, he will tell me, and give me the reasoning ability to articulate and understand it.

The spirit who was speaking to me did not offer his name, and I did not ask. I wanted to be careful to show homage only to the True God and Christ, not to any one else. I then felt myself sinking, as if falling through a bed. I was being pulled back.

With that, I woke up, my husband shaking me by the shoulders. Somehow my physical body was now lying on the front seat of the truck, although I had left it out in the mud. Three hours had passed since I had gone from the house to the tractor shed. The storm had passed, but left evidence that at least three other strikes had occurred on the pasture, besides the one that struck me.

"Welcome to the World of Healing"

At the emergency room I was hooked up with wires and given tests to check my heart. A thorough exam revealed that it had not been damaged. But, my eyes and ears were affected very badly, as was my sense of balance. I felt dizzy, but keenly aware of the reality of my experience. The only piece of jewelry I was wearing was a single diamond earring. A brown burn mark encircled the gold stud where it went through my ear. My skin tingled all over and was extremely sensitive to the touch, especially on my arms and in my hands.

The doctors told me that I had been very lucky; that usually an arm or leg gets blown off during a strike. People often die (and don't come back). They reasoned that because I was holding the chain-link with one hand and the wet wooden pole with the other, that the current had passed through me, instead of grounding in my body. I knew they wouldn't believe me if I told them it had been a Divine Strike, that God used this as a wake-up call, and that I had been before the Presence of God, and oh, by the way, Jesus spoke to me! They would have kept me a lot longer than they did, and probably in a little white jacket, in a locked padded room!

I spent a few days in bed, oscillating between a wild mixture of extreme happiness and unbelievable sadness. The emotions ran deeper than any I had ever felt. I was glad for the experience, but I had wanted to stay there! I kept re-living the event over and over in my mind, every detail emblazoned into my brain.

I was determined that even if I forgot my own name, *I would never forget this*. I tried painting what I had seen – oil paints on canvas. The colors, no matter how I mixed them, were not brilliant enough. Nothing could capture what I had seen and felt. I felt sad again. Then once more, happy for the experience. Then confused. What did it all mean?

After a few days, I was back to my chores, including putting salve on Star's skin infection. For six weeks I had smoothed on the medicine the vet had given me, but still the red blisters kept spreading and killing the hair all around his girth. Now I had ran out of medicine, so I just rubbed his belly lightly around the outside of the infection because he had grown used to the attention. I noticed that my hands were getting very hot. I thought it must be bacteria from the infection, and when I washed my hands under cold water it went away. I didn't think anything of it.

The next day, I walked up to rub his belly again - reminding myself to get new salve soon - and noticed that all the blisters had turned white and some were falling off. I once more rubbed around the infection, and my hands turned hot once more. The next day when I went out, *all* the blisters had fallen off, and there was evidence of new hair growing back. But, since I had been religiously trained that hands-on-healing died with the apostles (I had also been taught that near-death-experiences were just created by chemical reactions in the brain), I thought this was mere coincidence.

The next week, I took my cat in to be spayed. The vet said it would take 10 days for the stitches to completely heal. On the first day, she didn't want anything to do with me. But, the second day, she was in my lap as much as possible. She just would not leave me alone! Even yowling for me if I left the room. Every time I would rub her and pet her, I found that my hands would heat up again. On the third day, she tried pulling the stitches out with her teeth. On the morning of the forth day, I decided to look at what was going on, and found that the skin had healed so well that the stitches were puckering her skin up tight. I found myself embarrassed to take her back to the vet – what would he say? So I carefully cut the threads and pulled them out myself, *through skin that bore no surgical scar.* I began to understand what was happening…but, would this work on people?

The Wounded Healer

The next day, I said a prayer to God, laid my hands hot on my forehead, and on various parts of my body. Then, I made an appointment with the doctor. A previous mammogram had shown lumps in my breasts. A former doctor had told me I had fibroid cysts in my uterus, which could only be removed through surgery. Also, I had a torn rotator cuff in my shoulder, which had prevented me from sleeping well for the past six months.

24

I anxiously awaited the test results:
…the mammogram showed the lumps were all gone.
…the diagnostic ultrasound showed clear, the fibroid cysts had disappeared.
…also, I could sleep at night without any pain; my rotator cuff was healed.

God had blessed me with the gift of healing! This is what he had meant!

Hesitantly, I started sharing this new gift with my friends – and that's when I ran into trouble. *I found that I was taking the pain of their ailment onto myself.* If they had a migraine, I would get a migraine. If they had stomach pain, I would get stomach pain. That scared me – I found myself afraid to use the gift. Maybe I was using it wrong? Why would God give a gift that would cause harm to use it? I felt I wouldn't last very long in this work. And yet, I knew in my heart that God wouldn't give me something that would be unsafe for me to use. What was I missing?

I thought I might find answers if I watched the healing ministries on TV. For the first time in my life I wondered if they could actually be legitimate. I had never believed in this sort of thing – I had felt it was a fake, showy display to raise money and give people false hope. Now I wanted desperately to talk to one of them. Did *they* feel sick afterward? Had they each been told, "Welcome to the world of healers?" Was I part of this same group? What did God want me to understand?

I continued on this way for a time, confused by the gift. I thought maybe I would work only on animals; I did not feel their pain. Maybe I could work for a veterinarian, alone in a back room, quietly healing the animals. I didn't know what to do.

So, I prayed for understanding, and what I found was the Lord's words overflowing back at me. On and on the scriptures popped out of the Bible, the pages randomly falling open to pertinent information, my eyes emblazoned on the scriptures he wanted me to see. They popped out *as brightly as if they were highlighted by a yellow marker pen!* Dozens of scriptures! Here are just a few:

"For I know the plans I have for you," declares the Lord, "plans to prosper you and not to harm you, plans to give you hope and a future." (Jer. 29:11)

"You are the light of the world. A city on a hill cannot be hidden. Neither do people light a lamp and put it under a bowl. Instead they put it on its stand, and it gives light to everyone in the house. In the same way, let your light shine before men, that they may see your good deeds and praise your Father in heaven." (Mt. 5:14)

"...fan into flame the gift of God, which is in you through the laying on of my hands. For God did not give us a spirit of timidity, but a spirit of power, of love and of self-discipline." (2 Tim. 1:6)

Through his Word he kept reminding me that when the Lord gives his people a commission or Divine gift, *he does not do it without a specific purpose.* I knew I had to use the gift however *he* saw fit. I knew that gifts came with responsibilities, and I was prepared for that. I was going to be working for the Greatest Boss in the whole world! So many times I had been absolutely shattered, yet he had still held me gently in the palm of his hands. There had also been many times we had walked together hand-in-hand, and many times I had turned away from him, hid my face in shame, and withdrew my hand from his. Yet, his arm was still outstretched, and he still loved me...I was astonished. Everything I had done, and *He Still Loved Me! Unbelievable!*

And now, he gave me a real purpose, a job to do – he wanted me to work daily under his guidance! Work for *Him!* What a wonder Father we have!

He had gone through all this trouble to let me know my life's path. I had a purpose now, and I did not have to suffer in silence or ignore my plight. I could be strong again, *because his strength was in me.* Everything was made anew! I had *died to self at the foot of heaven and upon the earth* – and he had *resurrected me* up again as an adopted daughter, an heir of the kingdom! My father is the richest person in the universe; and now I was his princess. And I have *so many* brothers and sisters, princes and princesses all of us! We have all been bought with a price. And there is a price for us to pay to be with him. We must die to ourselves, and give all glory and worship to him! I was happy to do it.

"Let us then approach the throne of grace with confidence, so that we may receive mercy and find grace to help us in our time of need." (Heb. 4:16)

I was amazed that he was giving me a job where I would be working in direct communion with him everyday. He wasn't tired of me yet! I would also be making friends and helping people from all walks of life, social standing, color and religious background. *He opened me up!* I vowed I would never allow myself to be closed down again.

I asked to blow his direction as easy as the wind, and that I would go wherever he led me. One of my favorite scriptures came to mind: "The wind blows wherever it pleases. You hear its sound, but you cannot tell where it comes from or where it is going. So it is with everyone born of the Spirit." (John 3:8) I prayed to God to be used by the Holy Spirit fully, to touch as many people as I could, *to bring people to faith.* I had vowed to be a vessel empty, ready for him to fill. I did not care if it hurt. I would not fear. *His Will be done. His Will be done through me. "Here I am, send me!"* (Isa.6:8)

26

Reiki Healing in the God-Spot

One day, a trusted friend invited me to a Reiki ("ray'key") Open House near my home in Nashville, Tennessee. She said there were people being healed there. I cautiously went with her. I found people praying and laughing, and the laying on of hands. Their hands were hot like mine; and the people they were attending had come from the community, mostly the poor and the curious. Twice a month they would gather here in this upper room and invite any who wanted to come. I watched them, and it made me wonder. I felt comforted that there was a large painting of Jesus hanging predominately on the wall. On the desk was information about this Japanese technique, and I thumbed through it. There was a picture of a man, a Christian minister, who had given Japanese hands-on-healing this name of Reiki in the early 1800's, and had started many healing clinics. I looked at the picture and gasped. I knew this man!

This was the spirit with slant-eyes and rounded belly that was beside me during my near-death experience! The very same man! My Goodness! God works in very, very mysterious ways!

With this, I knew what my next step was; and I went through the training classes of Traditional Usui Reiki, receiving what is called the Reiki Master degree. Now, I felt energized and euphoric after the healings! I was not taking upon myself the other person's pain anymore. So, now I was using the "Gifts of the Spirit" offering "Healing Prayer" under the title of "Reiki Practitioner." But why had God led me up this path, one that I had never heard of before? Why was this strange name added to the calling of my ministry?

I have given *much* thought and prayer to this question. And this is what I have been given as the answer. And since he continues to use this vessel for even more powerful works, I know His Blessing has been upon it. I have learned not to judge where his Spirit places my foot, because wherever I am he places an angel to protect and shield me with a flaming sword of Unconditional Love. So, please do not judge too quickly, and give weight to the words of God; including "By their fruits you will recognize them…" (Mt. 7:16-20) At the least, please remember that even Abraham's son Jacob (who had been sold as a slave by his brothers) abided for a while in Egypt; it was for God's Higher Good and helped the most people. Jacob said "…God intended it for good to accomplish what is now being done, the saving of many lives." (Ge. 50:20)

Reiki is now recognized by the American Medical Association as a Complementary Alternative Medicine (CAM). It is used in many hospitals by trained nurses and doctors as a complement to normal health care needs. It has consistent and measurable results. There are more and more studies (including a double-blind study by NIH) and research being conducted to show it works. This form of hands-on-healing is easily accessible, and more and more accepted by the public. Reiki was "rediscovered" by Dr. Usui, a teacher and Christian minister at the DoShiSha Christian University in Japan. Reiki is also a healing modality that allows me to submit legally appropriate insurance claims for integrative healthcare interventions using ABC codes (this is not available for "Healing Prayer" at this time). This ability to bill insurance makes Hands-On-Healing more available for those who really need it, and legitimate as a recognized tool in healthcare.

I have also received my certificate from the California State Board of Nursing as a "provider." This means I can teach about the Divine Connection of healing (by the name of Reiki) to nurses for their necessary Continuing Education requirements. This helps the medical healers become even better healers – as they actively ask for the power of the Holy Spirit to come directly into their work, by their prayerful intention and touch.

To me, it doesn't matter what you call it; it makes sense that a God-thing would be accessible to all people, in all parts of the world, in all cultures throughout all periods of time. And that is exactly what we see. There are many titles for the formal usage of healing prayer being used as an access to the Holy Spirit.

About "faith healers," if you think about it, how many people do you know who would really go to a traveling convention to get well? For one, people have to have a certain amount of hope in God to even try it – to order a schedule, get the tickets, find the place, make accommodations and drive there. And there are so many people who are without hope, as hopeless as can be. Many feel alienated from God, and do not recognize when his hand is even reaching down to them. Even the doctors have given up hope on many. Practicing under the recognized "Reiki" title provides another tool to help them, in a clinical situation, regardless of religion, faith, or lack of it. And he still heals them. Who am I to limit God and tell him what to do? When we try to put him into a box, he breaks out every time!

I do not consider myself a "faith healer." I am not sure what that is - I have seen all kinds of people - including total atheists, and agnostics - have powerful healings manifest in their lives (and animals too). God wasn't called by their heartfelt faith or melodic prayer...*this is nothing that we can earn*. It is simply by his undeserved grace. He could choose to accomplish healings simply by individual prayer; and he often works in this way. *But, he also likes his kids to interact with each other, work together, need each other, and get along!*

He just allows me to be there when he goes to work! The Holy Spirit does all the healing. I just show up, and surrender myself totally to his power. Sometimes I may be led to offer some words of knowledge along the way. Often he allows me to be intuitive on specific health issues. As with all his children, and all his gifts, the more we choose to yield and get our own selves out of the way, the better he can work!

I have gone to several healing conventions and have watched from my seat with joy as people are healed by the Holy Spirit. I have seen over and over again that where there is a large group of people praying for his Spirit, great and miraculous healings flow out onto the floor, including spontaneous, immediate healings. I am fortunate that also in a one-to-one situation, the Spirit sees and helps people of all persuasions, equally at home or a clinical setting, and he still heals them. God in the mainstream, accomplishing his will as he sees fit.

It reminds me of how the apostle Paul was admonished to be all things to all people; it was necessary to reach as many people as possible in his day with the Good News of the Christ. First the kingdom was preached to the Jews, then to a mixed race, then the Gentiles themselves. (Acts 22 & 23) God puts his people in different places, with different responsibilities, at different times, to best accomplish his will. I'm OK with that!

A New Life, A New State of Being

The next couple of years saw many changes: I gave my husband his divorce, and I got re-ordained *very* simply as a nondenominational minister (I have a doctorate too, but we all know *real* ordination is only by God, the paperwork and the title is only for man!). I moved back to California, coming full circle to where I had been born, and where I still have relatives. I moved into a motorhome to be able to go wherever I was needed, and to keep my costs down so I could help as many people as possible. Through the Will of God, I (We) have helped *thousands* of people! *And I am happier now than I have ever been.* God has given me a unique purpose, and amazing people and interesting situations are brought into my life everyday. I have fewer material possessions than ever before, but I know where the true wealth lies. Now everyday is an adventure and a spirit journey for me! And, he takes care of my needs, and *very* often my desires too!

Please note - a person does not need to be struck by lightning to have healing hands. And, it has nothing to do with being a minister – it has everything to do with being a child of God, just like you. We are the same! There are many people who are called to become healers; and he gives this opportunity to them as a free gift. At first, the healing connection is widened just a bit larger than the one they were naturally born with. He sees how they handle the responsibilities and the blessings that come with it. Later, if they choose to progress as a vessel of healing, he will open them up some more, and he will see how they respond to that. Doors will open, or close, from there. Are they working for ego, or giving the credit to the One True Healer? Reiki *can* be a good step to connect oneself with the Divine, and with helping each other. Another piece of the God-Spot, and one that God himself chose for me, to help as many people as possible.

I am blessed to be working in several established clinics in southern California, as a full-time 'Worker for The Big Guy.' But, instead of the title "Healing Prayer" the term "Reiki Practitioner" is painted on the front glass door. I begin every healing by telling the client, "I will now be saying a silent prayer to God; since he is the only Healer here, *and I invite you to connect in prayer with him also."* This lets people know I am not the healer, and gives them an acceptance of responsibility and a sharing in the healing process. In this way, it is also not just something that is being done to them; *their active will is involved.* And, I give them the choice of hearing the prayers out loud. In this way they know I am just the extension cord – God is the electrical powerhouse.

"Again, I tell you that if two of you on earth agree about anything you ask for, it will be done for you by my Father in heaven. For where *two or three come together in my name,* there am I with them." (Mt 18:19,20)

It is true that some of my clients don't even believe in God, but he helps them anyway, and touches their heart and spirit besides their bodies! It makes them curious, at the very least, about this "Something" that is beyond their realm of understanding that is "mysteriously" helping them!

That curiosity can be a very good first step. And most often, I get to put in a few good words about this "Mysterious Something." I also hand out free Bibles. I know that the people who are brought to me, are *brought to me for a reason.* Jesus had said to me: "The Flesh Is The Test Of The Spirit." The brokenness of our bodies is a time when our soul can be very receptive and open; or, we can close our soul off very tightly. It is part of making the choices on our Spirit Journey. *It is often a time of rescued vulnerability; when the Love of God reaches down to save.* Often, I have seen illness simply as an incredible opportunity for tremendous choices, with lives being changed forever, for the very highest good.

Now my entire life is an adventure and a spirit journey! I praise God continually for every day, every moment, and every experience I have! I am always amazed how he brings his kids together. It totally *humbles* me to be involved in this kind of work.

This is nothing I earned. It is nothing any person could *ever* earn! Yet, I know that if he wanted to, he could make the rocks speak, so I am in good company. I know I have been hard-headed, extremely stubborn and completely sinful. Through difficult lessons and time he made me see my self-pity, false piety, and selfish desires. I also had a false form of love; I was giving love conditionally, with the aim to receive back. God's way is pure, Unconditional Love. I was also putting in God's place of worship other things, including spouses, and all of them were failing me miserably. Only he can fill up that yearning inside us, only he can fill the God-Spot. It is there to worship and connect *only* with him. My acknowledgement of sin made me see all these things clearly. He had removed the veil, and now I could see. I was free!

Redemption

I want to give you a little more of my background, a few more moments of my life, to let you know who I was before all this happened. We are all allowed periods of brokenness in our lives, and the choices we make govern our next step on the path. There are so many roads we could take, and if we don't learn the lessons we need to, we often end up circling around and being presented with them again! Then we wonder why the same things seem to repeat in our lives: it is because we didn't "get it" the first time! I have done this *a lot!*

Here is my life in story form; telling it in the "third person" helps me to see it from a perspective outside of myself, and to shelter myself from the rawness of the experiences. It is, out of necessity, a very condensed version. It is such a reminder to me how *much* we need the Lord. We are nothing of ourselves, it is only by his grace that we even exist in his sight! Even when we think we are "good," no one is good, but him!

Tiffany's Brokenness

Although Tiffany was barely forty years old, life had already been a very difficult journey. Although she had received Christ as her savior in the Baptist Church when she was eleven, and received water baptism in the Methodist Church when she was twelve, it did not prevent life's lessons from shaping her. By the time she was thirteen, she had been raped, forced to use drugs, a runaway, abandoned with strangers in various parts of the country, and had gone to several different schools. By the time she was sixteen she was living on her own, and was working two jobs part-time while still going to school.

When she was seventeen she contracted an unknown bacteria, went into a coma while visiting her grandparents, and almost died from an extended high fever. No hospital would admit her without parental consent because she was under age; and her parents were out of the country. She lost her photographic memory and her fingernails, and felt she was entirely alone in all the world.

Tiffany's career goals focused on wildlife management and working for the forest service. She envisioned working up on a mountain in a lookout tower watching for forest fires as she painted nature scenes, wrote children's books, and played her musical instruments. She felt being alone with God and nature was safer then being with people. Tiffany graduated from High School and watched the procession alone from the bleachers. She had no money for a cap and gown, and no family to sit beside her, as her parents were once again out of the country. Without any financial ability to go on to college, Tiffany put her dreams on hold.

She searched for God in her youth, and was attracted to several different religions. In her search, she would often invite two pastors from two different religions into a discussion and ask one single question, "If God is Love, why is there so much suffering in the world?" She would watch time and again as they either closed the Bible and declared it a "sacred mystery," or argued among themselves about the theology they were taught at seminary.

Becoming disillusioned with each religion stating that it was the only correct one, Tiffany decided to try to find the answer by herself; about why we suffer and become broken. It started a quest that took years of struggle and personal suffering to discover the answer to. It was not intentional defacement that Tiffany endured; no, it was just the best way for God to answer this question for her, by his allowing her to experience the spiritual lessons that trials brought to her development.

In the beginning, Tiffany went to the library and did vast amounts of research. First, she proved to herself that the Bible was indeed a Divinely inspired book. Then she found a church with very strict beliefs and felt comfortable with following restrictions, as her basic temperament had been shaped for needing to please those who are difficult to satisfy.

She married in the church one month after turning eighteen, to an older man who was a minister of the Word. She took her vows before God early, and also became a minister. She felt that with this foundation, all happiness would be achieved. They had four children in six years; but after nine years she was forced to go into shelter to protect herself and her children from physical abuse. Her church turned against her for leaving her husband, she was publicly reprimanded and scorned, and her young children were accused of lying about their injuries. She was forced to move to another area as the safety of the police Restraining Order was repeatedly broken. She lost the house that she had helped to build and in which she had given birth to her children.

Now, as a single parent with a ruptured disk in her neck, wearing a brace and having little outside help, Tiffany and her very young children endured various measures of poverty for many years. They often could be seen gathering aluminum cans off the side of the road to supplement the meager welfare and food program allotments, enabling them to buy gasoline and toiletries.

Often, Tiffany would feel angry at God, and would leave him for varying lengths of time when things went bad. When things were good, she would come back again. But, she would feel resentful and leave once more when trials once again confronted her. She felt she did not deserve the bad things thrust at her, that she had always tried to do good, and that he should have protected her from harm. It would take her a long time to learn that God does not prevent life's lessons from occurring; but what he does is help us survive them successfully. When lessons are especially tough is when we need The Teacher the most. But, Tiffany kept running out of the classroom; so the lessons kept having to repeat themselves.

Tiffany worked very hard, and by teaching herself basic computer skills and typing, she was able to work various jobs and took out student loans to start herself in college. Having learned to express her emotions through playing musical instruments and songwriting, she hoped to eventually be able to make a living with her music. She moved to Tennessee where she had been hired for an exceptional job, and rented a large house and a nanny to help with the children. When the job folded, she ended up marrying a consoling friend out of guilt, when she woke up in his bed after making her drunk one night. This man encouraged her musical talent, and she spent many lonely nights out on the road, and just as many empty ones at home. Tiffany had a measure of success in the music business, receiving a standing ovation at the Grand Ole Opry, extensive touring, some radio airplay and self-producing three albums. She divorced a second time, soon lost a second home, and dropped out of college. She spent many years working off incurred debts, and worked in numerous odd jobs.

Tiffany remained single for a long time, and after a while became engaged to another man. One month before their plans to wed, he tried to seduce her young teenage daughter. Tiffany broke off the engagement and soon became extremely sick, and was unable to continue work to support her family. She felt entirely alone and desperate. She found out that she was pregnant, and made a decision that still haunts her; she aborted the child, thinking it was the only way to continue to work to support the others. She had lost all faith in God to solve desperate situations. She felt her sin was too terrible to ever forgive, and in pain she turned her face away from him, hoping that he did not see. She had long ago stopped going to church.

Next, Tiffany moved into a relationship with a big business man who swept her off her feet, and promised to be a good provider for her and her children. By living together, she mistakenly thought that this would prevent any surprises later. After a year, they married, Tiffany still believing in God's sacred arrangement of matrimony, and having a hope for future redemption and years of wedded bliss. But, it was not to last, and Tiffany would soon become more broken than ever before.

What Tiffany didn't know, is that true surrender of the spirit is a godly sacrifice that Our Father can't ignore. Absolute vulnerability and brokenness always attracts the Lord's love and power. So, this time when God reached down to save *her, he brought her past the edge of death, let her know his true purpose for her, and baptized her with the Holy Spirit. And it changed her life for good, and forever.*

After all, he has repeatedly shown that he chooses to use the most unlikely people to give gifts to - that way no flesh can boast in his presence. And every onlooker knows - including the person anointed with the gift - that the power is not of his own accord, but by God's will. No flesh has the power to do the supernatural things that the Holy Spirit does, all to glorify The Most High!
(1 Co.1:27)

God had already laid out a wonderful possible future for her, once she had come back on track and had gotten past learning some preliminary lessons. Now, she was finally ready to move forward to the next lessons...using the gifts she had been given as an adopted daughter of the King and co-heir of the Kingdom. She realized she was precious and had been bought with a high price, and vowed to show her gratitude by love and obedience in anyway she could.

Tiffany wasn't feeling worthless anymore, and she definitely wasn't alone. She knew The One who really counted was always watching over her shoulder, and whatever was for the Highest Good in her spirit journey would be presented to her. As Tiffany surrendered her free will to His Will, she had a knowing faith that God would be directing her steps from supernatural places as the Holy Spirit manifested his glory. A new adventure had begun. A calling was heard. And peace beyond all thought was gained!

Tiffany was now happier than ever before, and was able to look back on all the lessons learned and thank God for them, knowing that everything was necessary to get to where she was now. By living in judgment herself, she has learned to become the non-judgmental channel that he requires for the Holy Spirit to do his healing work, having learned the lesson of forgiveness. She knows that the love of the Most High does not discriminate against those who are repentant sinners; and that no prejudicial barriers exist regarding religious affiliation, race, gender, social standing or financial ability.

Even when she didn't know what to ask for, God gave to Tiffany her life's work. Also, she is making a better 'movie' for when she comes before the Presence of God again. Plus she's sharing the gifts our Father freely gives to those he wishes to. Tiffany says a prayer of thanks everyday for that lightning bolt that came out of the sky – because when she was stubborn and striking out, he stepped in and struck her down!

CHAPTER 3

Prayer as Directed Energy
Free Godly Gifts, with Responsibilities

God. Man. God's relationship to man. Man's relationship to God and all that he has created. The very first book of the Bible, Genesis, meaning "origin," sets the tone for the entire revealing of God to mankind. We see the story of creation, how the angels applauded God for the splendor he had made, how everything was systematic and existed as an integral part of something else that had gone on before. We see animals and plants, and man and woman, neither sex exalted above the other, both made in the image of God, with the ability to reflect Godly characteristics. What else do we see?

We see Adam and Eve walking and working in the garden. They do not have on any clothes, and they are without shame. And what else are we seeing? What is this! "Then the man and his wife *heard the sound of the Lord God as he was walking in the garden in the cool of the day..." (Ge.3:8)*

They *heard* the sound! God was *walking as a man does.* Crunching leaves, breaking small twigs, stepping on rocks. *In the cool of the day*, before the sun went down, the One who lit the molten lava of the sun, the One who can hold the expanse of the known and unknown universes in his hands, the One that never had a beginning and will never have an end, *came to visit and just say "Hi!"*

God wanted their companionship. He was complete in himself; he did not *need* us. But, similar to a happy couple who chooses to share their love by bringing children into the world, *God wanted to share his joy!* What happened next?

By this time, Adam and Eve were already hiding. God knew what had happened, but he left it up to his kids to "come clean" and confess. He reached out to them, *he called to them, he walked over to them and he spoke to them face to face. God to Man. Man to God.* "The Lord called to the man, "Where are you?" (Ge. 3:9)

We know the rest of the story - how the kids blamed each other and how the neighborhood bully pushed his way into it. How God had to be a good father and tell them the repercussions of their behavior and banish them into the corner on a *big* "time out." Understanding God as Father in this most real and basic sense helps us recognize and identify what has happened in our family history, and what our place in that family is.

As you know, this is greatly simplified; but the point here is to see, feel and hear God in the original and One-to-one way he had *first intended*. There were no certain buildings that needed to be entered to access God. There were no special emblems or symbols that needed to be carried, worn, eaten or bowed to. There was no formal ritual needed to approach God. *There was no religion.* What was there?

There was trust. There was fellowship and time taken out of busy schedules to be together *every day*. It was working together for the higher good. *It was communication and seeking each other out.* It was family.

God is the same today. (Isa.45:5,6) He desires us to call him Daddy. He wants us to find time to say "Hi" and talk to him! Like all parents (remember we are made in his character likeness) we don't want our kids coming to see us *only* when they need something. When we see our dear Sammy only when he wants to borrow money or get the keys to the car, we don't really feel loved. Just used. Maybe we even feel resentful. We might even start occupying ourselves with other things when we see Sammy heading in our direction. It is not that we *don't* want Sammy to have the things that he desires, but it sure would go a long way if he would just come to talk and visit with us now and then, without having an agenda...

The same is true of our Heavenly Father. Do we only go to him only when we want to ask for things? Is that showing him love? No! Even those who have never chosen to look for God, or have actively rebelled, often will turn tearfully to God in times of peril. As the saying goes, "there are no atheists on a sinking ship." What do *you* talk to God about? When?

- **PRAYER God-Spot: The Grace of Direct Access.** *Know that* everything *that you ask, if it be according to God's Will (for the Highest Good)* will be answered. *All of these other God-Spot suggestions are just a tool to help us ask what we need to know and be sensitive to the answers.* **Prayer is one of the greatest gifts we have been given – without using this gift, we will not have access to any of the others!** *If we are in a state of "non-ego" before God, and are humbly submitting ourselves to him to accomplish His Will as his vessel, he will shower us with answers, ability, and added responsibility. Utilize your prayers for praise everyday; and do not push in your prayers for a very specific result – have faith that he knows the timing and best outcome for all those involved. We are just hand-made instruments in his symphony orchestra, hoping to stay in tune and interpret the musical arrangements placed in front of us to the best of our ability. He knows that we are imperfect and will make many mistakes; God forgives us much easier than we forgive ourselves. If we use our gifts for the intended betterment of His Kids (humankind) and His Creation (the earth), then he will keep training us with patience and new opportunities. We can have faith that even in our imperfection our efforts become a beautiful melody of love,* *floating gently upward to God, through the power of the Holy Spirit and the grace of our Redeemer Christ Jesus.*

Most churches and buildings of worship around the world today are not much more than a place where his kids go with long lists of "I wants." Whether they believe in the concept of "Santa Claus" or not, they often treat God the same way. They want to scamper up onto his lap, even if they have to push and shove someone else out. Maybe they will give him a fake hug now and then; but it is really just a ploy to "butter him up" and to tell their latest demands. How sad that often the personal religion of choice that spans all languages and cultures has one central theme…"I want."

But our Father beckons us to climb up into his arms for Unconditional Love, so he can hold us as gently as a snowflake on his outstretched palm. He wants us to cuddle and melt into his layered robes like a kitten does on a warm window shelf. It is his desire that we are not separated any longer. He wants us to know the Real Him. Are you ready? Or, are you only willing to see God in the parameters of what you were taught? What if God was different than that? Could you accept it? Do you really know the Person that you are talking to? Do you feel you are being listened to – and are able to listen to him in return?

God As Companion

God is the Patriarch of our family. Here is God in his original purpose, seeking us out. He wants to walk with us, and speak to us face to face, without our hiding. We each have the opportunity to be in a symbolic Garden of Eden; we make the choice everyday to go do our own thing or 'hang out' with God. If we do make the choice to visit, will we use our connection time with him as an excuse to whine, cry, beg and complain? Or, will we take the "I" out of it all and allow the "peace of God that excels all thought" to overtake us as our soul sings out in praise and magnification of his name?

In coming before God, approach him with openness and humility. You will experience genuine warmth and love being reflected back to you. A relationship has begun, between you and the Greatest Being in the universe. Treat it well!

Prayer is an extraordinary opportunity. It still amazes me that such a powerful connection with the Divine is available to all of us at a seconds notice, simply by our own *intention and desire.* It is our "cell phone" that has no busy signal, and never goes out of range. Sometimes, however, there is "static" in the line, which is made on our side. Clear reception has to do with our true reasons for "dialing up."

Use of Prayer in the Bible

James 5:13 says, "Is any one of you in trouble? He should *pray*. Is anyone happy? Let him sing songs of praise. Is any one of you sick? He should call the elders of the church to *pray* over him and anoint him with oil in the name of the Lord. And the *prayer* offered in faith will make the sick person well; the Lord will raise him up. If he has sinned, he will be forgiven. Therefore confess your sins to each other and *pray* for each other so that you may be healed. The *prayer* of a righteous man is powerful and effective."

Jesus is the number one example we have of Godly prayer in the Scriptures. His entire life was lived in an *undertone of prayer*, both silent and audible. Jesus often left to go to a *solitary place* to pray, sometimes even getting up early in the morning while it was still dark to do so. (Mk. 1:35) It was his custom. At another time, he "went up on a mountainside by himself to pray. When evening came, he was there alone." (Mt. 14:23)

Jesus also went to a quiet part of the garden to pray the night that he was given to the soldiers to be taken to Gethsemane: "he fell with his face to the ground and prayed." (Mt. 26:39) He prayed all the time, including speaking to his Father from the cross, "...forgive them, for they know not what they do." (Lk.23:34) And he told the disciples that night to continue to "Pray that you will not fall into temptation." (Lk.22:40)

His disciples were chosen through prayer, and all of his disciples were taught to pray, and to teach others to pray also. Jesus taught "The Lord's Prayer" as a good example of how to address priorities in the flow of prayer - the sanctification of God's name and his Divine qualities being first. (Mt. 6:9-13).

All throughout time, prayer was the link to call upon God. Moses, Abraham, Isaiah, John the Baptizer, all the folk of old used prayer for communication, including those in the New Testament. It was their lifeline, and the only way they could fulfill their missions given to them by God. They needed to keep those lines open, and their ears sensitive.

"And when you *pray*, do not be like the hypocrites, for they love to *pray* standing in the synagogues and on the street corners to be seen by men. I tell you the truth, they have received their reward in full. But when you *pray*, go into your room, close the door and *pray* to your Father, who is unseen. Then your Father, who sees what is done in secret, will reward you. And when you *pray*, do not keep on babbling like pagans, for they think they will be heard because of their many words. Do not be like them, for your Father knows what you need before you ask him." (Mt. 6:5-8)

We are admonished to pray in behalf of others, and to ask for their prayers for us, too, including prayers for the governmental authorities, (Ezr. 6:10) the peace of towns and cities, (Ps. 122:6) and for those who persecute us. (Mt. 5:44)

"Brothers, *pray* for us." (1 Th. 5:25) "I urge you, brothers, by our Lord Jesus Christ and by the love of the Spirit, to join me in my struggle by praying to God for me." (Ro. 15:30)

We are also encouraged to pray for *ourselves* (another example from Jesus). Please take the time to read John 17:6-25 where Jesus is in prayer to his Father, and eloquently prays for himself and his followers, with glowing terms of endearment, love and complete trust. This is truly the "Lord's Prayer."

Do Not Doubt

We are told not to doubt, for that shows lack of faith in God's desire or ability to answer us. "But when he asks, he must believe and not doubt, because he who doubts is like a wave of the sea, blown and tossed by the wind. That man should not think he will receive anything from the Lord, he is a double-minded man, unstable in all he does." (James 1:6,7) On the other hand, we are told, *faith* is the "assured expectation of things not yet beheld." (Heb. 11:1)

The word "Amen" means "And it shall be," or "So be it." When we end our prayers this way, we are saying that we *know* that we have been heard, and expect a result. It is our natural impulse to speak with authority, for God's word has power. We can have enough faith and knowledge about our Dad that the *Highest Good* for all concerned will be accomplished, at the *perfect time* for it. We need not wonder about it or doubt. Prayer is a gift of God, and by communicating with him everyday he will teach us how to speak, and how to listen. But, we must put forth the effort necessary to set aside time everyday for this discipline. We must cooperate with the gift. And he will change us, and open us up, through prayer.

"Have faith in God," Jesus answered. "I tell you the truth, if anyone says to this mountain, 'Go, throw yourself into the sea,' and does not doubt in his heart but believes that what he says will happen, it will be done for him. Therefore I tell you, whatever you ask for in prayer, believe that you have received it, and it will be yours." (Mk. 11:22-24)

Often you hear people put a "safety clause" in their prayers. They say "*if* it's your will," which could actually lay blame on God if the prayer is not answered within the time and way the one praying thinks it should! This type of praying is not honest nor effective, and may make people wonder if the God of Love may actually have a desire to *not* always have the will to help us. A better way to speak is: "as God Wills," or "God's Will be done." (Jas. 4:13-17)

Prayer is a time when we can close down the five senses and focus in on our receptive abilities, on our waiting on God. We talk, and he listens. He talks, and we listen. Real communication!

Where to Pray, & When?

In the scriptures, the Spirit of God said to Moses from the burning bush: "Take off your sandals, for the ground on which you are standing is Holy ground." (Ex. 3:5) And, in the temple in the wilderness, there were rules to be followed before entering to pray before God. In ancient times, even sacrifices were made, which were symbolic of various things. Coming before the Presence is always considered a time to offer respect, praise, confession, humility and ask for Godly interaction in our lives. Are we coming to him with the sacrifice of a pure heart? Are our motives unselfish?

"To some who were confident of their own righteousness and looked down on everybody else, Jesus told this parable: "Two men went up to the temple to pray, one a Pharisee and the other a tax collector. The Pharisee stood up and prayed about himself: 'God, I thank you that I am not like other men – robbers, evildoers, adulterers – or even like this tax collector. I fast twice a week and give a tenth of all I get.' "But the tax collector stood at a distance. He would not even look up to heaven, but beat his breast and said, 'God, have mercy on me, a sinner.' "I tell you that this man, rather than the other, went home justified before God. For everyone who exalts himself will be humbled, and he who humbles himself will be exalted." (Lk. 18:9-14)

There is a snare that we must not fall into, and it has to do with our habit of doing things. If you feel you *need* crosses, incense, a special chair, no sharp noises, etc. to be able to successfully pray to God, you are limiting yourself. You are making a beautifully simple process *unnecessarily cumbersome.* You're also setting yourself up for doubt and failure. By adding all these trappings of "special needs" before you can pray, *you end up creating reasons why it won't work.* Perhaps you couldn't find the right candle to burn, perhaps the door to the church was locked. Do you let your own religious customs come between you and God? Know that you can come to him within *any* circumstance and under *any* condition. Anytime and anywhere! Prayer is our lifeline to God - even in the lion's den, (Da. 6:1-28) or the furnace's mouth. (Da. 3:1-30)

Free Godly Gifts, with Responsibilities

As we have already seen, prayer *is the trunk of the tree that allows the branching forth of the fruit of Divine Gifts. As we increase in our awareness and ability to be a useful vessel, we acknowledge that with those added gifts come added responsibilities.*

Jesus told a story about a man who gave money to his servants to invest for him while he was out of town on business. To ten servants he each gave a coin. One servant earned ten more coins with his coin, and the master said to him "Well done, my good servant! Because you have been trustworthy in a very small matter, take charge of ten cities." Another servant had earned five with his one coin, and the master said, "Take charge of five cities." Then another servant came and said "Sir, here is your coin; I have kept it laid away in a piece of cloth. I was afraid of you, so I hid it. Here is your coin back." The master replied that the servant was wicked, should have at least put it in a bank where it would've gained interest, and had the coin taken away and given to the man who already had ten. Those standing by complained "Sir! He already has ten!" And the master told them "I tell you that to everyone who has, more will be given, but as for the one who has nothing, even what he has will be taken away." (Luke 19:11-26)

Think about what Jesus is saying here. If we do not take care of the gifts we have, *they will be taken away.* Also, *if we* use our gifts wisely, more will be added to them. *More responsibilities, yes, and more blessings too!* God expects us to use our talents so that they multiply. *Each of us is held accountable before God for what we do with those gifts.* Remember, please, that we are not just talking about the special gifts that God gives to his servants, but even the gift of our "breath of life."

"My Power is Made Perfect in Weakness"

Many servants of God have some sort of physical weakness that they must endure as they worship their Father. Even Paul, whom God used to heal others of their problems and even at times to even resurrect from the dead, was left with a health problem. He stated, "To keep me from becoming conceited because of these surpassingly great revelations, there was given me a thorn in my flesh, a messenger of Satan, to torment me. Three times I pleaded with the Lord to take it away from me. But he said to me, "My Grace is sufficient for you, for my power is made perfect in weakness." Therefore I will boast all the more gladly about my weaknesses, so that Christ's power may rest on me." (2 Cor.12:7,8) Even though we may have a treacherous mountain to climb, pray continuously. It makes the climb more bearable. Remember, it is not the easy walks of the meadow, but in climbing the mountain that makes you strong!

Even in financial or legal struggles, we need to maintain vigilant prayer: "Then Jesus told his disciples a parable to show them that they should always pray and not give up. He said: "In a certain town there was a judge who neither feared God nor cared about men. And there was a widow in that town who kept coming to him with the plea, 'Grant me justice against my adversary.' For some time he refused. But finally he said to himself, 'Even though I don't fear God or care about men, yet because this widow keeps bothering me, I will see that she gets justice, so that she won't eventually wear me out with her coming!" And the Lord said, "Listen to what the unjust judge says. And will not God bring about justice for his chosen ones, who cry out to him day and night? Will he keep putting them off? I tell you, he will see that they get justice, and quickly…" (Lk. 18:1-8)

1 Thessalonians 5:16 says, "Be joyful always; pray continually; give thanks in all circumstances, for this is God's will for you in Christ Jesus."

God Often Starts the Communication First

How has God communicated with you in the past? Have you recognized the times that he was trying to start a conversation with you? Most of us have been taught that we need to approach God first, before he will answer, guide or direct us. But, how many people do you know who have had a God-Initiated Supernatural Occurrence so dramatic that it shaped their lives from that point on? Are you one of them who acknowledged the knock when Daddy came visiting? Did you open the door and recognize it as being him?

Often he will keep knocking, and we fearfully refuse to open the door, or we just don't hear it. Yet, there are so many lessons we could be learning in our individual spirit journeys, guidance and directions that he wants us to take, opportunities he doesn't want us to miss. He endeavors to "keep the lines open" to us, an easy accomplishment if we are on the other end of the "prayer phone" actively listening and talking in return. But, he will also use a variety of means, "faxes, telegrams and e-mails" to get through to us when we are not "on the phone" with him. Like a Father will go through just about anything to make sure his kids are O.K., and keep in touch with them, so it is with Ours.

Falling in Love with God

I remember seeing on TV a music concert where the performers on stage were falling backwards into the audience. Standing straight up they would fall off the stage and onto the crowd; multitudes of hands catching and supporting them as they safely and quickly slid across the top of the people, hand over hand, to unknown destinations. The band members had total faith and dependence on these strangers to not drop them and to provide for their safety. Do we have faith like this in the Almighty God who made heaven and earth? Will you close your eyes in faith and totally surrender yourself, allowing God to hold you up in mid-air? Will you have the confidence in him that he has in you? When you see your life path going to unknown destinations, will you have the confidence to rely on his wisdom and know that there is a reason for it? What are you teaching your children? Do they have a secure knowledge of God's "support system?"

Children in the Light

We have a divine commission with regards to our children. We are to nurture them, taking care of them in every way, and give them love. We are also required to teach them what we know. Are you encouraging them to pray? Are you teaching them about God?

"Love the Lord your God with all your heart and with all your soul and with all your strength. These commandments that I give you today are to be upon your hearts. Impress them on your children. Talk about them when you sit at home and when you walk along the road, when you lie down and when you get up." (De.6:5,7)

We are to imitate the children in their innocence and lack of prejudice. We are to be teachable. The connection with God comes so much more natural to children, and that seed needs to be planted at the earliest possible age, so they are aware of Divine Guidance in their daily lives, and have confidence and a sense of security even when they are away from your protection.

"Be imitators of God, therefore, as dearly loved children." (Eph. 5:1)

Family mealtime is a wonderful way to develop good prayer habits in your children, letting them hear your heartfelt connection to God, and alternating in turn by also hearing theirs. Make a habit of sitting down as a family to eat. Buy out the time for it. This is one of the sacrifices we make to God, so that our own prayers will be unencumbered.

"Be very careful, then, how you live – not as unwise but as wise, making the most of every opportunity…" (Eph.5:15)

"Train a child in the way he should go, and when he is old he will not turn from it." (Pr. 22:6)

"Similarly, encourage the young men to be self-controlled. In everything set them an example by doing what is good." (Ti. 2:6)

All children are assigned a guardian angel. Jesus said: "See that you do not look down on one of these little ones. For I tell you that their angels in heaven always see the face of my Father in heaven." (Mt. 18:10) Have you ever wondered if the "invisible friend" your child has could be an angel, or a spirit? Often we as children are repeatedly told that what we see doesn't exist, and that we are foolish to believe in things we can't see. *Yet, aren't these the same sensitivities that we as adults are trying to learn now?* Isn't it better to encourage your child not to "grow out of it" at all?

God has used various means to communicate with children in the past – and continues to do so today! They are very good receptors. My earliest experience with the Supernatural Power of God was when he sent protection for me as a child. How many unproductive years were wasted in the middle part of my life, *when I had believed the lie that God doesn't interact with people today,* and stopped believing, refused to see, and plugged my ears to Divine direction! I have so many years now to make up. He has been so patient!

Monster Waves in Mexico – The Vision of St. Christopher

I had grown up around water – one of my first memories was learning to swim. When I was two years old, we had lived in Vista, California, where I was born. Father had built a pool onto the house and enclosed it. At the time, he worked for the "Vista Press" newspaper and would hold pool parties for the delivery boys.

I had been given an inflatable ring that went around my belly, and without my knowledge, my parents had been letting the air out, little-by-little, until it was totally flat. The fear I felt that day as the ring was removed, and I was told I could swim without it, is one of my earliest memories. I cried and cried, afraid I would drown. It takes strong emotions to actively remember events from that young of an age. I remember keeping my eyes as wide open as I could, and struggling toward my father a few feet away. I made it! I wasn't going to drown! My joy now was swimming all the time; and I remember pulling the rope on an inflatable boat around the pool, with the newspaper boys in it cheering me on!

Water was my natural element, I felt free in it, almost like I could fly. I still feel that way over forty years later, and that's the reason I became a certified scuba diver when I was just sixteen. Swimming produces such freedom of movement, in time and space, in complete weightlessness.

I was a tender ten years old when my folks put their camper upon the truck and we headed to sunny Mexico, and Mexican beaches. In the ocean, there are waves, and there are WAVES. Being very young, I don't remember where exactly we were in Mexico – but it was a beautiful place with a long strip of powdery sand and a very wide beach. There was a restaurant with palm fronds hanging over the side, built with poles and not much else. Chickens and dogs ran wild and needed to be constantly shooed off while a person ate.

I remember the waves that morning being large, and they progressed from there. Mother would usually occupy herself on the beach, father would be with her, or in the water himself. I was left to do my own thing, which usually was "catching waves." I was not afraid, although looking back I should have been. To this day I am sure (because of my early lack of supervision) I have been overly cautious at times with my own children, watching them too closely; whether they wanted it or not!

On that particular day I remember diving through the waves and bobbing up on the other side, surrounded by six or eight other kids, we were laughing and playing. Slowly they all left, and I was alone. I wanted to stay longer - I loved the feel of my body being lifted high in the water as the wave crested, and then diving back down and through again.

Facing the waves, and looking out toward the sea, I had no idea everyone had been waved out – and that the waves had become huge. There was a storm coming. I stayed in, realizing the waves were more than I had ever experienced before. But when I turned and looked toward shore, I didn't see my folks waving me out, or anyone else, so I stayed. In my child's mind, the waves were 20 feet tall. I don't know what they *really* were. But I do know the sound of the crashes were deafening, and I had to time it just right to not get caught at the bottom of a curl – I knew that hundreds of pounds of water corkscrewing my body into the sand would not be a good feeling. There was one particular wave that was going to break hard for me, and I had to wait to time it so I could hold my breath long enough to go through.

As I was gauging it, and it was cresting, I saw a vision of a man's huge face in the curl! With long thick hair like a woman's all around him, his eyes looked straight at me; I dove under, and the wave crashed over and was gone.

I felt a combination of being scared about what I had seen, and exhilaration. The face had been *kind and smiling*. I thought he wanted to tell me something - maybe I should get out of the water? I was starting to get tired now anyway. What would my folks say if I told them about the face? I ended up waiting thirty years to tell them the story. Seldom do people believe a kid, and how the kids know it! But, I would never forget that day – *this was my first time to see a Supernatural Occurrence. But was it from God?*

Swimming back towards the beach, I noticed a Mexican man and his son on shore staring at me. When I was about waist deep in the surges, the boy came out into the water to meet me. He kept looking me straight in the eyes and didn't say a word. He slowly reached out his hand; he wanted to give me something. Into my palm he placed a medallion of St. Christopher and closed my fingers tightly around it. I smiled and thanked him and waved to the older man on shore, who did not move or give any reaction, he just kept staring. The boy backed away from me, keeping eye contact almost to shore, then turned and hurried back to his father.

I put the silver chain around my neck and lifted up the medallion to look at the picture. It was a man with a *kind face and thick long hair*, in water up to his hips. He was safely carrying a child on his shoulders, and a cross was in the air beside the child. It made me smile, the vision had been from God! And now I knew the name of whom I had seen in the water - St. Christopher - and the Lord had even given me a souvenir to remember it all by!

I wore the medallion day and night, for over seven years. It was sand-cast and made of silver. It was precious to me. But I ended up giving it to a friend I was studying the Bible with; and she destroyed it. The religion she was affiliated with felt it was idol worship and that I was "marking myself for destruction" by wearing it. I still think of that day with sad regrets, when I took it off my neck, never to see it again. I do have a school photo of it hanging proudly, the chain shortened for the special event, the silver glint matching my full set of braces, as I smiled proudly!

Even as a child, I learned many things from that experience, things that I would later call, Life Lessons:

(1). When we are alone, even as children, we are never alone! God assigns Protectors to watch out for us, and validates it when they are from him.

(2). Complete strangers of different races and languages can communicate with us when God puts his message in their hearts, without a word even being spoken.

(3). Well-meaning religions can step in between us and God, often belittling or even condemning our own direct experiences with the Lord.

These life lessons could have helped me with many trials and struggles that I would face in later life. But this experience, even though being one of empirical knowledge (first-person experience) was pushed aside by those that I did tell it to as being a "child's fantasy," and even "evil." I *pray* that you will allow your children the Reality of God and Divine Intervention in their lives!

CHAPTER 4

Tools to Widen Our Divine Connection
A Buffet of Suggestions to Fill the Hungry "God-Spot"

The dinner needs to be cooked, the clothes washed, the kids fed and homework done. The stresses of everyday work, finances and relationships often make us feel overwhelmed. But when life seems to be crushing in around us, and there isn't enough time for anything, *that's when we need the God-Spot Connections the most.*

Utilizing the tools below, you will be able to make your life happier and you'll feel more in control, with less stress. Browse through this buffet and pick and choose items that will work with what you want to accomplish, in a way that you feel most comfortable in your *Personal Connection* with the Divine.

Ritual imparts sacredness to our lives. Birthdays, anniversaries and weddings are some of these wonderful celebrations that give us order and help us focus. Ceremonies and daily habits help us prioritize and re-evaluate our lives into a more meaningful and organized way. So, the time spent here in this chapter can save much time and wasted effort later down the line.

Many of the rituals listed below are considered sacred to those who practice them, and many of those who practice them are esteemed spiritual leaders, advisors and ministers. But, please keep in mind that your own personal adaptation or versions will *almost always* be successful. It has to do with *intention, discipline* and the heart-condition of *love!*

These suggestions are just man-made tools to help us "drill a hole through the Plexiglas," helping us to see more clearly our God Connection.

Also, keep in mind that the *tool* is not to be worshipped; all glory goes to the One and Only God. These things are just to be used as beacons, centennials and sign posts pointing to "The One Who Causes to Become."

Understand that you *do not need an official title or credentials* to become really close to the Lord. These are pieces of paper bestowed by men unto men – and they are often only a way to appease mankind's social and educational requirements. Only the Lord knows the heart, and he bestows his blessings, *true ordination* and wisdom, on those who hear his call and respond humbly. So, please officially "In-Power" yourself to customize these tools as you see fit; search for more on your own; develop your personal link with God, and in doing so see His Image and Likeness in *your* life.

Creating Sacred Space

Create a *Sacred Space* to go to when you need to be With Him. This can come in a variety of forms. Having a special place to visit will train your mind to focus much more easily, and your body to relax more quickly when you come to that place.

Arrange an *Inside Altar* in the corner of your bedroom or private office. Place a pretty piece of cloth and meaningful objects there – a favorite toy from your childhood, an artist's rendition of Christ, or a photo of your favorite place in the woods. Candles and incense help create a wonderful mood, which can be subtly altered by aroma choice or color of candle. Use simple things; a stone found on a trip to the mountains, a wooden cross hanging on a string, or a tiny hummingbird nest your child gave you. All things which hold a special place in your heart, inspire you, or bring back happy memories. The best times in our lives fill us with Love, and are a reflection of his Godly qualities at that moment. This sacred place should make you feel peace and love by just stepping into its boundaries. That feeling will help open you to accept even more love, from its Boundless Source.

Arrange an *Outside Altar.* You may want to gather and arrange some beautiful *Stones* or *Driftwood* into a circle or various shapes. You may want to use *Statues* (of saints, if you are Catholic), of various concrete animals or the renderings of angels. Hang vines and flowers, herbs and plants; wind chimes, fish ponds, or a trickling splash of a waterfall. A secret path lined with redwood chips or white granite pebbles might be intriguing. Some gardens have a gazebo set up as a sacred space – complete with overstuffed pillows and the ability to turn on soft, inspirational music. Be as imaginative as you wish! The first job mankind had was managing a garden!

If you find your inside altar becomes the new *favorite place* for the cat to curl up - and the squirrels outside *just love* what you've done with the place - just consider it a blessing! There is something there that attracts them as a place of comfort without fear, and I personally think that some *animals* could qualify as a "mobile" sacred space! The tranquility experienced with them lying close beside us often becomes extra-ordinary. Animals have a really good *Natural Connection* with God. Perhaps it's linked to their ability to give *Unconditional Love…*

Know that your sacred space is yours to visit whenever you wish. If you are away from the physical destination of it, you can go there with the intention of your mind, and wander through its paths in your imagination. In this way, even at the office you can relax in familiar surroundings, and no one can take this sacred time and space away from you, even in a hectic lifestyle.

Carry a Sacred Object

Carrying a *Sacred Object* with you wherever you go is like bringing your altar with you. You are never out of touch with that which is important to you: a piece of *Jewelry* from your mother or aunt; a *Medicine Bag* (don't forget the sweet scents of sage and lavender!); a *Coin* from your native homeland (or from the year you were baptized); an *Arrowhead* symbolic of spiritual wars God helps us win. Perhaps it is a carved *Wooden Object;* an *Engraved Stone* with an encouraging word on it; or a tiny, need-a-magnifying-glass-to-read-it *Bible!*

Remember when you were a kid and always got in trouble because you filled your pockets with crazy, special-only-to-you things? Here's your chance to get in touch with your 'inner child' and acknowledge the sacred at the same time. This works like tying a yellow ribbon around your finger – every time you see it or feel it in your pocket you will be reminded of the intention or memory you put with it! Have fun, it works!

Dedication

Most of the time a sacred space or object goes through a ceremony or ritual of *Sanctification* and *Dedication* before it is used. If it is a hardy object, it might literally be put through fire, ice, and water; presented to the North, South, East and West; buried for a time in the earth; or lifted above the head as an offering to God. It might be passed from hand to hand; each person saying a blessing over it as it goes around. There might be a reading of prayers, singing and dancing; fasting or feasting; anointing with oil; sprinkling with Holy Water; burning incense, or simply a moment of silence.

You can sanctify your *Home.* Invite a minister (or a person whom you know and respect to be close to the Lord) or research how to accomplish this and do it yourself. This sacred ceremony usually includes Blessing Prayers (specific to each area of the home), hiding bits of scripture (cut out from an old Bible) in unseen places, incense, sprinkling with Holy Water and Oil Anointing of door jams and windows. Sometimes it is combined with incense and smudging, especially if the history of the area is "unclean" or unknown. You may well be surprised how much "lighter" and refreshing a room can be without the residue of other people's energy tracings in it! This can also lead to an *Exorcism* of the place if an evil spirit (or even a ghost that refuses to go home) is found there. (Directions found in Connection Glossary – Deliverance from Evil)

You may want to dedicate and sanctify the *Land* your home will be built on. In a service of ground-breaking, there might be a walking out of boundaries, an invocation, song, a call and answer by a leader and the people in response.

Sometimes a *Corner Stone* is laid, with a variety of objects collected and placed in a weather-proof container inside it. Some of these items may be historical items of interest, others may be sacred objects. All should be items that reflect the people's best aspirations, hopes and dreams for the love, wisdom and Godly blessings that will be experienced in this sanctified ("set apart") new home.

Smudging and Incense

"Then the Lord said to Moses, "Take fragrant spices – gum resin…banum… and pure frankincense, all in equal amounts, and make a fragrant blend of *Incense*, the work of a perfumer. It is to be salted and pure and sacred. Grind some of it to powder and place it in front of the Testimony in the Tent of Meeting, where I will meet with you. It shall be most holy to you." (Ex. 30:34-36)

The Creator of heaven and earth asked for incense to be burned when he came to visit. And in Revelation 5:6-8, "golden bowls of incense" are likened to "the prayers of the saints." Indeed, during my NDE, misty wafts of prayers came up from the earth just like incense, and were drawn into the bright Presence of God.

At the Israelite ceremony of the Day of Atonement, instituted by God at the tabernacle in the wilderness, burning selected plants and herbs protected the High Priest from being killed! Once a year, the High Priest entered the Most Holy Place carrying a thick smoking censer of incense. Today we might call this *Smudging*. It was commanded to be *so thick* that the sacred objects of God, and His Presence, *could not be seen!* "He is to put the incense on the fire before the Lord, and the smoke of the incense will conceal the atonement cover above the Testimony, so that he will not die." (Le. 16:13)

It is interesting to note that a cord was attached to one of the priest's ankles, so if something went wrong during the fulfillment of the ceremony, the dead body could then be pulled back out under the curtain. "No one can see God and live." Smudging in ancient times meant the difference between life and death!

Smudging is also a Native American tradition used for consecration. Using a mixture of sage, juniper, sweet grass, or even just sage alone, the adobe or home is walked through from room to room, all doors open. Traditionally, a large abalone shell is used as the "golden bowl" and an eagle or turkey feather is used to waft the smoke up and out. Saturating the area asks for blessings of God to be there and purifies the home.

Meditation – Active Listening in the Stillness

"I will sing to the Lord all my life; I will sing praise to my God as long as I live. May my *Meditation* be pleasing to him, as I rejoice in the Lord." (Ps. 104:24-34)

Meditation is a common tool that many cultures use, for people to know themselves and to get close to God. Through meditation, awareness can be nurtured and trained. *Sense the stillness, and the stillness will awaken all your senses.* Sister Briege McKenna, a Catholic nun and healer, in her book *Miracles Do Happen,* said: "the discipline of sitting before the Lord is very important. It is only when your spirit is *still* and when the ears of your spirit are *open* that you can really hear the Lord and experience the wisdom and insights that come from the Holy Spirit." *She consistently puts aside three hours every day for this discipline!*

Even twenty minutes of prayer and meditation can noticeably benefit your life. The calmness, serenity, and peace you will exude may make your friends wonder what vacation you've just come back from! Besides the spiritual aspects, physical benefits abound also. Meditation has been attributed to lowering blood pressure, easing migraines, calming colitis and curing a host of other ailments.

Go to your sacred spot or a quiet chair and try to make sure there will be no distractions. Turn off the phones (including cell) and get Fluffy and Junior (your animal and human babies) out of the area. You may need to turn on some "white noise" if you are easily distracted by sound. This can be accomplished by turning on a fan, air conditioner, the TV to a non-station, or even a sound machine. *Sit* in a comfortable position. Lying down is often too conducive to sleep, unless you have a light on directly over you. Close your eyes and concentrate only on your steady heartbeat.

Now, breathe in through your nose slowly and deeply, and out through your mouth. We usually breathe too shallow - this deep breathing helps clean out stagnate air, stretch our lungs and oxygenate our blood.

Begin counting from one to ten, *starting over each time an unwanted thought crosses your mind!* Keep breathing. This may take some practice! The mind acts like a memo pad, constantly taking notes - what we need to do, what we did, what we forgot, what we need to plan...etc. Your job is to observe this taking place, *but not actively participate in it.* Just let it go, without sorting it out, without making decisions or controlling it. As you get better at quieting your mind, it will be easier to "take a break" from that pressure or stress whenever you wish to – "let go and let God."

Now, think upon *one word* that brings you close to Him, his awesome creation and wondrous works. Let that word absorb into your very being. Sometimes this is called a *mantra.* Is it "Love?" "Bliss?" "Family?" *Feel* every facet of the image that one word brought up. Hold it like a diamond in the palm of your hand, turning it this way and that in the light, seeing how every facet reflects the light just a little differently.

"I will *meditate* on all your works and consider all your mighty deeds." (Ps. 77:12)

There are numerous methods for meditation – here is another fun one, called "The Glass Elevator." After you have done your relaxed breathing and closed your eyes, imagine seeing a beautiful elevator in your mind. See yourself walking into this elevator and pushing the button for the first floor. Imagine the elevator rising and then stopping, and the door opening onto a beautiful scene of color – just one color. This first floor has *everything* in the color *red*. There are red balloons, red roses, ladies in red hats and soft flowing red dresses. There are red cardinals in the trees and even the trees and grasses themselves are a variant of red – there is shimmering red, muted red and dark red and light red. Feel and breathe in the red, knowing that every color is special and has a unique place in your life, with its own vibrational qualities.

After you have spent time here, imagining how all five of your senses feel, turn and walk back into the elevator, say "thank you" for the experience and close the door. Push the next button and go up another floor. Do this with each one of these colors: *red, orange, yellow, green, blue, indigo, and purple.* Be creative! Now, at the very top floor of these colors, past the purple, go to a place of *pure white light.* White light is a combination of all the spectrums, where all the colors converge into one. Open the door and go out. You see everything in white, with luminous, iridescent hints of color reflecting off the glow here and there. This is a most scared place! Here is where you can open your mind to be very receptive, and hear most clearly the accurate will of God, or what God wants us to hear from his messenger angels.

This is a place of connection, and of prophecies. One of the things that you may want to do here is ask questions and listen for the answers regarding your own physical body. Go from your head downward, asking the questions that you want to know: Am I healthy here; is there a structural problem (bones); what about chemical imbalances; hormones? How do the cells look; are there any tumors; what about scar tissue; is there anything that I should have a medical test for? Ask anything you want to know. Write down the answers. You can refer to them later, and see if you come up with the same information again when you visit the same places.

These answers are not going to be remembered long; since they don't *originate* in your own brain, but are simply sent through. So, you will not *retain* them in your synapse response. When you feel strongly enough about it, go get a medical test to confirm your answers. *Have faith that God wants to give you this information!*

"Ask and it will be given to you; seek and you will find; knock and the door will be opened to you. For everyone who asks receives; he who seeks finds; and to him who knocks, the door will be opened." (Mt. 7:7,8)

Know that this is a "place of white light," a Divine Connection with God that you can pull around yourself and your loved ones whenever you see fit. It is a protection and a blessing. When you are done meditating, *slowly* come back down the elevator, noticing the different colors of the buttons but not pushing them, yet taking the time to remember a few of the qualities of the stop you made there. Notice how you feel differently about God in your life now, and notice how that the God-Spot has filled up a little bit more. You are taking important steps in your Spirit Journey, and the "seeker will indeed find!"

There are many good books on the market about meditation. What I have listed are just a few basic techniques with which to start. This tool comes in all sizes, shapes and measurements. And, if used properly, I think you will find it includes a pretty good warranty!

Visual Imagery - Using the Five Senses

Sight, sound, smell, taste, touch – all of the five senses are designed to transport you into the true essence of this life's moment, grounding you into reality. But, the strong reactions you get from those same senses are what also make the strongest memories. Now, use these same senses to transcend past and present, and also allow them to take you into a future of your own making. What do you see? What would you create? You can use your imagination, or *Visual Imagery* to guide your senses.

Here is one way. Remember a happy time from your past. 'I am standing in a shallow mountain stream, the rocks are smooth under my feet and the water feels ice-cold up to my ankles (touch). I see the sparkles of sunlight dancing on the water, and the swaying evergreen trees in the meadow (sight). I smell the rich warm earth on the breeze (smell). The birds twitter with expectant glee from their new nests (hear). I bend down to the water and cup my hands, bringing the cold sweetness to my mouth (taste).' Are you there?

It may take a while to be able to really *sense* more than *one* or *two* of these things at a time, but the more you practice, the better and easier it will become. It is similar to being absorbed in a good book. Maybe the phone rings, and it takes a moment or two for you to acknowledge it, as you "get back to reality" and grab the phone. This is because you were totally absorbed in visual imagery.

Now, imagine yourself in the presence of Absolute Love. What would that be like? What lighting is around you, what color do you see? Do you hear anything?

What about imagining yourself as a character during the human life of Jesus. Or, how about the time of opening the ark to a cleansed earth after the flood, and being one of the first humans to start all over again? How would that first gust of fresh air feel? Or maybe, what about the future? What would the earth smell like in Hawaii in 200 years? How would you interact in other people's lives? What kind of person are you, what family do you have? In all of these sensory visions, ask yourself what you would see, hear, smell, touch and taste. Have fun!

Remember the best stories to use again another time. You can repeat the same situations, or continue on from where you left off. You hold the "fairy wand" in these wanderings. Be creative! It is similar to an active day-dream, and you are in complete control.

This tool is also very useful in pain management. Use in any situation where you need or choose to preoccupy yourself. This is excellent for chronic pain and cancer patients, and for women in childbirth. Become totally absorbed.

In childbirth, you may also want to absorb yourself in different future ages of your new child's life. See yourself and the child in specific situations, and bring in all the senses. What will the first day of school be like? What about baking cookies together, what would the kitchen look like? How about your child's face? You will feel less anxiety, be less afraid, and not perceive pain as easily. Meanwhile, your body will be able to relax and do more efficiently what it is designed to do, without you interfering and tensing up unnecessarily.

If you are house-bound or confined to a wheelchair or bed, visual imagery is an excellent opportunity, along with prayer and meditation, to escape and be free! *Nothing can hold back the human heart when Spirit is active!*

Diary of Prayer & Blessings

So often we forget the good things that happen in our lives – sometimes it may feel the bad is overwhelming. Also, many of us have little self-esteem, and don't actually accept deep into our hearts and minds the compliments and goodwill that others give us. Often, we don't even accept that God actively works in our lives! This is why it is so important to keep a *Diary of Prayer and Blessings*.

"This is the confidence we have in approaching God; that if we ask anything according to his will, he hears us. And if we know that he hears us – whatever we ask - we know that we have what we asked of him." (1 Jo. 5:14,15)

Keeping a diary of our prayers lets us see that God is active in our affairs. Sometimes, much time goes by before the Lord answers our prayers. Sometimes this is an answer in itself. It is not because he is ignoring us; but he is the one who knows the correct time for everything to occur. *He is never late.* By keeping a diary, we can develop the heart of wisdom and patience, seeing that he works for the very best in our behalf and for others around us.

Remember the old tradition at Thanksgiving time, where all sitting at the table passed a candle around and said out loud what they were thankful for during the past year? This is the part of your diary for Blessings. Have a book *full* of blessings, and actively read them whenever you wish. It will help give you confidence and joy!

At one seminar I attended, the presenter made a very good illustration. He had a large piece of white paper hooked onto a display rack, and took a felt-tip marker and colored a small black dot in the very middle. Then, he asked the audience what they saw. They all responded that they saw a black dot. He then told the audience that what they had seen represented merely a very small fraction of the area of the paper – that they were noticing the 5% black dot and ignoring the 95% white paper. This is similar with how we often forget all the good things going on in our lives, and instead tend to look at only the bad. There is much more to focus on than just the black dot!

Book of Prayers

This is very different from a Prayer Diary. The *Book of Prayers* is a simple book of plain paper that you will be writing people's names on to which you wish to send prayers. So many times we find ourselves trying to recite the names of everyone who needs prayers, and we feel guilty if we forget one name. Also, in church, it is often disheartening to hear the announcements of people's health problems when asking for prayers in their behalf. God knows both what they, and we, need. No personal information needs to be disclosed. Truly, this is the time that we can have faith in Romans 8:26, "…the Spirit helps us in our weakness. We do not know what we ought to pray for, but the Spirit himself intercedes for us with groans that words cannot express."

Having a personal *Book of Prayer* is one way that our intentions of love and connection with our neighbor can be demonstrated. At night before we go to bed, we think of any one who has been brought to our attention who needs help. Perhaps it is someone at the church, at our work, or even on TV or in the newspaper. Write his name down in the book, each one on his own uncluttered line. Be sure to write your own name in the book too.

Hold the book between your hands, in a prayer position, and approach God. "And the prayer offered in faith will make the sick person well; the Lord will raise him up. If he has sinned, he will be forgiven." (Jas. 5:15) Pray for the nations, the government officials, for the oceans and for the earth itself. Let God know how much you care to see "His will done on earth as it is in heaven." (Mt. 6:9-13) This is a wonderful way to give God all your cares and worries, having faith that he will work "for the Highest Good" for all concerned. Let the Holy Spirit groan for you. Know that what you are doing *really* matters!

Spiritual Retreats – Church Sponsored and Self-Sponsored

How often do we get to enjoy fellowship with others, learn God's will and give praises to the King of Kings? If you crave more than two or three hours at church and don't want to go home afterwards, then perhaps an organized *Church Sponsored Spiritual Retreat* is for you. Often these are up in the mountains, or in primitive surroundings, with very organized discourses on Bible-based teachings or acceptable social and religious protocol. There is usually a modest fee, and sometimes there is a separation of the "boys" camp and the "girls" camp. It can be a good way to make friends of the same mind and thought. Very little personal study is actually accomplished; most of the learning is through lectures and discourses. Being in a group mentality, one which is structured and holds to high moral standards, can be beneficial to many people.

A *Self-Sponsored Spiritual Retreat* is more like a sabbatical. Often a person will chose to be on his own, and will choose a private place conducive to learning. This might fit for a person who hikes up a mountain with a tent, Bible and concordance for a week; or it might be a person immersed in literature at the local library for the weekend. Sometimes, a desire for fasting, deprivation and isolation accompanies the learning experience. Often a "quest" is a stimulus for the retreat, perhaps to gain balance in one's life again, or perhaps to get an answer from God on a very big decision being faced. Sometimes a person will travel to the desert, or even to another country. It is also a time of self-realization, and is conducive to personal study; although some people use the spiritual retreat time for visiting others who may have the answers they themselves are seeking.

Fasting

One of the oldest ways to get to a point of God-Connection is through *Fasting*. There are many examples of people fasting in the Bible. Jesus fasted for 40 days. Fasting was often a way of humbling oneself before God. It showed repentance for sins, was used when in need of guidance, in meditation, in prayer, and to help endure tests. There were also four annual fasts that the Jews were commanded to celebrate by way of remembering important events in their nation's history. Many different religions around the world consider abstaining from food as a way to cleanse and purify oneself before coming before the Creator. It often makes one more open to listening on a spiritual level.

In recent times, fasting has also been studied and used as a diet or health practice. There are many books on the market about the subject, and it is recommended that anyone wanting to go on a fast be thoroughly checked by his doctor first. There can be benefits, and there can be indications that some people should *not* fast at all. If you are one of those who can fast, there is a lot of time saved in the day because you are *not* buying, preparing, eating, and cleaning up after meals. I also have found fasting to be a gentle rest for the entire physical system. But, keep in mind it can also be a time of slow reflex actions, slight dizziness, and bad breath as the body breaks down ketones in the system. It is often better to fast when you are away from the high energy pace of your everyday life. Some people are more able to have lucid dreams during this time. Some have visions. Many people in the scriptures did. Each person may have a unique personal experience, and that is one of the adventures and rewards of fasting. A sabbatical is a good time to fast.

Lucid Dreaming, Divine Dreaming

Have you ever had a dream where you knew you were dreaming, so you were able to take control and change the outcome? This is called *Lucid Dreaming.* To train yourself to do this, tell yourself right before you go to sleep that you are in *total control* of your dreams. Have a method that you have thought of beforehand that lets you *know the difference between awake and asleep.* One control measure might be to look at your hands, or to look at your feet. Often in a dream you will *not* actively notice these things, or you will see them fade out or crumble away. Also, ask yourself if you remember getting out of bed that morning. Ask yourself what day and month it is. These are more details that you do not normally know in a simple dream.

All these things should act as a clue that you are dreaming. Now, with focused intention you can change your dream to be a fabulous flight of fancy – you can wave your arms and fly, dance through the water with the dolphins, go to any place that you wish by imagining yourself there. Push off from the ground and rocket yourself toward heaven. Lucid dreaming *you* are in control of.

In the scriptures *Divine Dreaming* was used by God many times to impart prophecies, guidance, give understanding, Divine favor and warnings. In these kinds of dreams *God* is in control. It was also foretold that Divine dreams would be a gift of the Holy Spirit. "I will pour out my Spirit on all people. Your sons and daughters will prophesy, your old men will dream dreams, your young men will see visions." (Joel 2:28) There is *no doubt* when God gives you a Divine dream. It is not the natural, stress-relieving dreams that filter us in and out of unconsciousness. Also, we have no control as in lucid dreaming. And, often the dream will be repeated and we will feel a great motivation connected to it.

"Then the Lord came down in a pillar of cloud...he said, "Listen to my words: 'When a prophet of the Lord is among you, I reveal myself to him in visions, I speak to him in dreams...'" (Nu. 12:5,6)

There are also admonitions in the Bible warning that not all dreams are inspired, and that we should weigh carefully what is being told, and to check that it is not against the will of God. "Diviners see visions that lie; they tell dreams that are false." (Ze.10:2) (De. 13:1-4)

There are many books on the market about how to interpret dreams. The dreams from God will not need or have an interpretation found in a book. It is a rare and different kind of dream, and you will know it when it happens to you. He will be direct, or he will create a situation whereby you will be sure to interpret the information correctly. Please keep in mind that many people put way too much weight on every dream they have, and every symbol attached to it, when actually many dreams are just the brain unwinding and sorting things out from the day.

Communion with Nature

Sit in the rain, and listen to the storm. Watch it come and go, while you remain still. There is a great feeling of accomplishment in this. Feel totally enveloped by the raw elements (not during a *lightning* storm, please!) and try not to fight it. Run the gauntlet of emotions – cool shivering, moods of fear and wonder, the exhilaration of breezes, soft rain drops on your face. See and feel the power of God, and notice how every nuance is noticed and *all your senses are alive.* When the storm is over, or it is getting dark, congratulate yourself for allowing this time to experience the rawness of his mighty power, having seen the forces of nature at its bones and sinews, and acknowledge it with thanks.

Find a clear night sky, and bring a warm blanket and hot tea. Perhaps the moon is out, perhaps it is only a sliver. Perhaps you even bring a telescope. Tonight you will commune with the heavens and try to count the colorful planets and watch for brilliant falling stars. Notice the Milky Way and any satellites zooming across the sky. See if you can pick out any constellations that you know; and realize that you and all the scientists in the world see *only a fraction* of what is to be seen. Talk to God, and listen to the causal reply as his Glory absorbs you. Ask him about your purpose in life, and for a "wake-up call" in knowing when you have been brought to it. Don't be in a hurry to leave, let yourself drift off to sleep while imagining yourself floating closer and closer to the heavens. Have the excitement of adventure that a child has on a camping trip. Be open and trusting that the heavens themselves are your security blanket, and that you are being watched with the kind eyes of angels.

Being out in the wilderness is certainly one way to see, hear and sense the qualities of God face-to-face. Camping and exploring our beautiful State and National Parks is one of the most popular ways. Often this goes hand-in-hand with spending quality time with our families. Why not add to this the dimension of learning how God has dealt with people in the past, and what choices he gives us for our future? How about hearing the voice of God by bringing along a Bible and reading it out loud every morning before breakfast? In this way you will feel a satisfied fullness in your day that cannot be compared to regular food. You are accessing another way to fill the God-Spot!

Notice the trees, put your nose in their bark, and feel the softness of their leaves between your fingers. *Really feel, hear and see everything!* When you look at the trickling mountain stream or across the meadow of yellow and pink wildflowers, breathe it all in and absorb it deep into your soul. Be in the moment. You were created to enjoy the earth, and to wonder at his marvelous designs in his handiwork. It brings you closer to The Maker. *And your appreciation brings him closer to you!*

"For since the creation of the world God's invisible qualities – his eternal power and divine nature – have been clearly seen, being understood from what has been made, so that men are without excuse." (Ro. 1:20)

Communion with Animals

Animals are excellent companions, to be sure. But, did you know that they also are more sensitive to the spirit realm than most people? *Animals* see and sense spirits very plainly. Take special notice next time when Fluffy stares at a particular corner of a room or is looking intently at the wall or ceiling. This ability of animals to sense the invisible is nothing new, and was also recorded at Numbers 22:21-33 where we read:

"When the donkey saw the angel of the Lord standing in the road with a drawn sword in his hand, she turned off the road into a field. Balaam beat her to get her back on the road…then the Lord opened Balaam's eyes, and he saw the angel of the Lord standing in the road with his sword drawn…" The angel then said, "The donkey saw me and turned away from me these three times. If she had not turned away, I would certainly have killed you by now, but I would have spared her." At one point, the angel even had the donkey *speak* to Balaam in human language, to get a Divine point across. Wow!

God has used many different supernatural tools throughout time to communicate to his people. Who are we to say he is not allowed to do anything unusual *now?* But, whether animals talk to us in human voice or not *doesn't stop them from communicating.* Take time to be still, and listen. Why do they bristle at one person and not another? Do they sense something that you are missing? See how they respond to us differently when we are hurt or depressed. Animals can be great companions ("mobile sacred space"), and medical studies even show physical health benefits from spending time with them. These include stimulating our immune system and lowering risk from heart attack and high-blood pressure. This is one of the reasons there are now programs in many parts of the country that bring pets into medical wards, children's hospitals and elder-care facilities.

Who of us has not felt closer to God from the back of a horse? What about watching a red-tail hawk fly, or listening to a new batch of squeaky kittens? How we react to these relationships with animals also proves to all onlookers, both human and spirit, what kind of person we *really* are on the inside. We know that animals have no voice to get us in trouble, and domestic ones are often totally dependent on us to care and feed them. Their lives are in our hands. On a global scale, so are the lives of wild animals too. How are we doing in these matters?

Animals have natural sensitivity. They give unconditional love, and know when we are sad or sick, happy or angry. Given a chance, they will touch and comfort us, or let us sense their mutual empathy and concern or joy. If we sit quietly in the wild, native animals will often get very close to us, and on occasions may accept us in their habitat as just another creature created by the Almighty Father. Feel the unity, and appreciate that we were originally made as caretakers for the animals and for the planet. Respect them, and acknowledge that they are blessed creations made by God too.

Affirmations

"In Power" yourself, and become the best you possibly can. Often, we have a tape recording in our heads playing the same messages over and over again, and that recording is not always beneficial. *Realize your full potential as a Child of God.* Because these undesirable programmed thoughts have taken a long time to be instilled, they often take a bit of time to be replaced with positive ones. Be patient and consistent. Utilizing all these concepts together will speed the process. *Incorporate all the senses to "re-train your brain."*

Write down (sense of touch) a list of positive affirmations:

(1). *"I am beautiful exactly the way I am."*
(2). *"I am worthy to be loved."*
(3). *"I deserve to be treated with dignity and respect."*
(4). *"By grace, I am worthy to receive all that God has to give me."*
(5). *"I am forgiven, and I forgive."*

Make the list as long as you like, all reflecting *positive* ideals. Now, this is the most difficult and beneficial part - *stand in front of the mirror and say them out loud!* In this way we are also using our *eyes (sense of sight)* and our *ears (sense of hearing)*. This is the way we reach our heart and mind…it is O.K. to have an emotional release, go ahead and cry if you want, let the emotions wash warm though your very soul. We all have felt pain for *such a long time*.

Our Father doesn't want us to beat ourselves up anymore - he never did.

Use the list everyday - when you first wake up in the morning, and when you retire at night. See and feel yourself as God sees you: *Unconditionally Loved!*

Deliverance and Counseling

When you feel that evil is attached to you in some way and you are constantly thinking evil thoughts and harm toward yourself or others, and can't seem to shake it, you may need deliverance and/or professional counseling. When you do not feel in control of your actions, you may need qualified clergy to pray over you and ask God to "bind" the evil affliction or command the entity to depart. Even for those with very little "schooled" knowledge, the "heart" intention of fully submitting to God's will make you a tool that God can use to free you from constriction. Read directly from the scriptures, and use authoritive, strong prayers. A Minister's Guidebook is helpful. *Very few people are actually possessed.* Most have just attracted evil to themselves from past bad decisions, and it just won't let go. The scriptures talk about evil spirits, and how God is much more powerful than they are. One part of the healing ministry given us by Jesus is the ability to banish these attachments from our lives. Believe it!

"The name of the Lord is a strong tower; the righteous run to it and are safe."
(Pr. 18:10)

"Submit yourselves, then, to God. Resist the devil, and he will flee from you."
(Jas. 4:7)

In the area of bad inclinations and lack of self-control, sometimes we need a trusted friend or respected teacher to help us see things that we may not notice by ourselves. This might be in the form of professional counseling. Find someone trained to be unbiased and able to offer all facets of available choices. A listening ear and wise counsel might also come from a respected wise friend or clergy member. Be sure to test all things you are told by your God-Given conscious and intuition. Make sure the people you trust are in Divine Communion with God – *and not working from their own ego.* You need their words to be God's words, not their own opinions. Don't let other people run your life or make all the choices for you – remember that a wise counselor merely gives you many possibilities and the known "cause and effects" for each one. You must make the ultimate decisions, since only you will be taking the full responsibilities for them. Choose wisely!

Be with Someone Dying

Dying is like a birth. There is expectation and fear, and often a knowledge that it can't be stopped or prevented. There is also wonderment along with the sadness, for it is only the physical body that dies. Crossing over is harder for those left behind than for those who go. And, it is much easier for all involved if there is a spiritual foundation, trust and friendship with God. There is a knowledge that the fullness of the God-Spot ties us directly into the main current of God's powerhouse. He knows where we are, what we are doing, because a part of us is aligned with him. Whether we are sensitive to it or not, we are all *wonderfully connected with Spirit!*

Death is a *graduation* - we have accomplished many of the life lessons that we needed to learn along the way, and others have learned from us. Be joyful for the persons who are transitioning – they will soon be experiencing one of the greatest adventures of their lives! Remember that their consciousness and personality stays intact. *You are not really losing them! You just can't see or hear them as clearly anymore!*

Being in the presence of someone who is letting go is one of the most beautiful things you can ever experience. This is truly a complete surrender and brokenness that *attracts God's love and power!* There is often a peace that transcends upon the room – similar to birds outside becoming quiet before a storm. *There is the weightiness of God in the air.* For those who are sensitive, an awareness of angelic presence can be felt. Let your hands be a healing comfort to the one crossing over, placing one on the forehead, solar plexus, or arm. Direct your thoughts to the intention of love. Continue in prayer, close your eyes and relax. You are right where you need to be, there is no greater thing that you can be doing with your time. Just allow yourself to be here, let the surrender to Grace occur, and feel the heavens open up. Being around death will deepen your life. *Possibly, you will experience a glimpse of their relatives and friends waiting to greet the one crossing over, and at least one guiding angel too!*

Be with Someone Giving Birth

Surrender also happens at birth. When a mother is bringing forth life, and totally surrenders to the wonder of the inevitable, she is often at that moment her very closest to God. There is generally a feeling in a woman at this time of being connected to every soul who has ever been born; and that she is fulfilling a well-known and respected role in the circle of life. There is a change that comes upon a woman when she holds her new-born child that cannot be fully explained. She is often more "in the moment" (unless drugs have been used with the birth) than at any other time in her life. She straddles the place between sleep and wakefulness, bringing into herself the reality of this dream that has evolved into life! She has witnessed the miracle of creation in her own body, and is more available to God at this time than any other. With the blessing comes responsibility, to be sure, but she welcomes it with open arms, and tearful kisses. Seeing a new mother and child is a sight to behold. *This is the gentle tenderness of how the Christ holds us to him!*

Being with someone giving birth will give you the chance to see how unconditional love can be easily bestowed upon others, because the joyfulness of the one who created wants it to be so. The baby didn't do anything to earn his mother's love; it is a free gift of his mother, who took a huge sacrifice, in many ways. The mother will nourish, cherish, hold close, and take care of all his needs. The child will learn to show love to others, because of the warm example of his parents. It is the same way with God. "We love because he first loved us."
(1 Jo. 4:19)

Never forget the sacrifice and the joy that God has with us. We also didn't do anything to earn it. All he asks back is to be loved and listened to for our own benefit, and to share that love and what we've learned with our siblings. He is the best parent in the universe! Let us have the trust, confidence, faith and total submissiveness of a tender child when it comes to our "Abba" (Aramaic = Father), but also exercise the maturity of a wise parent in knowing our responsibilities before our God and his other children.

Go to a Healing Treatment

Feeling the power of the Holy Spirit working upon you to make you well in body, mind and spirit is a blessing beyond compare! There is a wide range of what a healing treatment will do – it may simply bring a sense of well-being and peace of mind, helping you sleep better at night, or cutting down on your aches and pains. On the other end of the spectrum, you will see the Big Hand of God; cancer cells dying, tumors shrinking, and chronic pain, maladies and disease disappear. I have seen miraculous things occur before my very eyes!

Sometimes the healing occurs gradually over a period of time; but sometimes it is an instantaneous healing, with a spontaneous "whoosh" of power. There are many names for healing; and many different ways that God allows for his Holy Spirit to touch the lives, hearts and bodies of mankind. And this fact is exactly how you would expect a God-thing to be: available in all parts of the world, to all peoples, through all periods of time. Of course it would be called by a variety of different names. There would not be a "corner" on it by some special class of people, who say that they alone are utilized for healing. Who can limit God? Who can tell the Holy Spirit where to manifest and where not to?

"There is one body and one Spirit – just as you were called to one hope when you were called – one Lord, one faith, one baptism; one God and Father of all, who is over all and through all and in all." (Eph 4:4,5)

If you are in question about the method of healing that is available to you, or the people or person administering it, lift it up to God in prayer. Talk to people who have had the method of treatment done, and see if they were touched by the God of Healing Love. There will be a brightness in their eyes, and a smile on their lips. They will not have to *guess* if God had a hand in their healing. *They will know!*

"...for I am the Lord, who heals you." (Ex. 15:26)

The Uniqueness of You - Finding Out Who You Are

Who are you? What do you like to do? What is your favorite color? Why? So many times we forget about our own uniqueness or just consider it vanity to know ourselves well. What is your favorite way to make eggs - as an omelet, scrambled, over-easy or poached? Have you tried a variety of ways to really know, or are you just in a habit and so consider that must be your favorite? Often we go along in life not really making the choices that we ourselves want, but to please someone else or just following a habit. Maybe it is something as simple as how we choose our eggs, or maybe it is as complicated as what religion we learned as a child. *How do you know what is right for you?*

The apostle Paul said: "Examine yourselves to see whether you are in the faith; test yourselves." (2 Co. 13:5) Sometimes we need to spend the time to re-evaluate how we do things, and why. We wouldn't want to wake up one morning and feel that our whole life has been "not really what we want to do." When that happens it makes us feel resentful and empty. When we try to please everyone, we find it can't be done, and that often we lose ourselves in the process.

What hobbies do you like? When was the last time you did one? What did you do as a child? If people were to buy you a gift, do they know what you like to collect? Do you? The Lord made us all different. We are perfect in our variety. Accept the differences in yourself and embrace them. Accept the differences in others too, and embrace them!

This knowing of oneself will take some work to do! The mind doesn't want to change its set patterns, even if they are not good ones. It will do anything to protect the old beliefs and find a way to adhere to its comfort zone, even in little things. It is one of the reasons that free coupons and samples work in advertising. Marketing firms know that once you have developed a pattern, you are more likely to stick to it, without actively looking much further. Now, they have you "hooked!" Re-make yourself. Set time everyday, even if it is only fifteen minutes, to ask yourself questions. Pretend you are a celebrity and interview yourself about every imaginable nuance. *If you know yourself first, what you like and dislike, you will see God's ability more clearly to guide and bless you toward your goals!*

Seeing God as a Real Person

Sing to God, write poems to him! Know that you can talk to him casually, and with respect, as you would a dear trusted friend. People often feel that they can manipulate God into doing whatever they want him to do, if they find the "magic formula" of words to say, then drone on and on, often within ear-shot of other people. Did that work with your earthly father at home? I doubt it! It doesn't work with your Heavenly Father either! Do not use all your time talking to God making deals or begging for things. He knows what you need before you even ask for it.

How many times have you just "dialed up" God and asked how his day was going? Do you regularly let him know what is going on in your life, and why you make the decisions that you do? Do you ask his opinion on this? He is the best friend anyone could ever have. He will never leave you or withdraw his hand from you. He loves you. He gave a high price as a ransom to be able to have you close again. Remember in the garden, how he sought out Adam and Eve to speak *face to face* with them. That was his original purpose. He still wants that connection today. That is why we are taking from the buffet as many tools as we can to help facilitate that. We want to be able to hear, see and sense as many responses from him and his designated messengers as we can.

It is two-way communication we have with our friends, mates, and relatives. How long do you think these relationships would last if we did all the talking and never allowed them a word in edge-wise? Think of God as a buddy who "hangs out" over your right shoulder. You are not talking to yourself. You are communicating with the Power of the Universe, and if you are listening in return, *you will know he's talking back to you.*

Visit a Variety of Churches

Even if you are happy in your home church, it is a good exercise to see the family of God in many places. There are many journeys of the soul; and seeing God break out in a multitude of various homes keeps us as humble children, never believing that we can keep God in a box of our own choosing.

My family and I will never forget the heart-felt singing and praise we experienced during one Sunday at a small Southern Baptist church in middle Tennessee. The congregation had been meeting in this little place for over a hundred years. We were the only "white" people there that day - we seemed a curiosity - but we were clearly welcomed as equal children of God. There were no musical instruments - they weren't needed - the robust voices sang beautifully in all different ranges and tones of harmony. The preacher was knowledgeable and kind. Shouts of "Amen!" and "Yes, Father!" came spontaneously from the pews. It was beautiful to see the Father praised in this way. It was quite different from the way I had been accustomed to seeing a service performed. My hands got hot as the Holy Spirit permeated the building. All of us clapped and sang, and I was asked to close with prayer. We were very thankful that we had been led by the Spirit to this little church on this Sunday morning. It touched our hearts, and gave us a new faceted angle to look at the gem of praise! I knew it made The Big Guy happy too!

Acceptance of Salvation

We are loved! But, we often waver in self-confidence and spend much time and effort in criticizing ourselves. We are bombarded with magazine and TV commercials constantly telling us that we are not thin enough, wealthy enough or young enough. We also deal with the constant programming in our heads that carries all the social conditioning we have received throughout our lives.

The reason we needed Christ to come and be offered up as a sacrifice for our sins is this: back in the garden of Eden we had two perfect people make the Free Will choice to rebel against God, even after God had told them where their choice would lead - to unhappiness and death. They cut themselves off from the perfect *connection* they had with their father. They "unplugged" themselves from the Universal Energy current. And, similar to a fan whose blades still continue to rotate a while before they slow down and stop, so it was with once-perfect mankind now living a shorter and shorter lifespan until finally they died after an average of only 70 years (this is why in Genesis you see Methuselah living 969 years, Lamech living 777 years, etc). It is similar to a dent being put in a mold - every piece that now came out of it would reflect that same dent. So it is with us, the defective children of Adam and Eve.

Depending on who you are, you might look at it as a bunch of "karma" that mankind could *never undo.* Darkness cannot exist around Light. How would this "curse" be taken off the kids and *each one* be allowed to make Free Will choices for themselves? *The scale needed to be balanced again,* hence, a perfect human who would freely choose to follow God, no matter what temptations were presented to him. That is where the miraculous, perfect life of Jesus came in; he balanced the scale by submission to God, even to his death. So now, each one of us can come into a position of *Grace* before God.

Physically, we still bear the dent. But spiritually, we are now allowed access to the Presence. And because of all that Christ suffered for us (when he could have chosen not to, by *his* choice of Free Will), we are admonished by the Father to "glorify the son." (Jo. 8: 54) This is also the same reason that Jesus told us "no one can come to the Father except through me." He opened the door, whether we acknowledge that fact or not. Knowing why we have a "dent" and that the scales are now balanced and how that occurred, helps us to understand why mankind in general has had a communication problem with Dad and why *we don't have to stay in the corner on "time out" anymore.* We are invited back into the family once again, and can even be allowed access to his "private study."

"Blessed are those conscious of their spiritual need, for theirs is the kingdom of heaven." (Mt. 5:3)

"Then Jesus cried out, "When a man believes in me, he does not believe in me only, but in the one who sent me. When he looks at me, he sees the one who sent me. I have come into the world as a light, so that no one who believes in me should stay in darkness...for I did not come to judge the world, but to save it." (Jo. 12:45- 47)

"For since death came through a man, the resurrection of the dead comes also through a man. For as in Adam all dies, so in Christ all will be made alive." (1 Co. 15:21)

Look for "Divine Coincidences"

The first rule in letting yourself be open to guidance from above is *looking* for it. Ask yourself: "What is God up to in this experience? What lesson does he want me to learn? What path is opening to me that is unusual, out-of-the-blue, what window is opening up?"

Often, I find God is right in front of me, opening doors and ushering me towards them. In my stubbornness, it has taken me a long time to develop faith enough to step foot on an unknown path without *first* knowing what the *final destination* was going to be. I was telling God, "Yes, I want you to guide my footsteps!" When actually I was saying: "I want you to remove the rocks in my *own* path!" There is a big difference!

When you find yourself pushing against an unmovable object, and everything that you do seems like "pulling teeth," maybe God is trying to tell you something. Also, when you find yourself saying, "Again? This is happening to me again?" It might just be because you *did not learn* the lesson you were supposed to learn the first (or second or third) time around! So, you have to be presented with it *again*, brought to the same spot *again,* and see if you make the same (stupid!) choices *again* (believe me, I know!). Or, hopefully, much *better ones!*

Pay Attention to The Subconscious

The subconscious has a language all its own. It uses feelings and symbols to talk to our brain to let it know what is going on. Often, it is like a foreigner trying to talk to us as we are frantically trying to interpret the words and put it in a form we can understand. We are always a little bit behind, and often doubt our own interpretation of its meanings.

This is where *another purpose of the God-Spot* comes in. The connection with God is a powerful source of accurate information, and the language can be learned and interpreted through time. The more we listen, connect to him and look for the meanings, the louder and more clearly his words will become to us. If we are strong enough to get our own preconceived notions out of the way, we might even be able to let God-Consciousness come straight through, with all of its purity and power and truth. A "knowing" compared to a "figuring out." *Bypassing the interpretation of the brain, you now allow direct access of the unity of the Divine Will. No words needed, just an absolute knowing.* Talk about being connected!

As you start getting glimpses of the meaning of the pieces of this jigsaw puzzle you are being given, you will start to see the picture forming in its totality right before your eyes. You will be able to see "The Big Picture." What do you see? How does it make you feel? Are you still missing some pieces? We all are. There is always something more to learn, and aren't we glad about that! We certainly won't get bored as we search out the deeper things of God, and learn to use the gifts he has given us. Be patient. You will be Blessed!

The Bible - A Supernatural Book

"Your word, O Lord, is eternal; it stands firm in the heavens. Your faithfulness continues through all generations; you established the earth, and it endures. Your laws endure to this day, for all things serve you. If your law had not been my delight, I would have perished in my affliction. I will never forget your precepts, for by them you have preserved my life. Save me, for I am yours; I have sought out your precepts. The wicked are waiting to destroy me, but I will ponder your statutes. To all perfection I see a limit; but your commands are boundless. Oh, how I love your law! I meditate on it all day long."
(Ps. 119: 89-97)

Who of us today would buy a new VCR or DVD and be able to hook everything up and have it play correctly, without even once referring to the instruction manual? How about your stereo console or computer system? This collection of 66 letters written under the united and inspired authorship of our Dad helps us to "hook up everything correctly" and play our lives in beautiful harmony and in full living color. No more static and fuzzy pictures for us!

If you have any questions about the Bible being the infallible and authoritive Word of God, I suggest that you go to a public library and figure it out. Use other books to learn about the secular history of surrounding nations - see if the prophecies regarding the future names, rise and destruction of kings, kingdoms and countries really came true. See if those towns really existed. See if where the Bible touches on science that it is accurate or not (ex: the ancients believed blood "ebbed and flowed" in the veins like the tide; the Bible says "it circulates").

What about the cohesiveness of the recently discovered Dead Sea Scrolls proving the Bible hasn't changed since it was written two thousand years ago. Are there any contradictions? No! Prove it to yourself one way or another! Think of this - *if it is even possible* that the Bible could be a Divine collection of works that is beneficial to us, and answers the deepest questions of all humankind, don't we owe it to ourselves *to find out for sure?*

Look at it this way. Suppose you were told that scientists had just proven that it was true that *alien beings did exist* in outer space; that they have been visiting our earth for years and manipulating events here; and that they had placed a book in the public libraries full of alien information about the founding of our world and all their activities in our historic events! Don't you think there would be a mad panic of people running out to buy one, no matter what the cost, dropping everything to sit down and read one? Wouldn't you want to know if these aliens were hostile or friendly? Well...the story's true!

God and the angels do exist in "outer space," they have been visiting and facilitating events on the earth for years, and the Bible tells how this planet and the people on it have been shaped by Supernatural forces in many of its historical events! Find out which "aliens" are hostile, and how our "Great Leader" plans to deal with them! Now do you feel the magnitude of this Book and the power of learning from it? Go get one and read it!

Games to Sharpen Our Ability to Yield
Developing the Sensitivity to See, Hear and Feel

Most people can be divided into two groups - those who seek God and those who do not. This is the reason why you are reading this book. *You are one who seeks!*

Perhaps in this book you have seen a reflection of a few gifts that you *already have*. Or, perhaps it has awakened in you a desire to ask for gifts that you *would like to have*. It is my hope that utilizing these gifts inspires you to seek a closer connection with the Divine. As a result, God will use you as a tool in wonderful ways to bring others to faith, and you yourself will also feel more confident and peaceful, as you fulfill your path of *gifting humanity*.

I have included in this chapter many different methods and games that will help you to develop your sensitivities; some you can practice on your own, some you can do with others. Please begin all games with a petition of prayer, since you are asking to develop these gifts and sensitivities *not for reasons of ego,* but to be a better channel for God to communicate with - and through - you. You are also allowing the small whispering voice of intuition to rise to a loud roar!

If you have ever taken the time to learn a new language or musical instrument, you know how much practice it takes and how dedicated you must be to be successful. No one expects to sit down at a grand piano for the first time and immediately start playing Beethoven's Fifth. But, some people will sit down at the piano and find they have a natural affinity for it – and that it comes more easily to them than guitar, for example. Others find the opposite to be true, and so on.

We all have Natural gifts, and you can ask for and receive God-given Supernatural ones too. There is nothing wrong with developing either; it is scriptural and highly encouraged. Just as some folks are stronger in one gift over another, so we can have sensitivities that come more naturally than others. Some may be better in listening to God, others in seeing visions, still others in feeling the Holy Spirit physically working through their mouths and hands. We are encouraged to progress in the work of the Lord: practice, practice, practice!

"But eagerly desire the greater gifts." (1 Co. 12:31)

Keep a Spirit Journal

This is a daily record of your feelings and intuitions, and to record your progress in widening your Divine Connection. It is also a sacred place to put the *songs and poetry that you offer to God.* It is not a book for anyone else to read. Personalize the outside of this journal with hand-made paper; cotton cloth; unique buttons; and colors of significance to truly make it yours. Keep it in a special place of respect where no one else will be touching or moving it.

Making a spirit journal is a physical manifestation of owning your progress. All the games that you play, all the God-Spots you endeavor to open, all the thoughts and feelings about your journey of what "fits" and what doesn't, all these should be part of your journal. *This is the diary of you, your relationship with God, and your gifts.* The reason I am placing it here at the beginning of this chapter is to highlight its importance. *From this day forward*, I encourage you to write in your Spirit Journal!

Scent-Association

What did Grandmother smell like? Whenever we smell that familiar scent now, does it remind us of her? This is scent-association. This is something invisible that puts a mental image in our physical brain. We can train ourselves to remember other things this way too. Perhaps Grandfather smelled like fishing worms on a hot day! Be specific in your training. Not all perfume should remind you of Grandmother (your Grandmother smelled only like "White Gardenia"); not all cigars should smell like Grandfather (hence the fishing worm reference could be a better choice).

Start now, before people in your life go before the Presence, to associate them with a scent. If they don't have one, buy a cologne or perfume for them. Smell it first, before you give it to them as a gift. Get it solid in your mind that *this* scent is for *this* loved one. If they cannot wear perfume or live far away where you will never smell it, you can still use this method. Simply get a photograph of them and set it on your dresser or a place that you will see everyday for a couple of weeks. Have the perfume open in front of it (with a cotton ball over the mouth), or saturate a cloth. You will begin to associate the aroma with the picture.

When they "graduate," you will know when they come back to "check" on you. Perhaps you will smell it while they are still alive and just thinking about you. You can even do this with your favorite pets, since I know they continue even after death to be connected with us (another revelation from the NDE). Also, sweat and body odors are natural scent-associations. How will people remember you?

Even the Holy Spirit has an aroma! I have read about the phenomenon of saints whose bodies smelled like roses when they died. But I wasn't truly aware of the scent of the Holy Spirit, until at a healing it was brought to my attention by a pastor's wife. She was concurrent in prayer with me, and asked if I used anointing oil with the healings. I said no, usually not. After several more times where the Lord let me be there while he healed, she confirmed that she was indeed smelling a most lovely flowery scent. She added that she had smelled this a few times before in her life, *always when the Holy Spirit had appeared.* Since then, I have had others mention how they just love the "incense" I use at the clinic. There is none!

Put a Memory to Rest

We clog ourselves up when we carry the burdens of the past. It makes it hard to hear God when we aren't being true to ourselves, or to others. Anger and all other destructive emotions need to be disposed of. Strive to live today free from guilt or worry!

"Therefore, if you are offering your gift at the altar and there remember that your brother has something against you, leave your gift there in front of the altar. First go and be reconciled to your brother; then come and offer your gift." (Mt. 5:23,24)

Take a clear water glass and fill it up with water. Go outside to a chosen plant. Think of the memory. Then dump the water out. Feel all the emotions of anger, frustration, pain, and now...forgiveness. See the benefits of release turned around to nurture one of his creations. Do this three times. It is symbolic of letting go, "...forgive us our debts, as we also have forgiven our debtors." (Mt. 6:12) Now, a variation of this is to write it on paper, and burn it, scattering the ashes outside. "For if you forgive men when they sin against you, your heavenly Father will also forgive you. But if you do not forgive men their sins, your father will not forgive your sins." (Mt. 5:14,15)

"Do not repay anyone evil for evil. Be careful to do what is right in the eyes of everybody. If it is possible, as far as it depends on you, live at peace with everyone. Do not take revenge, my friends, but leave room for God's wrath, for it is written: "It is mine to avenge; I will repay," says the Lord. On the contrary: "If your enemy is hungry, feed him; if he is thirsty, give him something to drink. In doing this, you will heap burning coals on his head." (Ro. 12:17-20)

You are developing transitional tools to change your life and heal your scars. It is your responsibility to let go of pain. There is no need for it anymore, and your process of movement is in place now. You have acknowledged Jesus as the sacrifice, not you. As Jesus told me at my NDE, *"Love Each Other."* This is the biggest thing we can do for each other. Reflect the love!

There will be times you will need to write a letter, make a phone call, or have a face-to-face to "make it right" with someone before you can let things go. *You need to forgive others and give forgiveness to yourself.* Now that you've done these requirements, give it all to God and *don't take back any of it.* Carrying around old energy tracings is like having dog poo on your shoe. Scrape it off and be done with it. You don't need it anymore, you've gone beyond all that!

Know Your Colors

Developing sensitivity to color is not difficult, but it does take time. For this game, you need various colors of markers, a package of index cards or the backs of old business cards, one manila envelope and several smaller "security" envelopes that can't be seen through. Also, have available several sheets of blank paper.

Start by choosing four markers: yellow, red, blue and green. Take four cards and on the back of the cards scribble a block of solid yellow. Do the same with the red, and so forth. Now you should have 16 cards. Add four more blank ones. You now have a color deck.

Take one of the yellow cards, and throughout your house find at least four other items that are predominately yellow. You can look outside too (flowers are a lovely choice for a color sensitivity). Put it as a little separate pile in front of you. Do this for the other colors and also for the "white" of the blank cards.

Now, quiet your mind and say a prayer to God, praising him for the wondrous variety and beauty he gives us in our lives, and asking for the gift of developing the sensitivity to know colors. He is a God of detail, and a brilliant artist, just admiring a sunset will tell you that! Which color do you think is his favorite? Why? My vote is blue, because of the predominance of it; the sky; the ocean reflecting it back. Then again, it could be green! There are so many shades and varieties! What is yours?

Take the yellow pile, and put the card in front of you. Look at all the yellow objects. How does yellow make you feel? Happy? Melancholy? Is it fast, slow, soft, coarse, dry, wet, old, young, spicy, sweet, etc. *Write down all your descriptions of "yellow" on the sheet of paper.* Ask yourself what the five senses think "yellow" is like. What does it smell like? What does it taste like? What would be the sound of "yellow?" (Note: if you have a musical instrument, assign each color to a specific note, if not, use a "natural" sound like a bird singing, the wind blowing, waves crashing, etc.) Although there are books on the market about "what colors mean," I want *you* to discover what significance these colors are to you, personally. *You* need to be able to identify them at a strong, in-depth level.

Now, do this with the other colors. If this seems too overwhelming, decide to "know" only one color per day. You can space it out to get to "know" each one. Now, put all the assorted items away, leaving only your colored cards. Shuffle them together, and place each one in a white envelope. Put all the envelopes into the big manila one. Reach in and pull one out. Hold it sandwiched between your hands. Ask yourself what color you feel. What sound, smell, taste, etc.

comes to mind? Lie out your sheets of paper, and put the envelope on which color you think it is.

The first impression is usually the correct one. The mind works quicker than the brain – the brain likes to have a concrete reason for what the mind is suggesting, and often confuses the matter instead of validating it. So, go through the envelopes quickly, placing them here and there. Now open the envelopes and look. How many did you get right? Through time, add other colors such as orange, lavender, brown and pastels. Get to know the whole color spectrum! This is similar to going from having a black-and-white TV to a color one; God will now be able to give you more details and specifics in what he asks you to do!

If you ever have doubts for the possible usage of colors, symbols, shapes (or the like) being used by God to communicate, just read the inspired books of Revelation, Ezekiel and Daniel. There you go!

The Colors of Healing

If you are blessed with his gift of healing, assign a color to specific diseases you feel in the person's body. Often, this will go hand-in-hand with a specific "vibration" that you feel when you have your hands on them. For example, I assign the vibration of cancer an "orange" color, aids an "orange-brown." Sugar problems are "blue," diabetes is "white-blue." Instead of trying to remember a specific vibrational frequency under your hands, it is much easier to allow God to "pop" a color in your mind to let you know what is going on.

Don't be surprised if this "assigning a color to a malady" facilitates your having immediate diagnosis of an ailment, even by just shaking a hand. But, as always, keep in mind that unless you are a licensed medical doctor, you cannot legally tell the client anything. You cannot diagnose. It must be viewed as God giving this information for you only, to sharpen your intention to heal and to be validated in the progress being made under his care.

If you feel strongly that the client should know what is going on (nearly-clogged artery, extreme blood pressure, cancer, etc) you can tell them, "I feel a lot of heat here; and heat is a by-product of work being done, so the Holy Spirit is definitely working on something here. If you don't know what this might be, I suggest you go to a medical doctor and find out." This should be enough to encourage them. Call in a week and ask if they've gone in for a diagnosis. This will encourage them even more because of your level of concern. Or you may even state, "in all good conscious I cannot continue to do treatments unless you see a medical doctor first." Of course, this can be a "catch 22" as God will often take care of the immediate problem, and leave nothing to be diagnosed! When this happens, you must not let the ego get in the way, but just be happy that the problem has been corrected. And, keep in mind, God uses doctors, machinery and medications to facilitate healings too!

The Shapes Game

This is similar to the color cards, except that you use one marker, usually a black one. Make several shapes on the back of index or old business cards. Draw a star, square, circle, rectangle, "X," and triangle. All you need is one of each, and focus intently on how the shape "feels, looks and listens" to you. Mix them up in an envelope or bag and reach in without looking. What shape are you holding? The shapes game and the color game is one that can also be adapted to a partner or group setting. Be imaginative! Have fun!

Sirens and Emergencies

People who are new at "feeling" things will feel big energies first – earthquakes, car accidents, heart attacks. The evening news may startle them when they learn that what they felt or envisioned actually happened. The subtleties come later. Learning how to feel often comes in "onion layers." This is why you may have a "knowing" when an ambulance goes by - you feel a car accident with injuries has occurred. The subtleties come when an ambulance goes by - and you know that an accident has occurred with a black and a red car, one male driver has a concussion from hitting his head on the windshield, and the female driver of the other car now has whiplash. Oh, by the way, it was caused from a child on a bicycle riding out in front of the woman, and when she braked, the male rear-ended her!

For those who have this "prophetic knowing," how will God use it? Remember that he only allows the gifts to be fully used in order to bring people to faith and to help one another. You can trust that if you allow him to open you up, he will put you to good use. *You will be utilized for helping life changes occur in people.* You will be facilitated in their times of brokenness, despair and worry to ease the fear and say the words of encouragement that he will give you to say, to open their hearts and minds.

Sometimes, no words need to be said - the Holy Spirit will silently do the healing. But, to be *fully available* to God to help with these big things, a personal solid foundation of faith in God and knowledge of scripture is necessary. "Always be prepared to give an answer to everyone who asks you to give the reason for the hope that you have." (1 Pe. 3:15) You will be used to minister. Perhaps you will be used as a healer (physical, emotional, spiritual) or as a consoling friend or relative. Do not be afraid. All that happens is between that person and The Big Guy - you are just the visible representation of his invisible Presence. But because of this precious responsibility, the reason for becoming as sensitive as possible to His Voice is clearly seen.

To develop your confidence in this ability, you might want to follow up on the emergencies and see if you are correct. But if you do, for safety reasons please be sure to stay out of the way of the emergency vehicles. I have known some people to buy a police scanner, and check their immediate impulses with the "rest of the story."

What is Right is Left, Right?

There are different hemispheres in the brain that are utilized for different things. The analytical left side and the imaginative right side are constantly battling and making conclusions. Usually our dominant left side wins. To stretch ourselves out from our usual way of perceiving things, there are different books on the market about "left-brain/right-brain" games. There are also "optical illusions" and "irrational figures" that stretch our awareness and stimulate our right brain into better functioning. These almost work as a brain/mind "warm-up" before we play our games. *They help to develop unfocused observation and help us to perceive reality on a multiple of levels.*

Another trick to help allow the *brain* to let the *mind* have control, is to get a photo of an animal. How about a cow? Now, take out a pencil and draw it, timing yourself as to when you are done. Next, take the original photo and turn it upside down! Can you draw it this way? It forces the analytical brain to shut down, since it sees everything as: "go 2 inches to the left, down 20 degrees, go ¼ inch left..." Now the mind steps in, and says: "wiggle a bit this way, down a little, waver that way, up a little, a little more, got it!" When I did this exercise, I was totally astonished to find that when I turned my "upside down" drawing back up, it was better drawn and more in proportion than the analytical one – and I had beaten the time clock too!

Another way to "cross your wires" is to use the *opposite* hand for normal tasks. If you are right-handed, try writing with your *left* hand. If you normally carry things with your left arm, use your *right*. When you see yourself stepping off with your right foot, use your *left*. Try doing the "Tia Adrianna Hug," which is hugging heart to heart, which is usually the opposite of the norm. You will find people remember it better because it is unusual – perhaps it puts more people "in beat" on your little street corner of humanity. And you thought you were clumsy *before!*

Broken Life-Forces

This is an exercise to sense things that are alive, and things that are dead or dying. At the very least, it will help you to know what houseplants need tending

77

to! At the other end of the spectrum, it may be used by him to give you information about a missing person. Please remember that all these little games that we are playing are to aid us to be facilitated for bigger things in the future.

Go into a flower shop and go to only the potted (live and still growing) flowers. Smell them, put your hands over them, and breathe in their essence. Ask yourself, how do they feel? Find two potted flowers that have the same sort of energy feeling. Purchase the same color, same variety. Take them home. Take one of the pots and cut all the flowers off, leaving as much stem as possible with each flower head. Wind a rubber band around the stems to keep them together, and stand them up in a vase. At this point, do not add water.

You now have flowers that are alive, and flowers that are dying. They are the same in every way except this. Smell the dying flowers, put your hands over them, breathe in their essence. Ask yourself, how do they feel? Go to the other ones that are still rooted in the pot. Do you feel a difference? Now, go out of the room and occupy yourself with something entirely different for an hour or so. Come back in and check on the flowers. How do they feel now? Do you feel the difference in the brokenness, in their letting go and the slowing down of the very vibration of the resonance of life? For a few hours, monitor what is happening. You may never cut a flower again!

Now, since you have experienced the "big-emotions" of life and death of flowers, add another onion layer of sensitivity. Have one pot fully alive, and once again cut the flowers off an identical one. Divide the cut bouquet in half, binding each with a rubber band. Put both in identical vases. Add water only to one. Now, you have one that is truly alive, and two that are in stages of dying. Over the next few hours, keep feeling the subtleties of what you have done.

For a test, ask a companion to move one group of flowers behind a door or shower curtain, somewhere that you can't see it. Quiet your mind and say your prayer. Which one are you feeling? Now, have it moved behind something more substantial, like a wall or concrete divider. Can you still feel it? Yes, you can! Because your sensitivities come from a God who sees both sides of the wall, and connects you with the information that you are asking to know. In this same way, he can show you a "message of knowledge" about the life-force of a missing person or child in any part of the world, or even your lost pet! (1 Co. 12:8)

Consciously Entering Altered States

Daydreaming is an altered state of consciousness. Often we slip into this state without even realizing it. We may find ourselves standing in the checkout line of the supermarket dreaming about the vacation we took last year, while our eyes are glazed-over, looking at a half-covered toothpaste tube saying *"...rest."*

As a kid in elementary school, I remember "awards" being passed out on the final day before summer vacation by my English professor, reflecting his take on the personalities and abilities of his students. Since I had been admonished constantly throughout the year about looking out the window instead of at my paper, I wondered what to expect. A hand-lettered certificate (which I still own) solidified what I was trying to hide - that my head was always in the clouds - I received the "Out of this World" award for "Daydreaming!"

Now, we need to learn to go into altered states consciously, by choice. This way we can be immediately open to God's instruction *without* needing 30 minutes of quieting our mind before we can hear him! Absentmindedness is a form of altered state, but we may not like how it affects us. We need to have control, and even daydreaming has the potential to be dangerous without it. How many times have we been driving along and realized we just missed our turn? Artists and musicians enter altered states consciously, but they have learned a high degree of focus and concentration to be able to do so. That's what we need to learn also!

It is common knowledge that people who have difficulties in one area, often have heightened senses in another. Those who are blind and deaf have some very definite abilities that help make up for the sense that is impaired or missing. *Guess what game we are going to play next!* Get out the blindfold and the earplugs!

Find an entire day you can devote to this without heavy responsibility or having to leave the house. And, before you put the blindfold on, it might be a good idea to take the breakables out of harm's way. Although you should be able to intuitively know the layout of your own home, you still might be running into a few tables! It is all right to have a companion in the house while you are doing this lesson, he will probably have to help you in the meal department. But try to do as much for yourself as possible, including navigation, bathing and answering the phone.

Keep a mental note of the focus and higher sensitivities you gain from the *other* senses, and not of the senses you are *lacking.* Does food taste different? Are you more in-tune with the sounds of movement in the house? Are you more cautious of damage to your body? Wait until it is dark that evening to remove the blindfold; and with no lights on, go to bed. Tonight, do you feel differently toward your companion, and do you touch more gently? Is the sensitivity of your own skin heightened? As you awake up in the morning, take time to write down the experiences you learned from the previous day, and praise God for the gift of sight, as you pray for the endurance and hope of those who have none.

Now, find an entire day on your calendar to do the same with earplugs and the lack of the sense of hearing. If you can still hear voices while wearing the plugs, then wear a set of additional hearing protectors. Also experiment with using a radio headset, with the radio knob turned to a non-station of white noise. Are you finding that you are trying to read lips when people speak to you? Are you intuitive about where people are in your home, or are you startled when someone rounds the corner? Again, go through the entire day, and write down your impressions when you awaken the next morning. What have you learned?

Developing Focus and Concentration

Take a piece of fruit and place it on the table in front of you. Walk around it and *really notice everything about it,* including any shadows and plays of light. Now pick it up and smell it, turn it over in both hands, and look at it from every angle. Is it smooth, soft, sweet? Take a knife and slice it open, and ask questions about it again. Does your brain remember exactly what it tastes like? Is your mouth watering for it? Slice it into many pieces and arrange it into a pretty design. Stand back and look at your art. Rearrange it and look at it again. Be very intent on remembering everything! Eat a piece, and savor the flavor. Take another piece and squish it between your fingers. What song would you attribute to this fruit? Why? Have you learned everything *all five senses* can tell you about this fruit? Now slowly clean it up, and note this experience too.

Now go into another room and look at the clock. For ten minutes I ask you to concentrate on the fruit you just experienced. You can choose to place the experience in order, or mix it up any way you wish. But the point is, only focus on this item for this duration of time. If you feel your mind wandering, reset your clock and start the ten minutes over again. You have many sensations to remember. Let your mind work for you, as compared to your brain. *Feel!*

The next day, take the memory of the fruit and focus on it for 15 minutes, then another day for 20 minutes. Is it getting easier? Then it is time to take you out of your quiet meditative situation and add some distractions! Try to accomplish five minutes while in a room with the TV on. Walk to a grocery store and try to focus for ten. Can you do it? Make it progressively difficult on yourself. Utilize your senses to help you remember. This strengthens concentration!

One Thousand One...One Thousand Two...

This is a counting game to help you continue to develop your concentration. Often our brain is involved in an underlying dialog of thought while we are doing something else or listening to someone. Even when *we* are doing the talking our brain is already far ahead of us, deciphering, reasoning, planning what to say next, and storing information. Now, consciously use this ability.

The next time you enter into a conversation with someone, start counting in your mind. When it is your turn to speak, speak. But, as soon as you finish and the other person continues on, pick up where you left off in your counting. Do this throughout the conversation. Each time, continuing your counting where you left off. You are developing an *undertone of thought*. It would go something like this, with "April" being the one developing her undertone, while still fully involved in the conversation at hand:

April: "George, how are you today?"

George: "Fine, April, how are you? How is John doing?" (April thinks: one thousand one...one thousand two...)

April: "He's doing good, working at his new location now, downtown."

George: "Yes, he was telling me about it. Sounds great! Is he getting the same benefits there as before?" (...one thousand three...one thousand four...one thousand five...etc.)

Now, instead of numbers, use an undertone of simple conversation with yourself. Talk to yourself about the plans you have for your garden, what you will plan for dinner tonight, etc. All the while, also concentrate on staying fully involved in the "outside" conversation. Some people do this whether they want to or not!

Next, have an undertone of prayer. Remember, prayer is two-way communication. *You are listening as well as speaking.* If you develop an undertone of connection throughout your ordinary daily routine, God will use you for extraordinary things! He will have constant access to you, and you to him! You will be actively altering your conscious use of the 10% of your brain while utilizing the 90% subconscious!

Connection through Sound

Have you ever awakened with a song in your head? Did it provide meaning to something you had a question about on the previous day? Have you ever anxiously heard your child's name explode in your mind in the middle of the day and had the urge to call the babysitter to check on him? You may be sensitive to hearing Divine direction. This is one of the hardest senses to ignore, especially when it's at full volume!

This connection will often cause an anxiety or uneasiness inside until you answer the call.

Many a person in the scriptures tried to ignore this voice, and did so to their detriment. "The word of the Lord came to Jonah...but Jonah ran away...but the Lord provided a great fish to swallow Jonah...then the word of the Lord came to Jonah a second time..." (Jnh.1-4)

One thing to remember, especially about the gift of Divine hearing, is that it needs to be written down or acted upon quickly. Since it is not formulated inside your brain, but merely passing through it, it will not easily be stored there either. How will you know if what you are hearing is just your own internal monologue or perhaps even an evil attachment operating? Apply the measuring stick of accurate knowledge and see the word "by its fruits." And, if you ever hear a "voice" telling you that you should injure yourself or someone else, or something incredibly ungodly like that, dismiss it at once. Remember the God of Love utilizes gifts to bring others to faith in him and to help us help each other, never to harm or hurt!

The "sound connection" is probably the best one for getting direct and specific questions answered by God. It can also be used for the "gift of prophecy." (1 Co. 12:10)

"Above all, you must understand that no prophecy of Scripture came about by the prophet's own interpretation. For prophecy never had its origin in the will of man, but men spoke from God as they were carried along by the Holy Spirit."
(2 Pe. 1:20)

Before you go to sleep at night, or in the morning before you get out of bed, actively listen to the sounds around you, and try to identify them. Now, focus your listening and hear your own heartbeat and the sound of your own breathing. The sounds of your own body were there all along, but you probably weren't actively listening for it until it was encouraged. *Often the whisperings of Spirit are drowned out by the noise of everyday life also.* That is why you need to distinguish sounds.

What if the Divine is talking to you during the day and you don't hear him? Most of the time he speaks in whispers. How about if he screamed at you with a warning? Perhaps you *feel* "unheard" promptings as a "gut-instinct." How do you feel when you go against those promptings? Perhaps you are missing out on angelic direction, a personal message from God himself, *directed to you!*

The God-Spot Glossary

Practice handling earth, wood, rock, metal and cloth. As you read through the God-Spot glossary, devise games that you can do to increase these sensitivities and to receive validation for them, thereby increasing your confidence and ability to listen to what information God may use you for.

The capacity to hold an object and receive information about people, places, things or events may be useful in criminal investigations, finding lost children, or stolen and misplaced items. All these successful stories can bring wonderful glory to God, and you should always tell everyone that you are working with where the Power comes from. If you want to be able to continue to be a worker, you have to acknowledge the Boss, or he may call you to work less and less. *Our own ego needs to stay at home,* under the rug - it has no place in this kind of work.

Keep in mind that God may not want us to have particular information, and may withhold some answers. He does this with the angels too! And, this is how it should be. We are not "all knowing," and we have faith that whatever task or information we are given is the best for all concerned. Some of it may be on a need-to-know basis only. We should also respect the confidentiality of the people we deal with, and not pander about personal information. Remember that the only part we have in this is making the Lord real to the hearts of men and women. This is what the Holy Spirit does through a yielded vessel.

Do we have to hold something in our hands to find out information about it? We don't. It is just a tool that our brain uses to help our mind connect and ask very specific questions. It is just like wrapping a ribbon around our wrist to remind ourselves to stop at the post office (or what ever you've designated it for), now every time we look at the ribbon we will think about the chore we are supposed to do.

It is a good practice to wash our hands between touching items. This "cleans the slate" and gives a definite focus to whatever information we are asking about. To help go from our analytical state to our subconscious/God-conscious state, first verbally describe the item out loud – this opens the brain to giving information, and soon the mind will follow.

It is the power of God, not our faith, which moves mountains. But, we have to have faith that God can and will do it. It is the same in believing that he uses mankind for special purposes on earth today, *and will use you!* Pray for the Supernatural Gift of Faith. (1 Co. 12:9) Even if our faith is not yet well-developed, God will let us see that there is power in what we do have, and that will encourage us to continue.

Jesus told his disciples," I tell you the truth, if you have faith as small as a mustard seed, you can say to this mountain, 'Move from here to there' and it will move. Nothing will be impossible for you." (Mt. 17:20,21) It is proper to pray for more faith. If you lack confidence or feel you have no knowledge or strength, make sure that you are not asking for *your* will to be done, instead of God's. Often you will be utilized as the "go-between" between someone else and The Big Guy. Do not trust in your own abilities. Trust in God, and let him do the work!

Love is the "electrical cord" of power that allows our connection with him, and faith is the "light switch" that turns on that power. May we manifest enough in our "little bulbs" to light the entire world!

Divine Protection

Have you ever sensed correctly the mood of a spouse, friend, or animal without any verbal interaction going on between you? Do you find yourself easily caught up in the moods of others, sometimes even having a hard time knowing if the emotions are truly yours, and not theirs? By having this feeling toward others, you are showing your love and sensitivity – and your natural empathy.

But, have you also found that you often feel drained after being around people, and seem to get sick more easily than others? Do you find yourself not wanting to shake hands or be hugged because the flood of information you receive is overwhelming? If so, you need to learn Divine Protection. You must learn the difference between Godly Empathy and Personal Empathy. You must know the difference between God's Will and Your Will.

In your own desire to help others so badly, you are forgetting your place. God has things in control. Worry is to be unsure of God's role in our lives. Everyone is presented with his own spirit journey, and is presented with choices and learning experiences along the way. You may be desiring and pleading with all your heart for someone you know to get over cancer, when actually God might be allowing this period of time for not a physical healing to take place, but an emotional one. Or both!

In the bigger picture, perhaps this is the only time in that person's life where family and friends have gathered around him, expressing love and support. You don't know. You do not have the schematics on it. And this is the true elegance of prayer – letting go of the results, knowing with confidence that our needs and those of others are being met. Show love, do any job the Lord gives you to do, and then let it be. As the saying goes, "Let Go and Let God."

The "energy" (your spiritual life-force) that you force from Your Own Will drains you. The "energy" (Holy Spirit) that you allow to go through you by His Will empowers you. Trust God and know that whatever occurs is for the highest good of the people involved, even if it leads to a conclusion that you may not understand. His view of the situation is much better than ours is, he sees the bigger picture, and he also knows all the choices made and factors involved along the way.

"For my thoughts are not your thoughts, neither are your ways my ways," declares the Lord. "As the heavens are higher than the earth, so are my ways higher than your ways and my thoughts than your thoughts." (Is. 55:8,9)

"Trust in the Lord with all your heart and lean not on your own understanding; in all your ways acknowledge him, and he will make your paths straight." (Pr. 3:5,6)

Play with Animals

Do animals seem to know you like them and come up to you wherever you go? As a child, did you have a special attachment to the family pet? Do you still have critters running all over the place, or try to spend time in nature or wild animal parks and zoos as much as you can? As you develop increased sensitivity as a child of God, you will also develop an increased capacity to sense an awareness of animals.

Remember the game we played with the fruit? You totally knew the fruit after spending time with it, seeing its qualities from all different angles. It is time to do the same with animals, to get a good mental image in your mind. For example: Pet your cat, smell her fur, and hear her purr. Watch intently how she washes herself and saunters across the floor and jumps up on the couch to a spot of sunshine. Feel and sense her with all five senses. Later, meditate on your memory.

As we have seen with the flowers, we can sense a difference about that which is dead and that which is alive. There is also a difference between inanimate objects and live ones. As you become more "in-tune" with animals, you will find you can almost guess what they are thinking. Maybe you can! Animals seem to be very "front-lobed" and carry all their immediate information in a very receptive place. It is similar to when an overwrought human is said to wear their emotions "on their sleeve." You can feel it!

Those who consistently work with animals are often seen to have an "almost human" communication going on with them. Whether they are known as a "horse whisperer" or a "pet psychic," people who truly enjoy their animals often develop a "knowing" about them. Many times there is a feeling of Unconditional Love reflected back that they may say they don't often experience with humans. I have experienced this myself. And, with developed sensitivity, you can aid this communication between you and the animals.

Just as a dog has the ability to hear higher frequencies than we do, some animals can also see higher vibrations than we, including visions of angels and spirits. (Nu. 22:21-33) I have also found they are very sensitive to *our* spirit, and can sense our emotions very well. Now, can this relationship be used in some way by the Holy Spirit to bring praise to God or help his kids? Yes! We see how people and animals work together even now to help others. Dogs are often used to find people trapped in fallen buildings, lost children in the wilderness, and skiers in avalanches. They are even trained to seek out drugs and poisons that would be used to injure others. Their handlers are trained to be "one" with the dog to accomplish these tasks. And communication with other kinds of animals (dolphins, chimpanzees, etc) is well underway.

So, why wouldn't God allow his Holy Spirit to have better connection between the animals and us? He often does!

Go to a zoo and find a quiet place with a medium-sized or large animal in a habitat, one big enough that he can move freely around. Find a comfortable place to totally relax, and hopefully to sit down undistracted. Watch the animal intently, and casually rotate your hands on your lap to open palms-up toward the animal. This helps you to focus your intention, as a kind of unobtrusive "radar screen." Pray to God and ask if this is something you should do, in that it might be something useful for later (maybe even to help calm an animal needing healing). Wait for a response, while you put all distractions out of your mind and focus on the "vibration" of the animal and the Word from God.

Ask in your mind, through prayer, for the animal to do something for you. See this as a picture in your head of what you want them to do (they don't understand "English"). With birds I always ask (through pictures), "stand on one foot while stretching your wing out on the same side." It seems to bring joy as much to them as it does to me! It truly seems to give them a thrill to actively allow games such as this! Maybe it is because they have also have joy in working with the Holy Spirit.

For larger animals, I ask them to walk toward me, turn to the right, go in a circle, and sit down. I vary it depending on the size of the cage and the "adaptability" of the animal. It truly seems they *like* this interplay - much better than their daily boredom and the constant "animal calls" of the curious humans passing by!

I have found the smaller animals have a very fast vibration going on, and are harder to focus on. The larger ones are easier to make contact with. It doesn't matter if it is a squirrel in a park or a songbird in your backyard, the smaller the animal, the more effort it will take on your part to be open to communication. If it is not happening, then don't worry about it. As always, you don't want to be doing something for ego or "see what I can do" purposes. If it seems to be heading that way in God's eyes, he won't allow the Spirit to connect. And, I think it can also be shut down by the animals. Especially at meal times or when there is courting to be done! Have fun!

What You Will See & Why –
Energy Tracings, Ghosts & Angels
You Are Protected in Unconditional Love

Angels are some of the most powerful and beloved creatures the universe has ever known. Both the Greek *ag'ge-los* and Hebrew *mal-'akh'* words actually mean "messenger" or "spirit messenger" and occur in the scriptures nearly 400 times. Angels were individually created by the will of the Most High; *they are not people who were once alive.* They were created before mankind even came on the scene. Angels are the most difficult to see because their frequency is *so very high.* They have to really slow it down to allow us to see them.

At the "founding of the earth" we see the "the morning stars sang together and all the angels shouted for joy." (Job 38:7) How many angels are there? The scriptures record what Daniel saw: "thousands upon thousands attended him, ten thousand times ten thousand stood before him." (Da. 7:10) And those are just the angels to attend and praise God! In the garden of Gethsemane, Jesus could have cried out to his father for *12 legions* of angels to protect him, if he had wanted to. Just *one* "legion" corresponded to the largest unit of the Roman army, consisting of 3,000 to 6,000 soldiers. One angel is known to have killed 185,000 people all on his own.

Angels also have particular duties, responsibilities and rank. There is the foremost angel, Michael the Archangel. There are seraphs (they have six wings), and there are cherubs. Then, there is a very large group of angels whose primary responsibilities are to act as message communicators between God and man, besides protecting (yes, we *do* have guardian angels) and reinforcing God's will and proclamations. (Mt. 18:10)

Angels have names and personalities too. Only two angel names are given in the Bible, Michael and Gabriel; since angels were dispatched by God, in *His Name,* not in their own. There are several references about people in the scriptures asking angels for their names, or wanting to worship them; but they were told by the angels, "Be careful! Do not do it! I am a fellow servant with you and with your brothers who hold to the testimony of Jesus. Worship God!" (Rev. 19:10)

Angels are sexless; they don't marry or procreate. But, they are generally referred to in the scriptures as males, although most paintings of them represent them as females. They were created with their own Free Will, or moral agency, as was mankind. God didn't want mindless robots operating around him. He wanted angels there because they *chose* to be, out of love for him. He feels the same way about us; and we were made "a little lower than the angels." (Heb. 2:7)

Because of that Free Will and ability to make one's own choices, there were angels in Noah's day who came down to earth and materialized male bodies for themselves. "The sons of God saw that the daughters of men were beautiful, and they married any of them they chose...the Nephilim were on the earth in those days, when the sons of God went to the daughters of men and had children by them." (Ge. 6:2-4) These angels who had left their responsibilities were then called "fallen angels," "evil spirits," or "demons."

The hybrid offspring of these willful angels were called "Nephilim" and one of the main reasons the flood occurred was to wipe out their hybrid physical bodies. They were a powerful race of giants, *half man and half angel,* bent on manipulation and destruction! They had supernatural powers. Did the memory of these superhuman giants in the minds of the eight surviving members of Noah's family ignite the great Greek mythologies of ancient times?

Satan himself had once been an angelic son of God, but because of misuse of Free Will, he chose to rebel, and thus *made himself* "the devil" (slanderer, rebeller). None of these *fallen angels* are allowed by God to materialize in physical form, ever again. But, they still manipulate behind the scenes. And, you may see them with your eyes as a mist or transparent form, but, *you do not need to have any fear of them!* Good always conquers evil, and God and his faithful angels protect us. He also gives *us* the power here on earth to *bind* them; they are powerless before our rebuke with his mighty power, which he gives to us through his Holy Spirit.

Angels communicate with each other, and they talk various languages, and they think for themselves. They are superhuman in power, and more intelligent than we are. They can travel at tremendous speeds, past anything we can compare on earth. But, there are some things that they don't know or understand, and they have an active interest in seeing how God works things out with us. Peter once stated: "Even angels long to look into these things." (1 Pe. 1:12) Angels also rejoice at the repentance of a sinner, and they watch the "theatrical spectacle" that we produce as we go about our lives, making our own free will choices, for good or for bad. (1 Co. 4:9)

Angels have many privileges, which have included giving messages that contributed toward writing the Bible. You see them in ancient times all over the place - announcing Jesus' birth; bringing him food after a prolonged fast; pronouncing his resurrection and ascension into heaven, and around his disciples and his church.

God's angel's didn't just "go away" after Jesus left the earth. They are still very active and well today. "Are not all angels ministering spirits sent to serve those who will inherit salvation?" (Heb. 1:14) We are still inheriting salvation today. We have a promise from God that we are continuing to be protected. "If you make the Most High your dwelling - then no harm will befall you...for he will command his angels concerning you to guard you in all your ways." (Ps. 91)

Since there are so many angels, and they still have an active role toward us, wouldn't it be wise to accept that they exist? As Christians, it would be heretical to *not* believe in them. That means *we must accept their role and be open to listening to these Godly spirits!* You would not want to miss a message from the Most High, would you?

Most of the time, *faithful angels* are also invisible, but they are allowed to appear and manifest to us at times. Sometimes they are a mist, bright light, and look like shimmering heat waves, or even as vibrational qualities of energy. Rarely, they are allowed to manifest in forms of matter, in human form. Remember what Einstein said? *Matter is just slowed down energy.* Believe me, they can do it, *if it is For the Highest Good,* and *if that is what it takes to get the job done*, then they will! But most of the time we will not *see* anything with our eyes – we will just have a *knowing sense* that we are not alone. And, it is *not* a sense of dear ole grandmother sitting beside you. No! *It is so much more!*

Sensing an angel presence is like *feeling a very high vibrational quality,* a pulling like a magnet. There is wonderful *warmth.* You also feel pushed toward what you are supposed to be doing, the way that you should go, or what you should say. There is a peacefulness of mind, and nervousness leaves. There is also an "I remember" feeling, a familiarity that our core responds to.

Always, while I am being facilitated by the Holy Spirit for a healing treatment, a large white angel wing dips down through the roof, and I know that the Lord's blessing is upon me, and I can begin. It is a comfort to see this vision. Angel's wings are not truly feathers, but shimmers of pulsating light radiating forth. Through the years, this angel wing has been gradually dipping lower and lower each time – at first, it was just a tip, then half a wing, now it is the whole thing, a shimmering "wing" of radiant light! It is awesome, inspiring, beautiful, and *huge!*

When I told my mother about the angel wing, she gasped for breath. When she was a young child, she remembers lying in bed very sick, wondering if she were dying. Immediately after asking this question, an amazing sight unfolded before her eyes – a beautiful white wing dipped down from the ceiling - and she knew it was a sign from God that she was going to be healed and would live!

Angels have a sense of authority, but of a "virgin" quality. They feel like they have a perfect balance of sensitivity and power. They are definitely what I would call "watchers." I have not met any with a perceptible sense of humor, but that does not mean that they don't have one. They are freindly and are greatly concerned about our welfare, but they seem all business about getting the job done. There is *nothing bad that can happen to your own spirit* when you are in the presence of a faithful angel of God. Sometimes, they will even actively prevent any *physical* harm from taking place in a dangerous situation. And, there is *always* one present when a person makes a transition from life to death, as a helper, comforter and guide.

If you ever have a chance to be with someone who is crossing over, then by all means take the opportunity. Besides being a caring companion to hold his hand and give encouraging words of love and hope, you will possibly be allowed to see the spirits of those who come to escort him home. There is always an angel in the crowd, along with a few loved ones, friends and relatives. How can you really see an angel or a spirit? Here is a suggestion you may find helpful:

The "Magic Eye" Blur to See Spirits, Halo/Auras

Do you remember the "Magic Eye" pictures that were published in the comic sections? There was also a craze of them in the 90's; posters abounded everywhere of dots upon dots that seemed just a mess of color. But...if you held your eyes slightly crossed when you were standing, staring straight ahead at it, after a moment or two the muscles in your eyes would relax and out would pop a 3-D picture! I used to love those things, especially the highly detailed ones where you would see dolphins jumping out of the sea, horses running through pastures, and birds flying through the clouds. *This is the same way to be able to first start seeing angels!*

Using this technique on people who are still alive will enable you to see what some call the "aura," or our own spirit energy within us. Our spirit energy is slightly larger than our physical body, and it is fairly easy for beginners to see a ¼ to ½ inch white glow around their hands. The more you practice, the easier it will get, and after a while you will begin to see pastel colors in this energy field. The colors on a person will change according to health *and* emotions – and just because you might see a gray or black spot on people doesn't mean they have cancer. Maybe they are depressed right now, or just having a bad day!

I have found this technique fun for looking across the church or classroom to spot people who are going to sleep – you will see their energy as a white mist growing and flowing larger and larger up and around their heads! When they wake up - slurp - it all comes quickly back in again!

I have wondered about the old master's paintings of Christ and the saints with the bright light, or "halo," painted behind their heads. Isn't that just the same thing that we are seeing today? Although then it was considered an honor and a blessing, now the word we use for it, "aura," is frowned upon and considered "New Age." I think it is just a language game again, that of semantics. A glow is

90

a glow is a glow. Seeing a spirit is the same now as it was before. They are still made out of the same stuff! And it is still all a part of the creation of God.

So, when you see angels, please do not run screaming in the opposite direction. That will hurt their feelings – they are not there to hurt or scare you, they are there to give you important messages, and to comfort and guide you. You don't want to make them feel like they are blowing their mission. Remember, you can call upon the angels of God whenever you like: especially if you feel the darkness of a fallen angel around. You need not be afraid! If you are in terror from being allowed to see an angel, it is possible that you may not be allowed to see one ever again, or for a very long time, because it was damaging to you.

If this is really what you want, pray to God about it, that you may have eyes to see; then don't go back on your word after he grants your request! Just breathe...in and out, in and out... and let the experience wash over you, knowing that a very holy creation of God stands before you!

There are many benefits to be able to allow God's world to become closer to you in this earthly one. Number One, he can use you more! He will use you to glorify his name in very unique ways! He will even allow you to work in a messenger (angelic) way, to relay information to others on important issues. There is no end to the adventures and missions you will receive! But, remember, if you are scared, it clogs up your channels, and shuts down your receptors. I am still dealing with this one myself, not because I am scared of any thing of God, but sometimes I find myself fearful of the reaction of simple humans, when I relay the information. Isn't that silly! It truly is only in the power of the Spirit that we as broken vessels can accomplish anything for him at all!

Angels are often called spirits, although they are different from average spirits (people who have transitioned successfully) and ghosts. And energy tracings are a completely different matter. Most people put them all in the same category, and think of them all as the same thing. But you are learning differently!

Energy Tracings & Energy Dustings

Energy *tracings* are not alive. They are things that you see, that have existed before. It is like a representation of that which was, but now is not. It is like a movie that runs before your eyes, where you cannot effect any change. There is no interaction between the characters and you.

Perhaps an easier way to explain it, is how science explains things. They say that everything that has ever happened here on the earth has been recorded as a vibration that has been sent out into the cosmic universe. They say that *someone with the right receiver* would be able to catch "I Love Lucy" even before it was put into re-runs! Nothing stops these waves from going on and on, traveling out further and further into the great expanse. They don't ever dissipate or stop existing. It is the same reason we see a star twinkle and go out, or even fall from the sky, *tonight,* when actually it went out thousands of years ago.

Seeing energy tracings is the same thing; except you can be "tuned in" and become that correct receiver yourself. Every time this has happened to me, as in all of these gifts, it was not for my own curiosity, but to be used to help someone else. You cannot ask the Holy Spirit to be available for simple amusement or "parlor games." If I did see something that did not seem to be related to something else, then I considered it a "trial run," for the Lord to see my choices and reaction to it, and to prepare me for the time I would be used. You will find many stories about energy tracings in the chapter on *Archeology Comes to Life.*

Energy *dustings* lay like dust particles on furniture. They are everywhere. Some places they can just jump out at you, because the vibrational frequency is so high. You are constantly being bombarded everyday by them. This is one of the reasons why you may go into a room or a building, and it feels uncomfortable to you. Especially prevalent in old places that have a lot of history. It is also the reason, if you had a happy home when you were a child, that you became so sad when your parents wanted to sell it; or why you want to go visit it again when you are grown. Perhaps there is a department store or grocery that gives you a headache every time you go into it. If you took the time to research it, you would find out that major energy events happened here.

Perhaps the store was robbed, or a man had a heart attack and died there. Perhaps that spare room that gives you the "creeps" is where someone's teenager used drugs (a quick, easy access through which evil energy attaches to a person by usurping Free Will), or a wife was beat up by an abusive husband. All these things are very high-energy events that leave their mark. The softer things that happen are dusted around too, but it takes a lot of sensitivity and practice of "sorting through the onion layers" to be able to find them. Good things are also high energy, and only a slightly different kind of vibration. Just like Thanksgiving can be a happy family time while also being a stressful one, filled with scores of details to be attended to. It is dusted all around.

Some things hold this energy dusting better than others. To this day I cannot hold onto a metal handrail without being overwhelmed by all the information on it. All emotions are overlapped on it. It is too confusing to understand any of it!

These energy dustings are often useful ways for God to communicate with us information that he needs us to know or to pass on. Would you like to help at a crime scene? Having an object under our hand helps our mind focus on the information, almost like a "touch-stone." We can get a sense about the people, and the event, and sometimes even "hear" the voices involved, as we open our sensitivities to it.

Ghosts – Spirits Not Letting Go

Ghosts are folk with unfinished business. Instead of crossing over to God, they are in a "holding pattern." Ghosts are always spirits from people who have died. *They do not know any more or any less than when they were alive.* If your aunt was mean when she was here on earth, she will still be mean as a ghost (*spirits who have gone to God have let go of all that tiresome stuff*). If she was the salt of the earth and kind-hearted, that is how she will be as a ghost. So, you do not have to be afraid of them! Let me repeat that, *you do not have to be afraid of ghosts!* They are people who have just shed their physical bodies. They have less power over you now than they ever had.

Please remember, *ghosts do not have all the answers.* Their information will be just as fallible as the next human. Whereas spirits, who have transitioned and come before the presence of the Lord, have access to Divine knowledge, and are sometimes used as messengers (an angel capacity) to tell you something. So, if you are given information, this is the priority list to whom you should listen: God, Jesus, the Holy Spirit, angels, spirits, *yourself,* ghosts, in that order. Test everything out first, using prayer (two-way God communication), and your conscious (God-given reasoning ability of right and wrong). And, listen to your gut-feeling (God-given intuition).

Ghosts are the easiest to see in all the spirit categories. Often you can tell right off that it is a ghost because of the ability to see all the nuances of his features. You will often see the wrinkles, the color of the eyes, the dryness of his skin. Once, as a waitress I went to pour coffee to one who was just "passing through." Boy, did I feel stupid! When I came within a few feet of the table I saw whom it was, and turned around and came back to the kitchen. There wasn't any one else there yet, except the cook, and did he give me a ribbing. "So, you pour coffee so much it's just a habit of going to tables when there's no one sitting at them, huh?" I smiled, and didn't tell him anything. But, I did go into the back room and say a releasing prayer for the drifting stranger. When I came back out, he had either gone "to the Light of God's Love," as I had prayed, or had just moved on.

You do not have to be worried that you will be walking around traumatized saying, "I see dead people..." as in the movie "Sixth Sense." Ghosts do not show up with any injuries on them. You will not see blood, etc. They will sometimes, as spirits will also, let you know *how* they crossed; and you may see or feel for a moment what happened to them, but you will not be seeing them constantly with those injuries. That is just Hollywood!

When spirits and ghosts are present, there are many tangible things your physical body can notice. Is the hair at the back of your neck or on your arms standing on end? Sometimes, you may see something moving out of the corner of your eye, or flashes of brightness that are gone when you look directly at them. Remember to do the "magic eye blur." Your spirit also has a *knowing* that their spirit is around. Also, as they need to slow down their energy to be able to communicate with you, you will often feel a coldness, even an icy chill at times. Also, pressure or heat at the base of the skull, or at the center of the forehead, can be a physical sign.

Often, ghosts will show up looking how they *feel* they look. You know, just like the person alive right now, who feels only 45 years old on the *inside,* even though he may be 70 years on the *outside.* Spirits do this too. Most of them appear how they looked when they were in their 30's; although if someone only knew them by a certain appearance (such as an old grandmother to a grandchild), then they will appear that certain way to be recognizable.

Also, a death that was sudden, and came as a shock, will produce the most ghosts. It is as if they keep repeating over and over again the last part of their lives, like a "Ground Hog" day re-run. Sometimes they just can't believe they are dead, and they will go on with the same chores and stresses during their day as if they were alive. These are the hardest to convince to go home. They do not believe that the angel God sent as an escort is real – even if the spirits of loved ones are there to help welcome them. There are those who will go hundred of years without improvement.

Many interesting experiences can come from working with ghosts. If the Lord sees that you are OK with it, he will allow you to help "tidy up" their loose ends and help them get on with their transition. You won't always be successful; after all, they had the Holy Angels who couldn't get them to understand what they should be doing, either. Possibly the one who died thinks the angel is part of a dream, and the reality of death is ignored. Often the humans around them want them to leave more than the ghosts do, hence the "haunting" or "haunted house" feeling. Here are a few examples of how we might be facilitated in bringing closure to these situations: (the names have been changed for privacy).

The Treasures in the Trunk

"Shelia" and her boyfriend had been renting the old house for over a year now. It was in a nice neighborhood, in an old southern town, and seemed like a good place to have a future. Shelia had made some little ripples in the music business, and right now she was really focusing on looking for unique songs and material that she could record. In this way, perhaps, she could stand out to the record companies and possibly get signed to a recording contract.

Shelia's other focus was her young son "Jimmy." He had been born prematurely and had several problems that could be with him for a long time. Even though he was almost five years old, he still wasn't talking more than a few words, and often just couldn't seem to focus on the reality around him. He was quiet and sweet, and showed affection easily, but also seemed easily distracted and "out of this world." So, for him, the ghost at Shelia's house was as real and visible as any playmate could ever be.

When I was first called, Shelia met me at the door and quickly let me in. "Now, you let me know if you see anything," she said. "I know something is here! It's driving me crazy."

Shelia brought me into the living room and nervously looked around. She could sense something, but the ghost wasn't in the living room - she was there in the kitchen, going through the motions of doing dishes in an empty sink. Jimmy was sitting on the living room floor, playing with a toy, pausing every now and then to turn in the ghost's direction with a big grin on his face. They definitely were pals. This always makes my job harder.

Shelia went on to tell me that the TV would often turn on in the middle of the night, with the volume up high – she would go to see if Jimmy had done it, but he would be fast asleep in his bed (you will find that ghosts and spirits like playing with electricity; it is similar to what they are made of, and is therefore easy to manipulate). I asked her about lights switching on and off, and she answered yes.

She also said that often she felt an icy coldness as she walked through the house, and in one spot in particular where she thought there had been a door replaced with a wall. She had actually resigned herself to these things; since she was afraid to tell anyone about it, in case they thought she was crazy. But, now she was being awakened in the middle of the night and early morning by a feeling of someone lying beside her, when her boyfriend wasn't there or had already gotten up. The final blow came when she couldn't open the door to the bedroom; after a few inches it just wouldn't budge, like something was propped on the floor against it. She was also afraid that "what ever it was" might hurt little Jimmy; his bedroom stayed so unusually cold now. I assured her that the ghost had no intention of hurting her son.

I asked if she had noticed when all this had begun, and she said things had been fine for a long time - just little problems now and then - but it had greatly sped up in just the last month.

I had said a prayer of protection before I came, not knowing what I would find, which is my way of saying to God "Alright, I'm going in! Let's keep the communication lines hot here!" But the Holy Spirit assured me things would be fine without additional "shields" (angels). "You be the power, I'll just be the mouth behind the words, ok?" I said in my head, with the intention of being heard by My Greatest Love.

Shelia walked me around the house and through the rooms. The ghost was very aware that I was aware of her, and actually stepped through me to get to the "door" (wall) when I was passing by it. I never like it when that happens. But, it does give me a very detailed description of them for that split-second that their spirit is in your flesh (dear reader, there you go getting scared again, stop that! God won't allow anything bad to happen to you, he is your protection and you are on a mission here)!

We went back into the living room and sat down, the ghost reappearing through the door, and moving back into the kitchen. She looked to be in her early 40's. She was dressed simply in a flowered cotton yellow dress, and had on flats and stockings. She had her dark hair neatly tucked up onto her head with bobby pins. It was not a tight bun, and seemed to be fairly short. She was of average height, maybe a bit taller.

I asked Shelia to stay there in the living room and I moved to the kitchen, where the ghost politely waved me in. I smiled at her and told her my name, and I could see her mouth move to tell me hers; but I couldn't quite get it. She motioned to her lovely kitchen and I saw it the way it used to be – she had projected it from her mind. She decorated it just like she had had it, blue and white being her favorite colors.

She took me on a tour of the rest of the house, and I saw the bedroom where she and her husband had slept (the same room where Shelia slept, and the old bed was in the same spot) and all the (antique) furnishings, including a beautiful quilt on the bed. She herself had died in that room. It felt like her husband had too, in this same room. She also wanted me to know that she was the owner of the house, and that she had been here for many years. I got the impression her husband had died many years before she did, and that she had also taken care of him through an extended time. The ghost looked out the window to the street outside. I looked too, but didn't see anything old – everything still looked modern, without anything being "superimposed" over it.

The ghost showed me something that she considered very important. There was a large *wooden chest* image on the floor in her bedroom. She kept making reference to it, and knocking on it, she wanted me to know it was important; I told her I understood, and she smiled.

We moved on, and I let her go ahead of me, where she passed through the (walled up) cellar door that *went down to the basement*. It seemed like something she was automated to do whenever she was close to it. When she came back up again, we went straight into the boy's room, where Jimmy was sitting on the bed.

96

He watched her come over to him and sit down beside him, putting her arm up over his back in a hug. He smiled from ear to ear.

"Tiffany, is everything ok?" Shelia called out. "Do you want Jimmy back in here?"

"No, we're fine, be out in a few minutes." I called back. I leaned against the wall and looked at the two on the bed. "You know, Jimmy," I said, "she is *not* your mommy."

He looked at me and nodded. He knew that.

"You know, Miss, that you will have to let him go and continue on your way. You have your husband waiting to welcome you, and think of all your friends who are waiting to see you again."

I let her know about my near-death experience (the lightning strike), and told her of the wonderful love that was waiting for her before the presence of the Lord. She heard the words, but she didn't seem to be listening.

I thought I would probably be seeing her again, so I left it at that. I know how these things are – first I have to do my part before they do theirs. And that chest was unfinished business.

I came back into the living room and told Shelia what was going on. She sat there with her mouth open.

"Shelia, is there anyone around here who would know who she is, and anything about that old chest?" I asked. She wasn't sure, perhaps one of her neighbors would know, she would ask. " I wonder what is inside that chest? She's not going to leave until we figure this out." I asked a Blessing on the house and *all* the folk who live there, and then I went home.

Two days later I got an urgent phone call from Shelia. "Tiffany, you must come quickly!"

Shelia had talked to her neighbor, a young woman close to her own age, who as a child, remembered the "old woman next door." When Shelia had first described the woman's appearance, she shook her head no, no, that wasn't her. Then Shelia mentioned about the woman dying in her room. Yes, the neighbor said, the old woman had been found dead in her room. She had been missing for a while, and when they first found her, it was hard to get in the bedroom because her body was on the floor in front of the door. They had to push the door hard to get it open. Also, her husband had died many years earlier, and the neighbor thought that had happened at home too.

The neighbor said she remembered seeing the old woman working long hours with the flowers in the front yard, but mostly she saw her in a rocking chair on the porch, writing. Shelia asked about the wooden chest. She didn't know anything about it, but she would ask her mother. Later on, the mother told her that the woman had given her *a chest full of letters, poems and songs.* And, oh by the way, the description we gave her of the "young woman's" appearance? It was exactly how the mother remembered how the old woman had looked when she was young!

The mystery was solved! The woman had been a writer! She wanted Shelia to look at her songs and the things she had written! She had such a need to communicate that she could not complete her transition without her things being shared with someone who could really appreciate them, instead of being locked up in a chest. It had been her life's work. So, while Shelia was heartily looking for songs, the ghost was heartily trying to give them to her. My goodness! *That* is a country song in itself!

There was such relief on all sides, for both the dead and the living! I praised God and finished with a simple prayer for the ghost. She would go now, and she did. I wasn't there to see the final parting, but I'm sure Jimmy was sad to see her go. But, everything that happens is for the Highest Good, and both needed to move into their future. This would also help Jimmy grasp *this* reality better, instead of being quite so open to both worlds. A tender place to be at any age!

There are many occurrences where you might be asked to help *ghosts* successfully continue their journey, but there might be times where *people* don't want you to "interfere." Sometimes they consider ghosts a conversation piece, and take every chance to show them off. I think this is selfish, and sad. Why wouldn't all people want the very best for these weary travelers? When the Holy Spirit takes the lead and propels a person to take the initiative to try to help, you have to go against what anyone else says and "just do it." God knows the best timing on all these things. *He never gives up on any of us* – and just as in life he brings people into our path at different places to see if we are ready yet to make new choices. He does this with ghosts too.

More Ghosts, Southern Style

There was a restaurant in middle Tennessee that was known far and wide for its "chittlins," catfish dinners, and homemade pies. To the locals, it was also known for its ghosts. A sensitive person would often be able to easily see them the very first time they walked in the door. This is how slow their vibration was and how grounded they were to the earthly realm. All the restaurant workers knew about them too, and it seemed to be a ritual for many to spend a few minutes of the evening after work, just sitting around drinking coffee and talking about the ghosts. I worked as a server here part-time.

The conversations had not been specific, and no one seemed to know how many ghosts there were, but speculation had it that it must be the old owner keeping an eye on the place. People had been known to quit after dodging pans mysteriously thrown at them across the kitchen. Guests had told the cashier many times of hearing someone crying in the bathroom, thinking there was a live person with black shoes and black stockings in the middle stall needing help. There was a pantry that stayed exceptionally cold and gave people the "willies," and the waitresses would always make a point of asking one of the busboys to get the needed items, instead of going in themselves. The cooks and servers who had been there for a longer period of time just ignored the conversations, letting the newer ones have their thrill.

One night, about two weeks after joining the team, I decided to join in on one of the conversations. They knew I had been given the gift of healing, since God had already used me for helping with knife cuts, carpal tunnel, burns, and a jammed wrist. It already seemed I spent more time in the back helping the staff than out front doing my job! But the manager was happy for it, because people didn't need to take time off work, they had a "doctor" on call! They didn't know that working with the Holy Spirit often allows a person to be used for other things. So, when the time seemed right, I offered to the discussion that there were three ghosts, two women and a man; and went on to describe them. *I hoped increased knowledge would lessen fear.*

The male ghost had been a cook or was in the kitchen most of the time, and yes, he would get very angry because he felt people weren't doing their job (I had noticed this especially when some of the boys would sneak outback and smoke marijuana during their breaks – his anger was so thick you could cut it with a knife!). He was older, and average height; and his head was balding and gray where it seemed to have been black before. He was the one who stayed in the back of the restaurant, and in the kitchen area.

There was also a female who seemed the perfect re-creation of what a Hollywood ghost would be. She was graceful and floated across the room everywhere she went. She spent most of her time out front, I never saw her in the kitchen area. She was very proud of her appearance and had her hair piled very high on top of her head, and wore bright red lipstick. She looked to be in her 40's. She seemed perfectly content to be spending all of her time in the dining rooms, smiling and greeting guests and walking with them to their tables. She blended easily in with the servers and the busboys, seemingly happy with all of it. Wherever she was, the immediate area around her was superimposed with the pictures and items and colors of the restaurant the way she remembered it. I tried talking to her once about "going home," and she just smiled back at me and pointed out "Today's Specials" on the menu!

I thought for a long time, trying to figure out what her unfinished business could be - since she seemed so happy here. Maybe that was it; she just didn't know how much better it was before the Lord.

The woman in the bathroom was another story: I had a hard time even using the facilities because of the pain of her sorrow. She would wail out loud and cry, mumbling words I couldn't understand. No one who worked here used the middle stall, they were all afraid. She definitely was wearing black shoes and black stockings; a little fancy, I thought, for someone who would be eating here. Curiosity made me wonder about the guests who actually sat down on that stool. Did they leave feeling depressed? Servers would come in to the bathroom and count their tips to trade for larger bills, and get all flustered, having to count it over many times. Her energy was very distracting. I even watched a few small children come in and behave strangely - to the point of their mothers asking them "what is wrong?" Children have a "knowing" when ghosts and spirits are around. And who is to say that this sphere is not where many of our little one's "invisible friends" and "special playmates" come from?

As the discussion was developing, more of the staff sat down to listen. I asked some of the folk who had been there a while if they could validate anything of what I was saying. No one spoke. I told them the purpose for my sharing this information, from Whom I got it, and our obligation to help ghosts when we can. I was hoping that perhaps less people would quit now, too. Time would tell. The one thing for me that happened immediately, was being pulled aside the next day by the owner for a private talk!

"I heard about that conversation last night. How do you know these things?" he asked.

I started off by telling him we were all off the clock at that time, as far as I knew. I was thinking, "Oh no! Here goes my job!" (I was offering healing on a donation basis at the time, and it was all by word of mouth; hence the need for the part-time job). I told him how the Lord uses me for things, and briefly described the three ghosts again, to make sure he had heard the information correctly.

He nodded his head. "Well, let me tell you something. Two years ago I had two parapsychologists come in here with a room full of fancy equipment, and *tell me the same things."* I smiled.

I asked him if he wanted me to tell the ghosts anything, and that I would like to do a cleansing ceremony, after restaurant hours, and ask them to go. He said, "No, they aren't bothering anyone. I was just curious about how you knew about them. Just let them be."

I was shocked. I had never been confronted with this problem before. He owned this establishment. Having the ghosts here had brought him notoriety before, maybe they would again. He definitely did not want me to "mess with them."

I pushed a little further. I said, "But it is so much nicer where they could be; especially the woman in the bathroom. Wouldn't you like them to move on? It is no problem for me, I really think you should let me do this!"

He didn't even hesitate, "The woman with the red lipstick is Mrs. S., and I like having her around. This used to be her restaurant, and how you described her is just how she looked when she was younger. If she wants to be here, then this is her heaven. Just leave them alone." (I found out later that she never missed a day of work, and that when she died at an old age, they even buried her with a tall wig on and in her bright red lipstick, just the way she had always worn it).

I didn't know what else to say to change his mind. What was I to do? I went to God in prayer. This was the restaurant owner's land, his property. And I was under obligation even as his employee to "obey the boss." The answer came back clear:

"I AM THE BOSS! I placed you here for many things, and this is one of them...!"

I Love It when he makes things so clear! The next night found me coming to work early and "casually" hanging around the entrance to the back door. I was trying to do a purification ceremony outside for the "cooking ghost." I was interrupted many times. I knew that it would have been better inside, but there was no way I could do it around all these people. I ended up not doing anything out of the *Minister's Service Manual* and just tried to tell him about the heaven that I had seen, and how much better it was there than here; just by projecting my thoughts and prayer. I did Mrs. S. the same way. I hoped that was enough for now, and that the Holy Spirit would send an angel and some friends and relatives to help convince them (again) too.

The ghost in the bathroom I had more time with. Who is going to come into your own stall and ask what you are doing? She was also the one for whom I felt the most motivation. I sat in the stall next to her, and looked at her stockings and feet. They were almost so real I could have touched them. She told me of her pain, and "how he didn't love her," and "how could he do this to me?" The words were audible enough, but she showed me no pictures in my mind of anything. She was continually crying and sobbing uncontrollably.

I let her know, as I did the others, that she had already let go of life in this world; she had died, and her flesh was no more. From there I did the ceremony and shared with her my near-death experience of coming before the Presence of God. It seems I get used a lot in this field, maybe because I am a *human* who has been there and can share the experience, helping to dispel some fear of theirs – perhaps from a different angle than an angel could.

Before my eyes the stockings faded and disappeared. The crying stopped, and a glow of warmth settled in around me; coming down my head and flooding my entire body. It was the Holy Spirit, telling me we were successful. She had gone! I said a *Thank You* prayer and praised God for being used in anyway he sees fit.

The next day, one of the long-time servers approached me and told me about who she thought the woman in the bathroom could be. The story goes that a woman and her fiancé were driving down the freeway together, on their way to a party. He had been drinking, and they got into a fight. He pulled out a gun and shot her at point-blank range, in the stomach, opened the car door and pushed her out. She was found dead, not far from the road, as if she had walked for a bit first.

The restaurant is just at that exit from the freeway. Perhaps she thought she was still alive and just kept walking; couldn't comprehend what had happened to her; and hid herself in the bathroom to cry and never came out. It had been many years since the murder. Everything fit, and I'm sure this had been the ghost from that incident. Now, she was at peace, and had found the only True Love.

The other two ghosts remained until I stopped working there a few months later. Now, though, they took notice of when I was there, and avoided me like I was the plague. When I asked the Lord about it, he said my job was done here, and that they would be given another opportunity later on.

Sometimes, a ghost is brought to you for a dual purpose, for the closure of someone living, and for someone dead. Such is the case in the next story, and it was a time when I was still learning how to "hear" and new to interpreting what I could "see." But, when the Lord wants his work done, he gets the messages across.

A Father Asks Forgiveness

An urgent message was left on the answering machine from a person whose name I didn't recognize. Returning her call, I spoke to "Rose," the young woman on the other end. Could I see her tomorrow? She was in desperate pain and suicidal. If I couldn't help her, she didn't know what else to do. She had been to many doctors for her pelvic pain, and had had two operations. Still she had pain, too terrible to even keep a job. She had quit work and was living back home with her parents, although she was nearing 30 years of age. She just couldn't go on. We made the appointment, and I encouraged her to look forward to our meeting, and to hold tight until we could meet. We would meet tomorrow, everything would be better then. Did she need some phone numbers? I had some helpful people she could talk to *right now*. I offered her the suicide hotline number. She said no, that she would be ok. I encouraged her and got driving directions, I would be going to her house in the morning.

Suicide! I'm her last hope! Nothing like a little bit of pressure, eh! I am glad that it is *God* who is doing all this, and that I don't have to worry about the next day; it is his work! But, he does have me offer words at times to help in additional ways, and I always keep a listing of telephone numbers that I can pass on. These include the listings for the suicide hotline, domestic violence and shelter programs, police, and various counselors, etc. It is a good idea for everyone to carry around a listing like this. You never know when it could come in handy. There are many well-trained people who are ready to help others *in any way they can.* Healing comes in many ways.

That night, I was in bed reading when I felt the "whoosh" of a spirit go thru me - I was being visited. I knew that the Lord only allows things like this to happen when he arranges it, so I was not afraid. I looked up and saw the mist of a ghost, not very clear definitions though, nor facial features, but a ghost nonetheless.

I asked for whom the visit was, thinking it was for someone whom I had previously had a treatment with that day. There was no fluctuation of any kind in its energy pattern. So, I went down the list of names I had scheduled for the next day. "George...(no change), Elsa...(no change), Rose..." All of a sudden, a power surge hit - the phone rang half a ring, and the lights flickered. "Ok, it's for Rose." I said out loud. I knew there was a need for the ghost to communicate with Rose, but I was new at interpreting these kinds of messages. How would I understand? How could we talk to each other? I was so afraid of misinterpreting something, that I was actually clogging myself up.

So, being the inventor that I am (sometimes to my detriment!) I first got out a can of foaming bathtub cleaner, and sprayed the closet mirror. I informed the ghost he could write in here what he wanted to say. All that happened was the foam slogged to the bottom of the glass and made a mess to clean up. That wasn't going to work!

Next, I lit a candle and put a post-it note on one side of it with the word "yes" written on it, and another on the other side saying "no." Then I said, "ok, if you are male, bend the flame to yes" – and the flame bent over to yes!

Then I said "OK, this might sound funny, but if you are female, bend it to yes." And the flame bent to "no." Then I was able to proceed with many questions, while I wrote the answers down. This man was Rose's father, and he was incredibly *sorry*.

More than anything, he wanted forgiveness from his daughter. He had been sexually abusive toward her as a young girl. He wanted me to tell her that he loved her very much, and "please forgive me." He definitely had unfinished business with her, and had not been able to cross over to the Lord. He was *very sad.*

I asked him many questions, and filled three small pages with "yes" and "no" answers, just by watching the flame. Sometimes he put a vision in my head, when I needed more information, and when I was not asking a question, the flame stood straight up, without flickering.

I still wanted more. I wanted concrete evidence that I could give Rose that her dad had visited me the night before her healing. This was going to be some heavy stuff – I needed absolute warranty!

I asked him how would she know it was he who was contacting her - *so he went through me* - and for a moment *I felt* what he looked like. He had a broad, wide nose; long black hair from the midline of his head to his neck and balding on top; a beard, and a deep echo voice. He was Native American. I took out a pencil and drew a quick picture.

When I asked how he died, I felt a tingling down my left leg. I asked if anything was wrong with his leg; he said "no - yes - maybe." I said I couldn't do "maybes," it had to be either "yes" or "no." I asked if he had a bad left arm, or had died of a stroke, and he said "yes, yes, yes" three times. I also had gotten the nickname of "Red," the word "kitty" and something about a frog. He was an alcoholic. I asked him if he had been trying to contact Rose and he said "yes."

Next, I got angry with him and said, "Shame on you for waiting until you are dead and having to wait until a stranger comes along to apologize for you! Isn't there someone else to speak to her *here* instead of me (grandparents, friends, etc)?" He said "no."

Then I told him that I had enough information, that I wanted him to leave now, and not to come back again unless I asked him to. Having his gloomy presence there was *not* the same feeling as an "Aunt Betsy's ghost baking cookies." When I looked up, the ghost/mist had disappeared. After his presence was gone, I prayed for guidance and visualized the Lord's Love and enveloping light surrounding me, growing and growing until the entire room was cleansed. Everything was clear.

The next day I showed up at Rose's house. This was a whole new experience for me, about passing on information like this. But, I had faith that it would be the right thing to do. I reasoned that now the healing done would be on all fronts because of this: a *spiritual* healing for both (perhaps giving the information would let her father continue on) if Rose was able to show forgiveness; an *emotional* healing tied into the pain in her pelvis; and perhaps a *physical* healing for any scar tissue, etc, that had occurred from the (possibly unneeded) surgeries.

I rang the doorbell and waited. Who should answer the door but a small-boned, pale-skinned and slender blonde! "Oh no, I really blew it this time" I'm thinking to myself. "How could I get all that wrong?" She showed me to the kitchen and offered me some tea. I hesitated.

"First," I asked, "Could you tell me if your father is dead?"

A moment of quietness; then slowly, "Yes...why?"

"Because he came to visit me last night." I replied. She leaned against the counter to keep from falling.

I started reading her the pages of notes. He says, "I am so sorry...can you forgive me...I tried to visit you...please, I love you...I want you to be happy..." I went on and on.

I stopped and looked up, her eyes full of tears. "Do you understand all this?" I asked.

"Yes," she said. "He had a very red colored face, that is why he is saying "red." His face is exactly as you describe him; wide nose; dark eyes; and he was Indian. My mom wasn't. I dye my hair blonde, or else it would be dark."

I sighed relief to myself (why do I doubt when I am being used for The Lord's work?).

Then I said, "He also said he died of a stroke...he said 'yes' to that three times."

Rose broke into weeping. "Yes," she answered, "Do you know how huge this is?" she sobbed.

"Yes," I said. "God has arranged our meeting. Now you can forgive, let go, and get on with your life. And your father wants to move on too." I told her he probably won't or can't move on to the light of God until she truly forgives him, and that she needs to talk to him tonight, when we were finished with the healing treatment.

Rose said she could do that – she *could* forgive him! I did a healing treatment on her and found scar tissue and adhesions from the surgeries. I felt anger toward the doctors. I hoped there really had been something wrong, and not their just having taken advantage of her emotional pain.

105

One Week Later - Rose called this morning, and had a surprise to tell me. That night, after the treatment, she had a long talk with her "ghost dad." She also had sexual relations with the young man she loved, and for the *first time* in her life she had *no pain!* She said she felt like a new woman. She had put a deposit on an apartment, and was looking for a job. Now, she could see herself getting married and even having a family. She was so happy!

I am sure her spirit dad was too, now that the transition could finally take place; and he could move into a situation of which only Divine Grace could afford the high price. Divine Grace and a daughter's tears, of forgiveness. A cleansing for both of them, and deep healing on many levels.

Spirits

Spirits are the life force of people who have died and successfully transitioned to the Lord. They often take the time to show up once or twice to let us know they are OK on the "the other side." It takes quite a bit of effort to manipulate this energy, and it seems like it takes a bit of practice too. On the average, I have found spirits are easier to be seen either *immediately* after their death (like on the same day – they still have the angel's energy helping them to finish up and let go) or after a small waiting period. I don't know if they go through a "settling in" process or what, but after approximately two weeks they learn to slow their frequency down enough to manage being seen for short periods of time.

The spirits that you see will often be people that you know. Especially if you were close to them and had a connection of love. More often, you will sense them. Perhaps even catch a whiff of grandpa's aftershave or mama's perfume. As with ghosts, you may feel cold and have the other bodily receptors activate.

Spirits often are sent in a "messenger" way to tell you something, or to act as a warning. They are also allowed to communicate through dreams. Sometimes they just barge right in and make themselves known. They did the same thing, numerous times, in the Bible.

Jesus as Divine Protection

If we believe in God and angels, then we are compelled to also believe what the scriptures say about demons and evil spirits too. We have already seen where the demons came from – they were angel sons of God who rebelled against the guidelines and heavenly responsibilities they were given, and created bodies for themselves, having relations with earthly women. They thus aligned themselves with the first rebellious angel, the one called "Devil" (Hebrew – "Slanderer") and "Satan" (Hebrew – "Resister"), the one who challenged that God didn't operate in the best interests for mankind and the heavenly realm. Later, a third of the angels were ousted from heaven by Faithful Angels and the Archangel Michael. They are permitted to operate on the earth today, for a short period of time. (1 Pe. 3:19-20)

The devil was a beautiful angel with high responsibility who started wanting all of God's glory for himself. He had started out perfect, as an angel created by God. (De. 32:4) But, as a free moral agent, he made his own choices along the way, and he chose to act against all that was good and holy. (Jas. 1:13) All through the scriptures he is seen as a person, and not as some evil abstract. As Christians, we are enlightened through the Bible to realize that Satan exists, but that *he has no holds on us.* Jesus expelled wicked spirits from people, and gave this same authority to his followers, the apostles and the disciples, "In the name of Jesus." (Lu. 10:17) We work for the God of Love and Divine Power. Satan's purposes and manners of operation are shown clearly to us from the scriptures, but the Lord enables us to fight him with His Name and the spiritual weapons he provides.

"Finally, be strong in the Lord and in his mighty power. Put on the full armor of God so that you can take your stand against the devil's schemes. For our struggle is not against flesh and blood, but against the rulers, against the authorities, against the powers of this dark world and against the spiritual forces of evil in the heavenly realms. Therefore, put on the full armor of God..." (Eph.6:10)

Do not fear! The Lord will hold you in the palm of his hand - working for God is a place of Divine Blessing and Spiritual Protection. I have included a guideline in the back of the book if you are brought to a situation that the Lord wants you to remove from the area and cast out; this a God-Spot gift too.

In dealing with all these responsibilities that may come your way, know that you are using your Divine Gifts in the best possible way. You are helping his kids find their way again, and true freedom. "The righteous cry out, and the Lord hears them; and he delivers them from all their troubles." (Ps. 34:17) Our Mighty God! Everyone we meet has a "why!" There is a reason for us coming into each others paths. There is no such thing as plain coincidence, just Divine Intervention!

CHAPTER 7

The Healing Connection – Miracles in the God-Spot
Healing Prayer, Reiki and Medical Intuitiveness

"He said to them…and these signs will accompany those who believe…they will place their hands on sick people and they will get well." (Mk 16:18)

"Now about spiritual gifts, brothers, I do not want you to be ignorant… there are different kinds of gifts, but the same Spirit…to each one the manifestation of the Spirit is given for the common good…to one there is given the gift of prophecy…to another gifts of healing…all these are the work of one and the same Spirit, and he gives them to each one, just as he determines."
(1 Co. 12:1-11)

The Bible is a complete book about healing! He touches us physically, emotionally, spiritually, and delivers us from evil. God has our holistic health care plan all laid out! In fact, Jesus said, in fulfillment of Isaiah's prophecy, that those who refused to recognize healing as a divine miraculous sign were considered "blind, deaf, and deadened in their hearts." (Jn. 12:37-40)

Healing in the past was considered a sign of God's Spirit manifesting its power in our behalf. Even before the time of the miracles of Jesus, God enabled many of his people to have healing abilities. And even then, they were manifested in a *variety* of ways. Just as today, it does not seem to matter what method was used – they were all channels through which God's power could be seen and felt in people's lives; both for the facilitator, and for the one being healed, their friends and their family.

Many Styles, Many Methods, One Spirit

In the scriptures, we find people were healed with the laying on of hands; prayer; people touching the healer; long-distance healing with just a word; healing for someone who interceded for someone else; mud; spittle; cloth; poultice; water; oil; bones and even the shadow of the healer touching someone. Why wouldn't our unchangeable God use a variety of methods today? He does!

"I the Lord do not change." (Mal. 3:6)

"Jesus Christ is the same yesterday and today and forever." (Heb. 13:8)

Jesus said that after his death and resurrection, the Holy Spirit would be poured out and even greater works would be accomplished. (Acts 2:17-33) What a blessing! Are we helping to accomplish that which was prophesied?

It only makes sense that Divine Healing, being one of God's Gifts, would be seen in all parts of the earth, in all different cultures, and throughout all periods of time. There would be no "corner" on the market. Who can box in the Holy Spirit? Why are we then so surprised when gifts come to us called by different names? Are we going to be prejudiced against them, and 'chop down the tree before it bears fruit?'

Timothy was told by the apostle Paul: "*Fan into flame the gift of God, which is in you through the laying on of my hands.* For God did not give us a spirit of timidity, but a spirit of power, of love and of self-discipline." (2 Tim. 1:6) God gives all Christians gifts to minister with, and we are told that all of us should *"eagerly desire the greater gifts."* (1 Co. 27-31) We are commissioned to heal the sick among us, and as believers we are asking God to develop what is already inside us – the authority and power of the Holy Spirit.

We must actively *yield* to be successfully used by him. *Surrender.* Some of us may also have specialties that help one disease or problem better than another. Do you see that Paul helped Timothy receive the "gift of God" by his laying on of hands? *Do not be afraid to ask others to help you come before the Lord in sacred trust and ceremony.* God asks us to take action to show we are serious with our prayers.

Jesus said: "Have faith in God...Therefore I tell you, whatever you ask for in prayer, believe that you have received it, and it will be yours." (Mk. 11:24)

"Praise the Lord... who heals all your diseases." (Ps. 103:1-3)

Some Ways the Holy Spirit Does Healings

Sometimes in the scriptures, we find that healing was gradual, and at other times it was instantaneous. It is the same way today. Never put a barrier on this Wondrous Energy! The Holy Spirit is Limitless! You don't even need to know what the problem or disease is for the Spirit to cure it – what is occurring isn't wishful thinking or hypnosis or mind control. It is not the "power of positive thinking." *It has consistent, measurable results. And faith by the sick one is not always a factor,* yesterday or today, about whether someone gets healed or not. There are many instances in the scriptures where those *without* faith were healed. *Faith does not heal – God heals!* (Jn. 5:5-13) This is why even people without faith in God, babies who have no knowledge, and agnostics and atheists, receive healings. So do animals. Why?

All this brings glory to the One Gracious Father. None of us could ever *earn* being healed. It is a gift from God, to *draw us to him* and *manifest his will in our lives,* as a witness to our spirit and those around us, so that we may *all* glorify him!

Often a warm glow will descend down upon the one being healed. The one being facilitated by the Holy Spirit for the healing will also feel the glow – for me it starts at the top of the head as a feeling of effervescent warmth and sparkle, then slowly descends down through the rest of my body (like warm honey!). It is always accompanied by a feeling of peace and bliss – it is that feeling of communion with God that I live for! I find that if even a few days go by and I have not been utilized by the Holy Spirit, that I become anxiety ridden and nervous. I need my "fix!" Working for the Lord is the best addiction in the world! The healings make me feel peaceful beyond words, calm and as warm as stepping into a Jacuzzi. I always feel a healing too, and totally loved!

The Holy Spirit seems to bathe all the individual cells with a "cosmic energy soup." It also stimulates recuperation time and seems to promote "cell memory" of how the original cell structure is organized. As technology advances, more and more clinical studies are becoming available citing research on different methods of what the medical community often calls "Energy Modality," "Healing Prayer," or "Spiritual Healing." Some, like Reiki and Therapeutic Touch®, have gained enough attention to be considered a Complementary Alternative Medicine as defined by the American Medical Association, and practitioners are actively utilized in many hospitals (and is being used by nurses and doctors too!).

Falling under the title of "Reiki Practitioner" has made it possible for me to call upon the Spirit to heal full-time in clinical environments. I am considered by the California State Board of Nursing as a provider for Continuing Education for nurse's requirements. I am also in a pilot program for being able to legally submit appropriate insurance claims for integrative healthcare interventions using ABC Codes (Reiki is listed but not, as yet, Healing Prayer). It is wonderful to live in a time when That Which Is Invisible can be seen through the eyes of science as "really there!" For those with the eyes of faith, this is not needed. But, for those who may not have an understanding of God's power, it is invaluable as a factor in helping them decide to submit themselves to something in which they had not believed. *Sometimes a healing is the first time in their lives that people have felt the presence of God working in their behalf!* And, since the Lord heals at all levels, often a spiritual and emotional release accompanies the physical one. Indeed, if the spirit is not touched, what's the point?

Sometimes, in the case of bacteria or a virus, the symptoms may initially get worse. The natural duration of the disease is being sped up – and cells are actively cleansing themselves and pushing toxins out into the bloodstream, where they are still needing to be released from the body. Drinking plenty of water after a healing always helps. Some people are also a bit dizzy, and should wait and walk around a bit before they drive home.

After the Holy Spirit is initially finished, the Spirit's energy is still in the body for several days, continuing to heal the one being helped. It is similar to unplugging a fan out of the wall; just like fan blades continuing to spin, it takes a while for them to slow down and stop. During that time, healing still continues through the rest of the day or even throughout the week. People often feel very peaceful and relaxed, as all the Wonderful Energy of God that has gone through them leaves a lovely residual effect!

The ones helping with the healing also receive many "perks" from working so closely with the Lord. *A feeling of being connected to all living things occurs* – we seem to know where every bird is in the trees, where every squirrel is under the bushes! Colors themselves seem to be brighter, and hearing more intense. A sense of *well-being* and *peace beyond words* descends upon us, and *truly blissful sleep* comes from knowing that we are fulfilling the Divine purpose for our lives.

If you chose to work as a vessel being yielded, you are choosing to work hand-in-hand with the Very Persona of God. You may even notice that during a treatment your own breathing is altered to become slow and thin, almost as if your own life-force were yielding to leave room for the Spirit of God within. What a feeling! You will see his guiding hand as people and situations are brought in to your life in such a way that could *never* be possible before. "Divine Coincidences" abound, as you grow used to "blessed uncertainty," having confidence that God knows the destination of your path, has put your foot firmly upon it, and all you have to do is plunge straight ahead. Run after him! He will work out the details! Such a sense of freedom could never be imagined, until you see it in your own life. Everyday is an adventure as you keep your head in the heavens, feet on the earth, and arms wide open!

Prayer is Absolutely Necessary

It is best for those calling upon the Lord for healing to be in a constant state (in an undertone) of silent (or audible) prayer. Indeed, what can be accomplished without prayer? And inviting the one to be healed to *also approach God in prayer* accomplishes many things. For one, *the people themselves are taking an active step in reaching out to God,* perhaps for the first time in years, and are acknowledging an *acceptance of responsibility* in the healing process. For example, if the person wants to be healed of lung cancer, the acceptance of responsibility may be to actively throw his cigarettes away and stop smoking. If a drug addict or alcoholic wants to be cleaned of toxins, the acceptance of responsibility would dictate that he does not use these substances anymore nor associate with those who encourage him to do so.

The true elegance of healing prayer is being able to let go of the results, knowing what will be accomplished is for the Highest Good. The flesh is not the main concern - that is only a temple for our spirit to live in. The important thing is our spirit journey - learning by the obstacles in our life that we gain success only when we lean upon the Lord. We know and have the confidence that all of our needs are being met, *in God's own way and in his perfect time.*

"Trust in the Lord with all your heart and lean not on your own understanding; in all your ways acknowledge him, and he will make your paths straight."
(Pro. 3:5,6)

Not all people are going to be healed physically. Perhaps an emotional or spiritual healing is going to occur first, or even in place of, a physical one. We do not know. Even though we may want and pray earnestly for the ability to heal a problem, we must realize that *we* do not use the Holy Spirit - it is *he* who uses *us!* Realizing that *we* cannot heal everyone, that *we* can't always do what *we* want to do, shows us that *we are only instruments,* a tool. We have no control over what God does. And, in saying that, please note that it is not your fault if results do not seem openly noticeable. It is not our job to defend God, he can do that himself. It is our job to *proclaim him.*

By telling the person that you are approaching God in prayer in their behalf for the healing, they also see that *you* are applying to a Higher Source, and that there is no special thing inside you – you are not the one doing the healing. Your job is to be a yielded vessel, and not "clog up the channel" by any preconceived notions or prejudices about race, gender, social standing or religious affiliation, etc. Just keep out of the way and let the Big Guy come through! You are only the power cord, the jumper cable, between this person and God. Just a vessel of clay, a fleshly body, just a lover of God wanting to help his kids be touched by his Divine Hand.

Why does God allow the gift of healing between people? We know *he can go direct* by Divine Prayer, without any "middle man," and he often does. He doesn't need a lump of flesh to yield himself to him for the Holy Spirit to work. So why does he use "healers?" Simply this - he is a good, loving father who wants *all of his kids to work together, love each other and to get along!* Just like he decided that man and woman should come together to create a child, he actively wants us to interact together for the common good and to help and encourage each other. He doesn't *need* to give us gifts at all, but he does. He always amazes me!

Medical Intuitiveness – God's "Sonar"

Often I start a healing treatment at the clinic without even knowing what is wrong with the person. If there is time, I move my hands respectfully from one place to another, from head to foot. Then, as I find things, they gain confidence in the work being done. They gain validation as my hands get hot and find the problem spots on their bodies without them telling me. In this way they know it is not "power of positive thinking" or any kind of "hypnosis." This also sets what I do apart from psychic healing, wishful thinking or mind control.

Although there are practitioners in Reiki (as in every other kind of modality) who may not be acknowledging the Holy Spirit as their Source, or combine it with questionable practices, overall, I have found Reiki to be a very pure connection for God to work. As in all things, please keep in mind the test of "by their fruits you will recognize them," as discussed previously, before you seek *any* healing practitioner.

I have found that some places where my hands "get hot" are injuries or broken bones that go back thirty years or more. This is the main reason for a full body hands-on-healing, so the person feels the place of injury being acknowledged. The Holy Spirit does not need this method to activate a healing - my hands may be touching one spot only, as on the forehead or chest. The Holy Spirit will work if you are only holding onto a toe or a finger - such as in a hospital bed with very little skin exposed. He will even act with the hands being held over *or just towards the body,* without the person being physically touched at all!

Healing often occurs for people in the same room, across the street, across the town, and across the world! Since he knows what needs to be done, and it is by *his* power that healing is done anyway, he will often use our Godly intention (prayer) to facilitate healing through many means, *time and distance not being a factor.* It does not matter where the physical body is, he knows! You can also send healing prayer to a future time if you know of a stressful situation going to occur, or send healing prayer to a time in the past that needs to be overcome and let go of. Do not forget to send healing prayers in behalf of yourself, it will keep you balanced and strong. *God is the Father of time and quantum physics: past, present and future are simple equations in his hands.*

Jesus said, "Therefore I tell you, whatever you ask for in prayer, believe that you have received it, and it will be yours." (Mk 11:24)

Medical intuitiveness is not a necessary item for healing to progress. Just as with the hands feeling hot against the body where there is a physical injury, or an emotional one, being intuitive just gives more details to the *convince the brain what the mind already knows.* Sometimes the vision of spirit is so clear when I am being used to work on someone, that I can readily see through the skin, down past the muscle and tendons, and through to the inside of bones. Often I will draw diagrams of what I see on my charts, especially if it is a tumor, cancer, or an artery blockage.

Different things *feel* different under a sensitive hand. There are different vibrational qualities attached to different problems. Through time, I have been able to assign "colors" to different vibrations that I feel, in this way it makes the diseases and ailments easier to remember. At first I didn't know anything at all - I would pick up a certain vibration, and find out afterward what it was when the person would say "I have diabetes," or "I have heart disease." Then I would keep that vibration in mind and assign it an easy memory color pattern. When I felt that same vibration again in someone else, I would softly venture the question. In this way I learned. I am still learning, and come across new things all the time.

I have also found that there are some types of drugs and medications that make the vibrations in the body difficult for me to "see" through. Two of them are cocaine and morphine-based medications. I am *not* saying that healing cannot be done through them - who am I to limit the hand of God? I am just saying that the vibrational level is *so extremely high* that I cannot feel the Spirit moving under my hands, or the "intuitive knowing" that he sometimes allows.

Some things are now very easy for me to detect, cancer being one of them. It seems that the vibration of cancer is so all-invasive that even just touching a person's hand is all that is needed to know that the disease is somewhere in the body. I assign it an "orange" color. Aids is "orange-brown." The list goes on, with several color combinations coming from fine-tuning the knowledge given. But, I also make mistakes and misinterpret vibrations. Especially, new problems that I am not yet familiar with. I use the medical intuition openly when the person I am working on knows beforehand about the disease or ailment. Giving the additional information can lead them to a greater belief in the God who sees what is hidden. *I refuse to use it as a "parlor trick" to impress.* This would be *unjust use* of the power of the Most Just, whom I *really* do not want to offend!

"For you created my innermost being; you knit me together in my mother's womb. I praise you because I am fearfully and wonderfully made; your works are wonderful, I know that full well. My frame was not hidden from you when I was made in the secret place. When I was woven together in the depths of the earth, your eyes saw my unformed body. All the days ordained for me were written in your book before one of them came to be." (Ps.139:13-16)

Not being a medical doctor, I do not diagnose. But, I do encourage people to get things checked out when I find something "wrong." Comically, this can be a "Catch 22" because often the Lord heals the ailment and takes care of the problem when I initially see the person – then there is *nothing* to diagnose! But, the main thing is that the person has been healed, not that my ego is satisfied. May His Will be done!

Some things will feel different under my hands from just the difference between hot and cold. Often, a tumor will feel like a cold spot – almost like a lump of scar tissue, with edges that fade out into the warm surrounding area. A broken bone will feel like a definite cold line, with sharp contrast to the surrounding bone. A fracture is much more subtle to feel – a soft cold line, with minimal contrast.

The first time I "looked" at the brain, I thought I was going to faint! An entire city under a cap of bone! The pulsating of blood and electrical "synapses" passing back and forth and through the coiled up folds looks like translucent earthworms! What a complex and marvelous machine, capable of so many things! I also found that places where a stroke had appeared, or damage caused by accident, were easily identified in the soft tissues. Emotions are also easy to perceive here, and placing the hands on the head relieves many stresses and fear. This "head" position (there are actually five) is also a good position to aid the one who is crossing over in death. But, as always, please remember that The Spirit, like Divine aspirin, goes to where it is needed. We, as mortals, need not be too concerned about hand-placement.

Here are a few letters and stories you might enjoy from my files, the names have been changed for the sake of privacy. You will see I may call the healing by different names at different times – but it is of "the same Spirit." (1 Co. 12)

93 Year Old Woman Escapes Surgery with Healing Prayers

(As received by letter from V.H. - Reprinted by Permission)

The gift of touch and the touch of healing is truly a gift from God that a person can be anointed in. I wrote this letter to show that God still uses people to do healing work, just like in the days of Jesus, through the Holy Spirit. Then it was a sign of God's Love and Power working for his people, and I believe He still uses it today because I saw it in my life!

This is what happened when God moved one of His Gifts into our lives in a mighty way, and the woman who brought the gift, who I can truly call my dear friend.

Reverend Doctor Tiffany Snow and I met in a special and unique way while she was still in Tennessee, and she has been a blessing and teacher to my family since she moved here to California this last summer.

My mother is 93 years old and she has a keen sense of discernment for people. When she first met Rev. Snow she immediately took a liking to her. Because of this bond, she looked forward to each session with her. With each session, healing in and through mom's body was occurring. Both eyes were clearing, one eye had nearly been blind, and her ability to walk greatly improved. The power of prayer and God's mercy and grace stretched our belief in healing hands by touch.

In September of this year, my mom was diagnosed with a spot (4 cm) on her right lung, and abnormal pap cells. Suspecting cancer, the doctor, Dr. G. M.D., FAAFP., was recommending a biopsy and possible surgery. At mom's age this was an impossible vision to foresee and one my family and I questioned.

The night before my mom was scheduled for a cat scan, Dr. Snow came to visit. Upon greeting my mom with a hug she informed me that my cousin and I had to be powerful prayer warriors this evening.

As Dr. Snow gently laid her hands upon my mom's head and on different places of her body, and started her healing prayers, God used her in a powerful way. The presence of the Holy Spirit not only filled the room my mom was in - He filled the entire house with His Glory! The power of prayer was awesome as we also had several prayer groups across San Diego County uniting with us for healing of mom's body.

There is no other explanation, but we knew that whatever occurred after this evening it would be God's will, and I was okay with His decision.

Mom's visit on Thursday morning at the imaging center in Riverside was intense, not knowing, but believing a miracle had occurred on that previous Tuesday night. The doctor entered with mom's chart and test results saying "Ladies…someone's been praying." My cousin and I replied, "Yes, we have." The doctor said "No! I mean let me read the test results…!"

The only word I remember is "benign" and the praise began as the tears flowed. The doctor informed us that "only a residue" was left in the area where the spot had existed and they would treat her with medication for the cervical area. No surgery was needed!

This stretched my faith in healing - when we allow God to use us and with Dr. Snow as a healer anointed by God, because of her Love and respect for God and her desire to be obedient and a vessel empty and ready to be filled. This miracle has touched the lives of so many people who know my mother – friends, relatives, doctors and nurses. I am hoping it will inspire you to Praise God! And to know that His hand is never too short to reach us, we are never too old to be helped. And that He is able and wanting to show us Love in every way - if we are just open to it, He can Heal us.

Crippled Hand Revived

When I lived in Tennessee, a man in his 50's came into the restaurant where I worked. As I poured his coffee he pulled out a miniature Bible and started reading it while waiting for his meal.

He looked up and smiled, "I can see by the light in your eyes that you have Jesus in your heart."

"Thank you!" I replied, "And I appreciate seeing a person reading the Bible in a public place."

"What church do you and your husband attend?" the man asked.

"I visit many churches," I said, "and I *am* dedicated, not to a man, but to my work with the Lord. I am staying single to do it properly."

"What work is that?" he asked.

"God lets me be there when he heals people." I replied.

"Oh, please! Please!" said the man, "I need a healing. I have a terrible migraine and have been in pain for days!

"I can't." I said, "I am working right now. But after work I could say prayers with you."

"No, no!" the man said, with a look of despair on his face.

Well, right then I knew I was about to jeopardize my job again for the sake of the Lord, as I was compelled to take one hand, then the other, and say a prayer to God for this man in pain. I touched his shoulders, his head and his chest. He started blubbering and crying out loud. I felt my job would be over – all the other tables were looking strangely at us.

"Why are you crying?" I asked. "Did it hurt?"

"My hand!" he said, as he looked at his left hand curling and uncurling; "My hand! I haven't been able to do that for 24 years! I have arthritis, and look at it stretch out! My headache is gone too, praise the Lord! I don't know what your name is, but I am going to call you Angel, thank you for the healing!"

I leaned over and whispered in his ear, "You do not need to thank me. You know who did the healing, *it was the Lord.* Let this be our secret."

Well, the Holy Spirit knew I had limited time with this man, and facilitated an instantaneous healing within a span of a couple of minutes. And, another miracle - my manager and the other servers didn't seem to have noticed! But it was a good witness to many observing tables. I saw this man several more times, though he never needed another healing. Often he would bring others with him who needed The Great Doctor, and we made plans to heal them after hours.

Speedy Recovery from Mononucleosis

My daughter Sierra was working part time and finishing up eleventh grade in high school. Her final exams were just a few weeks away when she was diagnosed with mononucleosis and told not to come back to school until it was completely over. She was also told if she missed her finals, she may have to return next year and take the courses all over again. We were told it would take six or seven weeks for her to get completely over the sickness, and that it was not unusual for it to take much more time than that.

This news was absolutely devastating to both of us. She was put on medicine and put to bed. Meanwhile, we both came before the Lord in prayer every night, placing our hands on her belly and on her forehead. I knew that God's healing goes to wherever it is needed. I did not need to be right on the spot for it to work.

At first, Sierra got much worse. Her throat clogged up so much I was afraid that she couldn't breathe – even swallowing was painful and difficult. This lasted for a few days. Then, she got better…and the disease was gone! From beginning to end it took a little less than two weeks; she was able to go back to school with a clean bill of health – and satisfactorily complete her final exams for the year.

Healed in the Night

"Denise," an employee I was working with, suddenly became very sick and had to go home early. She was vomiting and dizzy. She had had problems like this many times before and the doctors had given her medicine but not a reason for her distress. That night at three A.M I suddenly awakened out of bed with her on my mind. I said a prayer for her to be relieved, and went back to sleep.

The next day, Denise was back at work again. I asked how she felt, and she said she felt very good. I asked if it had happened during the night, and she said, "Yes, when I got up in the night I felt better."

"By chance, do you know what time it was when you got up?" I asked.

"Yes, I remember looking at the clock. Why do you ask?" She said, with a quizzical look on her face. "It was about 3 A.M."

During the next year that I knew her, she had not had any recurring problems with this undiagnosed illness.

Finger Ripped to the Tendons

"Lacy," a humble woman of little means, worked as dishwasher at a busy truck stop. I worked there also. She was loved by everyone who took the time to know her, although she struggled with a learning disability that she had born with, over fifty years previously.

One evening she ripped open the side of her little finger on a piece of metal in the kitchen. It bled heavily, and everyone, including me, encouraged her to go to the hospital, but she refused to go, giving as her reason that she could not lose the money or take the time off work.

I came over and looked at it; and saw that the flesh had been torn all the way down to the tendons, and was hanging off to the side in a lump. The tendons were showing but looked intact. The bleeding still continued heavily, with paper towels being replaced regularly. I asked her if I could hold her hand and say a prayer for her, and we found a chair in the back where it was quiet. We were able to come before the Lord for about 15 minutes. She then announced that she was fine and wanted to go back to work.

I removed the last bloody towel, and gently washed around it with clean water. The bleeding had stopped, and Lacy said the pain was gone. I put hydrogen peroxide on it and a band-aid. A few hours later, I noticed Lacey scratching her finger; often a sign of healing. I took off her band-aid to change it, and it looked bluish and white. She finished her shift, which meant putting her hands back into dirty hot water, and the band-aids did not want to stay on. We found a long plastic glove she could use, and we both finished our workday.

The next evening I asked Lacy how she was feeling, and she was very excited to show me the injury. She did not have a band-aid on anymore. The torn lump had mended back onto her finger *and all the area had turned pink and healthy*. There was no sign of infection, and she had full mobility without any pain. Just a thin pale line remained where the jagged tear had been. She said she thought she had been injured to show unbelievers that I was a "healer" – I told her that God doesn't hurt people or work that way; and that *he* is the healer, not me. It is true that many people who worked or frequented there were joyously told about the healing that the Lord had done for Lacy, and it rippled to helping facilitate more healings and spiritual conversations.

For the next few months that I worked with her, whenever I saw her on break she was engrossed in reading her favorite book, the Bible. In that way and many others she is smarter than many people I know.

Emotional Healing for Black Belt Instructor

The first time I met "Jason," the Holy Spirit let me see that the real reason he taught Tai Chi, had a Black belt, and was a "trained warrior" was because of a previous emotional injury. I could see through the eyes of Spirit a very definite gray triangle at the back of his head. Physically, he was in good health. I had been asked to talk about Reiki to his Tai Chi group there at the YMCA. As part of my presentation I offered hands-on-healing in a little room off to the side. Jason came in and I put my hands on his head and closed my eyes, listening in the stillness for any information from the Spirit that I should pass on.

Jason said he had received energy healing before, and that I had the strongest energy he had ever felt. I asked him if anyone had ever used prayer with his previous healings, and he said no. I told him that the reason this healing felt different is because I recognized the Source, and that the Spirit of God is what truly heals. I also told him that we must let go and forgive ourselves and others for injuries and pain of the past. I told him why I have faith in God to heal.

My hands were extremely hot on his head, and I felt an emotional release coming on, although he showed no outward emotion. I saw the gray mist dissipate and fade into nothing. I knew the pain of the past that he had been carrying for so many years had been absolved.

I told Jason what I had seen. He then told me that his father had been overly strict, and had been verbally and physically abusive. Often the father had hit him. He especially remembered the time he was hit with the end of a water hose on the back of the head, exactly where the gray triangle had been. Jason left the treatment feeling much better; and with a knowledge that he didn't have to fight back anymore. If he just asked Him, God would fight his fights for him, *and would always be in his corner.* Now, Jason seemed encouraged to progress in his spirit journey; and with a new awareness of what the God-Spot was, and the need to fill it with the right things.

Brain Tumor Shrinks

Not all healings end up with the expected results. We must always remember that each person is on his own path, and will make their own choices, for good and for bad, along the way. The Lord never retrieves his outstretched hand, but so often we take our own away from him. This is what happened with "Rachel:"

Rachel had an inoperable brain tumor and was on several medications. I didn't know when I was called to help her that there was a tumor involved – I knew that she was sick and couldn't keep her balance when she got up from the couch. She fell down a lot. I knew that she had a lot of pain and had a lead weight in her eyelid to keep it down. I also knew that her kids and grandchildren came over all the time to take care of her and see how she was doing.

When I started the prayers and put both of my hands over her ears, that's when I I noticed the tumor deep in her brain. I told her something needed to be checked there – hoping she already knew about the problem. I was relieved when she verified it. This is what was messing with her balance, and with her eyesight. She said this was her second time. The first tumor had been in a place where they could remove it with laser surgery. This one, they couldn't. I drew a picture of it on a piece of paper, showing two lobes and a web of tentacles around it. She verified the size and shape to be what the doctors had shown to her.

I visited Rachel at her home every week for four weeks, twice a week. Under the power of the Holy Spirit I felt the tumor reduce in size, pull back its tentacles from one side, and "turn color" in my mind's eye from beige-orange to light brown. It became like melted bubble gum. Her ability to walk and keep her balance improved. Her eyesight became better, her skin tone more balanced. She had other things wrong with her too, and the Energy from God was taking care of it in its own time. Her hands and knees were almost pain free and her mobility had greatly increased.

Rachel told me how much better she felt; and how she had been talking to her neurologist and how he wanted to meet me, which was not what she had expected. He had been her surgeon for over six years, and had seen Rachel go through a lot. The doctor said there were signs that the tumor was better; and that he was tremendously impressed with the mobility she was having. He scheduled new tests. He encouraged her to *"keep doing whatever you are doing."* Rachel invited me to come to her next tumor support group meeting, held monthly. She also said that she had been getting out more and able to do some things with her husband.

She also expressed that her daughter and grandkids weren't coming around as much anymore, now that she was getting better.

At the next appointment, I showed up and no one was home, and with no note. Later I talked to Rachel on the phone, and she said it was OK if I stopped coming over because they really couldn't afford to pay a love offering (donation) anymore. I suggested that if they just covered my gas, that would be enough. I said I wasn't going to let money keep me from being used to heal her, and expressed the desire to continue on a regular schedule, until the Lord said, "it is enough."

But, it seemed *I wanted to heal her more than she wanted the healing.* I found I couldn't win – she identified with the tumor too much. And, *I was wanting My Will to be done.* My ego was now tied up with beating this thing. During our conversations she would say things such as: "I wonder if the grandkids will still come over if I am well?" "I have the tumor because I am taking upon my own body anything that might hurt the grandkids - it's better me than them." She had a core belief that she held deep inside; that she was keeping her kids and grandkids healthy in *"having"* their diseases. She also felt that they would *ignore her* if she weren't dying!

When I went to the next appointment, no one answered the door. I once again called her on the phone, and we had a nice conversation. I spoke to her in plain terms. I told her Christ was the martyr for us – we don't need to carry sin or illness on our own body for anyone else – we are denying the sacrifice of Christ by doing so. I showed her ego was getting in the way, and that she was afraid of getting well because she would lose the attention that she received in her weakened state. I quoted scriptures and promised that her family would enjoy being around her *even more if she were well!* I asked her to think of all the things they could do together! But, I was hitting my head against a wall. She had retrieved her hand, and the Lord would not heal her against her will, or, for *my* will. Nothing was going to change her mind.

I felt flattened for a few days. I had a lesson to learn the hard way. I don't know how the patience of our Lord, who is so long-suffering, can endure us! My ego was involved, and I had to let it go.

When I next heard of Rachel's condition, I was told that she had taken a turn for the worse and was in bed again, unable to stand and barely able to see. I was sure the tumor had come back with a vengeance. Even though Jesus says, "Vengeance is mine; I shall repay" saith the Lord." (Ro 12:19-20) He had been healing her…but she didn't want him to. It still makes me want to cry. But, it is her Free Will choice.

Christ the Only Healer at World Religion Day

I had been invited to a World Religion Day convention held annually in Nashville, Tennessee. Speakers from all kinds of religions were there. Each was invited to give a discourse on his beliefs, with an encouraged tie-in expected from each religion about World Peace. After every three speakers there would be entertainment, and one was a drumming and dancing group under the direction of master drummer "George" of Burundi, Africa.

In George's introduction, he explained he had been told by his doctors not to jump (a integral part of the traditional dancing) because he had just had brain surgery two months ago! He said as he lay in the hospital recuperating, all he could think about was being able to come to this convention and perform his best, thankful to God that he was still alive. He and the other drummers (all of them children) put on quite a spirited show! There was very creative drumming and colorful native attire, with all the drummers jumping and springing up very high, over and over again, *including George.* Everyone clapped, and after his program ended there was a break for a meal gathering. Many people went up to him to congratulate him and his group on their performance, and to ask how he felt. He assured them that he felt wonderful, and thanked them for their concern. I kept an eye on him, being led by the Spirit to keep close.

After the initial adrenalin wore off, about 20 minutes later, he began to fade. His smile was forced, and he seemed distracted. I came up and introduced myself, and let him know that I was there to help with his pain. He looked all around and then back to me. "Yes, I would like that," he said, nodding. We found the door to the projector room open, and went in.

I explained to him how the Holy Spirit works, and that this was through the grace of Jesus Christ, and to the glory of God. I told him hands-on-healing often went by many names through the world, and that it had also been a sign in the early Christian church for the new believers. I asked him if there was hands-on-healing in his country, and he said there was healing, but it was different, and there were also curses.

I let him know that it was the Holy Spirit that had told me to be ready to help him tonight.

George was a very tall man and sat down in the chair in front of me. The back of his head showed an incision scar that started at his top neck vertebrae and went up several inches from there. He told me of how he had been born with his brain adhered to his skull. As a child it had grown more and more painful, until he thought he just couldn't take it anymore. Then, he had an auto accident, which actually made him *feel better* for a while. But, then the headaches started again and so did the pain, increasing and increasing until he came to America and had the corrective surgery done.

Shortly after we started, George said he felt an electrical surge from the right side of his brain. "I am amazed!" he said. My hands were as hot as fire embers on his scar area – heat is often a by-product of work being done, so I knew the Spirit was on to something! George then took my left hand and moved it onto his forehead. "This is where I hurt when I get mad," he said. "But I am not hurting *anywhere* now! It is amazing!"

George also said, "I feel blessed because God always puts special people into my life to help me with things!" He hugged me and asked me when we could get together to do this again.

I assured him that anywhere he went in the world, he could find Christians to *heal and pray* for him in Jesus' name. Sometimes we are located in the yellow pages

124

under "Holistic Health" services; "Alternative Health;" or "Complementary Alternative Medicine." You can even find Christians who are under "Therapeutic Touch®;" "Reiki;" "Spiritual Healing" and "Energy Medicine." I'm sure there are even other listings too. I encouraged him to ask to make sure that they use Prayer with their modality and acknowledge the Source. And, I encouraged him to use his intuition and God-given discernment to know that the source they are referring to is the Only Almighty Father of Unconditional Love.

"There are different kinds of gifts, but the same Spirit. There are different kinds of service, but the same Lord. There are different kinds of working, but the same God works all of them in all men." (1 Co. 12:4-6)

God is Stronger than Chemo and Cancer

When I first met "Charlotte," her sister "Karen" had brought her to me for pain relief. She had received a mastectomy and reconstruction by surgery that cut the muscle off her back and wrapped it around to the front to be reattached. She could not raise her arm without considerable pain. She had lost a lot of weight and had no appetite. She wore a wrap around her head, having lost her hair due to the chemo. Both she and her sister were both Godly women who frequented church.

After the first healing treatment, Charlotte felt so relieved that she started flapping her elbow up and down like a bird, and announced, "I'm hungry, let's all go out to eat!" Whereby she proceeded to down a hearty southern meal. I was astounded!

As time went by, we were together for several healings and wonderful spiritual discussions. But, when the time would come for the chemotherapy again, she would have a bad reaction. Once, the day after a chemo treatment, Karen called 911, and me. Since we lived in the country, the ambulance can sometimes take quite a while to get to where it is going – but I happened to be driving in town right by her road when she called. I made a quick detour and found Charlotte lying on the bed unresponsive. Karen said Charlotte had been throwing up all morning.

Charlotte seemed like she was in a coma. Her eyes were sunken with darkness, she felt cold to the touch, and it seemed her heart and blood was barely moving. I placed my hands on her head for a few seconds; then her solar plexus; then her feet. Her body felt barely responsive to the groaning of the Spirit; she had already shut down so much. Again I placed my hands on head, stomach and feet. I call this the "shock therapy" treatment. I kept in prayer and repeated all three positions again and again, feeling the energy grow stronger and stronger, eventually cycling wildly and hotly through her body.

When the ambulance got there thirteen minutes later, Charlotte was sitting up on the bed waving them off and saying, "Go away, I feel better now. Really. Go away!" Both her sister and I implored her to go to the hospital anyway, I told her God uses doctors and medicine as his tools too - we had to force her to go! They took her out on a stretcher.

Later, I found out that she felt so much better on the way in the ambulance, that the hospital wouldn't even admit her or keep her overnight because her blood cell count wasn't low enough! After she had been at the brink of death! God is Good!

Charlotte was not able to continue her chemotherapy treatments because of the adverse reactions; once more time she tried it, and once more she almost died. She was not given much of a future by the medical doctors. But, it is now over a year later, and her faith in God and his desire to heal continues to prove all of them wrong.

(Here is a letter as received by "Charlotte.")

"Hello My Angel Friend Tiffany;

As you well know, I was as low as one could go; just short of dying. The chemo nearly took my life twice and the last time; I was barely alive. We have to go all the way down in order to go all the way up. PTL! One has to have been there to know what a wonderful feeling it is. You and I know this feeling. Out of everything bad, there comes good. Look at YOU; using your personal life here on earth as an example to lead others. What a blessing it has been to have had the pleasure to know you and have those precious Godly hands of yours touch me. I will always remember the times when you made me feel so much better. May God Bless You Abundantly Always!!! I know he will.

It was one of my life's greatest joys to listen to you talk and have you touch my sick cancer-stricken body, with those lovely healing hands that God gave to you. I know you continuously praise God for striking you down so that you can be His servant. Most people are angry at first and some never heed to God's way for us to live life. I'm so grateful that I can truly say that I never became angry with God for my getting cancer. I asked him for acceptance and the endurance for the things that which I could not change. I know that God heard and granted my prayer for this. There has been such a multiplicity of peace within me. PTL!

Now, I feel good…just like before I was sick. I have opened up the salon again and am cutting hair for all my friends. My hair is growing back and is a beautiful silvery salt and pepper. Everyone whom I meet cannot believe that I look so good now. It is not me…IT IS A GIFT FROM GOD!!! PTL!!!

I am writing my poetry again and have even started a website which keeps me in touch with those who have supported me, and as a way to support others. I feel so Blessed! I am so thankful that our paths crossed. I know that God meant for this to be. When you are down to nothing, God is up to Something!"

A Time to Sleep, A Time to Mend Bones

"Jack" had been on pure oxygen for six months, but still walked well, around all the tubing covering his living room floor. I had come to their home to do a scheduled treatment on his wife "Cleo," but found she was in the hospital recovering from a broken ankle, and I would have to visit her there. I volunteered to help the husband before I headed down to the hospital, and he agreed but he was very skeptical.

I put my hands on his head, shoulders, lungs (hot), stomach, liver, abdomen and knees. I asked him to bend over in the chair and started working his back. I felt a cold line down my entire hand, with definite edges to it and heat all around it.

"Jack, do you have any broken bones?" I asked, with my hands still placed on that spot on his back.

Yes," he replied. "Two ribs fractured - the ones your hands are on."

"Did you see the x-ray?" I asked. "Because I feel I could draw you a picture of how this looks under my hands." He didn't know what they looked like. I drew the picture anyway.

"Have you had your heart looked at recently? It looks like there might be a problem there." I questioned.

"Yes and no," he said. "I had angioplasty done recently."

"It looks like there are still constrictions there." I said.

"Yes, but the doctor says it's not bad enough for more angioplasty yet," he answered, with good confidence in me now. The treatment ended well, and he encouraged me to visit his wife next.

I went straight into Williamson Medical Center – no one seemed to see me – past the pink ladies; up the elevator; down the hall, past the nurse's station. No one stopped me or even looked my way - I was thankful that I did not have to explain myself. Cleo's door was closed and I gently opened it and stepped through. She had a tube up her nose, and was on her back with her foot wrapped with gauze up to her knee.

"Hello," I said. "Your husband told me what happened. We did a healing treatment, and I came to see if we could help you feel better too."

"My pastor left ten minutes ago," Cleo began. "I love my husband, my kids, grandkids, everyone, but I haven't been able to sleep but 45 minutes in the last day and a half…"

"I know you love everyone, Cleo, you have a very loving and God-praising heart." I said.

"But I am allergic to everything, and the pain keeps me awake. I can't even take…" And with that I placed my hands on her belly and she was gone, in mid-sentence she went to sleep. As Cleo was now asleep, I continued my prayers out loud. She had the only occupied bed in the room. Next, I gently took my hands and touched her hands, then moved to her foot.

By now I had realized that I had forgotten to eat breakfast or lunch (an unfortunate habit), and it was 4:00 in the afternoon, and I was feeling dizzy. I was pretty sure it was lack of food and not from doing the treatments, although I always feel a euphoric effect from the Healing Spirit, similar to emerging from hot spa water.

I was working holding my arms raised slightly above the heavy metal in the bed footing and railing (there was a swing-lift attached to it, hanging above). I was feeling inadequate, and remembering that God uses weak vessels to show his strength and power, and I kept praying and holding my hands in different positions above her leg and foot, which had puddled blood under the skin, abrasions, and broken veins. Her toes were unwrapped and blue, and I was feeling "I'm not strong enough Lord, let my hands be Your Hands…and I saw her *foot bones literally move* underneath my hands; and I wasn't even touching her, just holding my hands in midair, and it startled me…and the swelling noticeably reduced *right before my eyes.*

I felt relief, and a certain amount of trepidation. What had really happened here? All had been done in secrecy. It was just between the Lord and Cleo, and me. I had never seen bones move before, but knew that whatever had just happened, was for her greatest benefit. Perhaps the sleep was permitted to be deep enough to not wake her up from any pain of manipulation. Had there been no "setting in place" by the doctors? Was this movement just for my benefit and validation of work being done? I do not know. All I know was that I saw a mass move underneath the gauze. Perhaps it was the hand of God.

After an hour, with Cleo still sleeping, I left the room, and silently made my way outside to my vehicle, and was reminded of how hungry I was. The words of Jesus were brought to my mind "My food is to do the will of him who has sent me and to finish his work." (Jn. 4:34) Still, I was happy to find the bag of almonds I had stashed away in the car! I dismissed the thought that the movement had been "only in my mind." Especially was this so when I visited Cleo at home after her "much shorter than expected" hospital stay, and witnessed the expected "several months" of recuperation, cast and crutches reduced to merely a fraction of the time!

Dogs and Horses and People, Oh My!

"Nelly" lived near the Tennessee River, not far from Kentucky. It was a good 100 mile drive North of where I lived. I had been in fervent prayer about letting go of the safety net of a part-time job, to go full-time into the healing work on a "love offering" basis. Nellie called the day after I had quit my job; and where she had found my phone number I still don't know. I barely had gas money for the long drive; but I knew I would not let fear, or lack of money, hold me back.

Although it was a beautiful drive, several times I got lost trying to find the correct fork in the highway, on the correct back-road, by the correct mile-marker or sign-post of some quaint historic town! It was about the most backwoods that I had ever been. Thoughts of dusty-faced children shouting to each other, "Ma, there's someone comin' up the holler!" echoed in my head like a sequence in an old movie.

Nelly had a nice little farm off one of these back roads. I was relieved when I pulled into the driveway and received a welcome wave - verifying that I had completed my cycle of "lost" adventures for the day. The dogs decided they would receive the first treatments, which I did, since they are attracted to the Spirit and often won't let me help others until they have their fill. Next, Nelly received a treatment, and gave an offering for her sister, "Carey" to have a treatment for her birthday gift. They both enjoyed the healings very much, with reduction of pain from many places and a variety of other problems relieved.

Then Nelly brought me out to the barn, and showed me a male spotted horse. His hip was stretched and depressed down, but a lot of muscles had grown up to make the difference. Some arthritis was in both front knees, although the horse was only eight years old. His head was very hot – as were his lungs. Nelly said she has treated him for allergies. He "accepted" a healing, by moving his body weight against my hands as the treatment began, instead of backing off or moving away. It seemed to go well.

Animals, babies and small children have a natural connection to God, and they are such good pure channels for the Spirit to work through. Many people notice that animals are sensitive to the "energy" of people around them, and they either like them, or not. One of the great things about animals is that there is no "clogging up" or thoughts of "I wonder if this is working" going on in their heads.

129

There is just yes or no. The only animals I have worked on who said "No," were those about to die. They chose to not continue to live anymore, and would not accept the healing power. I am so glad that God allows us to work on animals too! So much suffering has been alleviated.

The main reason I had been called out here was to work on the horse in the next stall. She was a beautiful chestnut mare, with pale mane and tail. She had a dislocated front left shoulder – I felt no broken bones (which Nelly verified the veterinarian had also told her). She had gone "spread eagle" on the ice last January, (four months ago) and had not put any weight on it since then. In the pasture, she would actually "hop" around on three legs. It was definitely "popped out of joint," with the bone jutting out in a crazy angle, and a huge dip in the skin behind it. I could sense torn muscles and stretched ligaments where the chest attached to the leg. She was in a lot of pain, constantly.

The two vets (and one horse chiropractor – common in Tennessee where so many expensive Walkers are raised) gave very little hope. One possible therapy was to lift the horse up in a sling full-time, until the ligaments shortened. The cost was prohibitive. Or, it was suggested to put the horse down (kill by injection, because of the pain). The chiropractor said he could adjust her, but needed more than the helpers he had with him that day to do it. There was not much comfort or hope from any of them, and it had already been so many months.

I remembered the bone moving under the gauze for Cleo at the hospital - I knew it would have to be Divine intervention, in a similar way, to adjust this poor horse. I placed my hands on her head, started the prayers, and then went to the point of injury. I felt the desire to press hard enough to try to make it go back in place – something the doctor had tried to do with the help of three people. Instead, I just did a soft touch with steady, smooth connection and stayed in one place for a few moments. The bone shifted under my hand and moved back into place!

I released my touch, and it "fell out" again. Once more I held my hand to her shoulder, and the leg "went back in" with tight "snapping" sounds. I left my hand there for a few minutes. After I released it, it stayed in place for a few minutes more…then it came back out again.

This time I placed both hands on her chest and shoulder, and left them on for about 20 minutes. Again, her bones popped back into place. I stayed longer. She adjusted her weight away from me and the other three legs and placed her weight *onto* the wounded leg. She gained confidence in it, and even rested her *back* leg for a while, bringing a larger portion of her body-weight to her shoulder. She was using it for the first time in months! She tried to walk with it, I moved away and the joint popped again – but Nelly made the observation that she seemed to stand straighter, and with her hooves together now. It did seem like the ligaments had shortened a bit to help keep everything aligned better. Her

130

head felt better too, she was not pulling the heat in, needing pain relief like before. And it seemed like her eyes were smiling! Horses are so intelligent. Why wouldn't they be able to show an expression that is universal to all cultures, languages and tribes around the world, the wonderful smile!

I also did a treatment on an older white dog – so many dogs have arthritis in their joints, it really amazes me – even some young dogs have it, depending on the breed. I also found fractures in the middle of her back (I was told, "Yes, she was stepped on by a horse"). She also had cataracts, and her intestines "felt" slimy. But I did not feel any parasites. Nelly said she had been giving her the wormwood herb for one week, and had seen parasites in the stools, so she knew it had been working. And her eyes had stopped tearing, which she said usually means the worms are gone. All that made sense to what I was feeling under my hands.

Now, the word had gotten out up the canyon, and we were invited up the road to an older woman's house, "Betty," to "get the ringing out of my ears that I have had since an accident in childhood." Nellie asked me if I was thirsty, and dropped me off to run to the store (the store was miles and miles away!). After doing the first five head positions, the ringing sound did not go away, but Betty said it had lessened considerably, to a low "dim" sound. The Lord let me discover carpel tunnel (which she knew about), arthritis and a heart murmur (also known) and constriction in one of her arteries.

There was a group of people now in her living room, watching what was going on – I felt a sluggishness in her system too (the slow vibration from excess of beer or wine – hard liquor vibrates fast), and asked her when was the last time she had gone to a doctor and had everything checked out. She said it had been many years. I whispered in her ear, "do you drink?" She couldn't hear me - I tried to say it a little louder but was very conscious of the crowd. I cupped my hands together around her ear. "Do you drink?" "No!" she said. I continued whispering slowly and clearly in her ear: "Well, if you don't drink, and your body is this sluggish, and feels like this, I would say you really need to see a doctor as soon as possible. And your heart should be checked right away. Will you please go see one?" I encouraged, knowing she wouldn't go, but knowing I needed to encourage her anyway. "I don't drink!" she said out-loud in front of everyone and pushed a wad of money into my hand. I saw a few people turn to each other and nod, look back at me and smile.

As soon as we had left the house, I heard unknown voices laughing and talking behind me, "Yes, she does! We all know that!" "She does too drink!" And when Nellie got me back into the car, she smiled and said, "Yes, she does," and added, "we just don't let her know that *we* know! I'll try to get her to a doctor." I found myself with a familiar problem, wondering if the doctors would find anything now, or if God had already fixed it. I smiled at the woman's unfortunate declaration, so boldly spoken out-loud, letting everyone know what the whispering had been about!

Nellie handed me a paper bag with a diet Dr. Pepper in it and peanut butter crackers, saying "Don't throw the bag away, your money is in there." She looked at me and said I seemed a bit tired. We could see more folk another time. I knew she was right; I had only been working with the Holy Spirit for less than a year, I was still adjusting to the mighty flush of power surges going through my physical body. The healings made me feel relaxed and euphoric, but doing so many in one day was stretching the envelope of my "yield-ability" at that time. This is *always* a good thing. I find after I have been "stretched," he uses me for even greater work for a longer period, the next time.

Nellie next handed me a silver-turquoise ring. "Can you feel anything from this?" she asked. Knowing that an energy-dusting occurs on everything, I wondered if this was another way that the Spirit wanted to communicate anything to his kids today. I really try to be open to His Will, not always knowing what particular turn in the path it might take, or why. I held the ring to see if I could feel anything. I prayed for ability to bring people to faith, and be a spokesman to their heart in a way that would be acceptable to them. I remembered being so tired. I closed my eyes and did the *Metal and Jewelry God-Spot:*

"I feel a little girl...your mother...your mother gave you the ring." I said. "And you, are you going through a divorce?" Nellie's eyes got big.

"You are dead right," she said. When Nellie was a little girl, it had been her favorite ring that her mother owned. When she grew up, her mother had given it to her as encouragement, since Nellie was now in the process of going through a divorce.

Now I knew why the Lord had used the ring. We were able to have a nice discussion about divorce, encouragement and the love of God, always being by our side to help us through everything. *If we just allow him to,* he is our strength.

"She is clothed with strength and dignity; she can laugh at the days to come." (Pr.31:25)

"I can do everything through him who gives me strength." (Php. 4:13)

I got into my vehicle, and started down the road; looking in the rear view mirror I saw all the folk who were still standing on the road, waving and wishing me well, "Bye!" "God Bless You!" "Thanks Bunches!" "Come Back Again Soon!" The assorted dogs in amongst them, waving their tails, the horses on the other side of the fence, leaning over (they still seemed to be smiling!). It really felt like time had

132

stood still and I was leaving a Kentucky holler back in the 1940's. What a shining adventure this day had been!

It took me a while to get back on the main road, and as my concerns of financial obligations closed in on me, I pulled off the side of the road and looked into the bag. I knew I would be happy with whatever the folk from this poor rural community would be able to share. My jaw dropped in shock as I lifted out handfuls of large bills, a cash donation totaling $260! All my problems would be solved for several weeks! I raised my voice in blessing to the Lord who made all the gold in the mountains. My heart full of thanks for these wonderful people, who *allowed* themselves to be moved by the Spirit of the Lord, knowing that *they took out of their own needs to help me with mine.* Selah!

Several months later, I received a letter from Nellie after I had moved to California. One of the things she was happy to tell me was about this beautiful horse. She had made so much improvement that she was not only springing around like the other horses, but also ride-able – the belief was that the healing had been gradual, but had started on the day I visited. Nellie had successfully begun a new life too, and is being trained as a CNA, and is looking forward to being trained in Reiki at her course completion, to be able to help others as fully as possible in their healings. I congratulate her!

Spontaneous Healing - Kicked Out of Church

We were invited to go with a friend to a new church, and I readily agreed. My daughter and son and I would often visit different churches, of various beliefs and customs. I find it is very similar to finding shimmering jewels on the bare ground. Lifting up one stone and holding it to the light, turning it this way and that way to look at the glistening facets, one can see the beauty of each precious one, without judging it in comparison to the others. Big or small, with different shapes and different colors, and found in various locations, the rubies, diamonds and emeralds will far outweigh the accidental pieces of clay and sandstone you may pick up. If our eyes be clear, the individual perfection of that stone will be clearly revealed when held up to God's love light of truth.

"Do not judge, or you too will be judged. For in the same way you judge others, you will be judged, and with the measure you use, it will be measured out to you. Why do you look at the speck of sawdust in your brother's eye and pay no attention to the plank in your own eye? How can you say to your brother, 'Let me take the speck out of your eye,' when all the time there is a plank in your own eye? You hypocrite, first take the plank out of your own eye, and then you will see clearly to remove the speck from your brother's eye." (Mt. 7:1-5)

This large Christian church had a wonderful service and joyful praise! With heartfelt desire they were calling upon God to bless their congregation, calling upon the Holy Spirit to descend, and Jesus to guide their hearts and minds. My hands were getting hot just sitting there – I knew that the Spirit was willing! I wondered what would happen, and how he would communicate with his people that *he was certainly here.*

On this particular day most of the brothers were absent, having gone to a retreat. The wives of the ministers and servants were taking care of the service, and I offered myself to one of the wives to help when the call went out for those who would like to be prayed for. There would be about four or five sisters helping. The minister's wife thought that it would be fine, and I stood beside her at the end of the service so as to respect her position of authority, as people started walking up.

A woman in her 50's came up, and started pouring out her heart to the minister's wife. She was having problems at work, and also had diabetes. She felt hemmed in on all sides. The minister's wife started praying for her, and anointed her with oil. I was standing by and listening. The Spirit chose the mid-part of the prayer for me to put my hand on the woman's heart…and she fainted dead away! She locked her knees and fell flat backwards to the floor, bumping her head with a "crack" sound as she went! She had been "slain in the Spirit." This was my very first time to be used by the Holy Spirit to facilitate this.

It startled me – I looked at the minister's wife and said, "I'm sorry!" (I promise not to not apologize for the Holy Spirit ever again – it was just my first human reaction). The wife was just staring – I dropped to my knees and started praying over the woman's body, keeping my hands lifted a few inches away. A crowd gathered, and I praised God, and blessed him for hearing the cries of his people. *Four or five minutes later,* the woman finally came to, and started *laughing joyously,* without restraint. She was just lying there, laughing, and not moving a muscle anywhere else! I whispered in her ear, "God has heard your pleas, he loves you. You are never alone - spend the rest of your day praising him!"

She finally sat up, and was helped to stand, where I led her to a chair and talked to her about God's love and guidance in our lives, and how everything that happens to us can be an opportunity to shape ourselves more into his likeness. Her face was as innocent and glowing as a newborn child. I knew the Lord had removed her illnesses, and I simply told her that also her stomach would feel better.

I could tell that I needed to disappear now. This had evidently not happened here before, and it seemed to cause quite a commotion. I would like to have stayed to see what else the Spirit would do, but felt compelled to leave. I did not want to be a side-show or cause attention to myself. I was here to worship God and focus attention on him. As I was walking away, I saw the minister's wife go over to the woman, and I heard the woman say, "She knew that my stomach hurt, and God has healed me!" I rejoiced for the joy in her heart. This had been a powerful witness to the All Mighty and Powerful God!

I took my children to a local park and sat on a large rock, feeling the comfort and connectedness all around me. How my heart was pounding with joy! I felt like I had completed twenty healing sessions – there had been so much power shot through me! What bliss and exhilaration I was experiencing! Looking around me, I could see everything keenly that had the blood of life running through its veins - the birds in the trees; the squirrels in their burrows, even the fish I could sense under their spot in the water. Nothing could hide from me. It was "medical intuitiveness" in a unique way – a "life-force intuitiveness," if you will. I praised God for this opportunity to be used in the church for his will. I asked forgiveness for any undue attention that it gave me, wishing only to be a reflection of his love.

Two days later, on the same day that the FBI asked me to send my 9-11 information (another chapter) I received a phone call at lunch from the minister's wife. I asked her if I could call her back, that I was at a restaurant about to eat a meal with my family. She then proceeded to verbally attack me, calling me a wolf in sheep's clothing, and also *by whose authority* do you do this? Who are you associated with?" She ripped into me from all angles, saying I can't be going to the churches to heal, and that I was not submissive to the headship in their church; but that possibly, if I am repentant and come under their authority, I might be used later on, "under close supervision."

I answered her with scriptures the best I could, and let her angry words, prompted by fear, wash over me like water off a duck's back. I had expected a welcome to come back, and to hear a kind word of praise for the Lord who chooses to work with vessels of clay. Instead she repeated, "Do you understand what I am saying? You cannot come back here! Do you understand? You cannot come back!"

I was laughing to myself as the Lord brought these words to mind: "Blessed are you when people insult you, persecute you and falsely say all kinds of evil against you because of me. Rejoice and be glad, because great is your reward in heaven, for in the same way they persecuted the prophets who were before you." (Mt. 5:11,12) I rejoiced that I was being persecuted with almost the *exact same words* uttered by the chief priests and teachers of the law almost two thousand years ago against Jesus, when they said, "Tell us by what authority you are doing these things," and "Who gave you this authority?" (Lk. 20:2; Mt. 21:23; Mr. 11:28)

It also reminded me of when Jesus had healed a demon-possessed man who was blind and mute:

135

"But when the Pharisees heard this, they said, "It is only by Beelzebub, the prince of demons, that this fellow drives out demons." Jesus knew their thoughts and said to them, "Every kingdom divided against itself will be ruined, and every city or household divided against itself will not stand. If Satan drives out Satan, he is divided against himself. How then can his kingdom stand? And if I drive out demons by Beelzebub, by whom do your people drive them out? So then, they will be your judges. But if I drive out demons by the Spirit of God, then the kingdom of God has come upon you." (Mt. 12:22-28)

My children were upset when I relayed the information that we would not be returning, and why. Being in their teenage years, their sense of right and wrong created an immediate flare of indignation over injustice. I told them to laugh it off – that the conversation had just been prompted by fear of that which cannot be controlled (how to control the Holy Spirit?).

The church had prayed for the will of God. His Holy Spirit fell out on a believer, and when they saw it occur, it scared them and they denounced it! It is so sad when God is put in a "box" as if to control him to conform to a church's programs and level of understanding. That is not how he works! He does what he wants! The sacred secret is...he often does what *we* want, too. Hence the old adage: "Be careful what you pray for."

Although I felt glorious for being put in the same category as these wondrous souls in the past, I also felt very sorry that the woman and all the people who were joyful witnesses at the church, would now be *confused* at what they saw. Also, it proved to be a temporary stumbling for my friend who had invited me, and she stepped down from her position at the church, saying: "How can they say one thing and do another; and to tell a daughter of God she can't come back to the church – and over the phone instead of in person!" I agreed with her, but also reminded her that people are very fearful, and that God still has to use imperfect people to do his will. Just look at me for an example of that! But perfect love drives all fear aside. We need to keep such ones in our prayers.

I thought it interesting that this happened on the very same day that the one of the top security agencies of the government (FBI) had expressed great interest in what I had to say (even after I revealed that it was all by the power of God), and the church, which is supposed to be the top security agency of the people, expressly did not...

The Mother Said, "This Is the Boy I Remember!"

Seven-year-old "Jason" lay on the table fidgeting a bit – his mother "Lily" was sitting in a chair nearby. I didn't know why they had come, but that they had come from far away by referral. Under the muted lights and with soft music I put my hands on his head, and moved them into the "third" position. Through the eyes of prayer, the Lord revealed a tumor nestled deep at the base of his brain – directly between his ears, and straight down. I asked Jason to imagine floating in a big warm swimming pool, and enjoy the warmth and freedom of the "water." I knew he was feeling the Power coming through to him, and I did not want him to be afraid. The center of my hands felt like there were laser beams attached to them, and pulsation was occurring – I knew we were doing good work.

After half an hour, I sent Jason out to wait with his family, and spoke to the mother, asking why she had brought him here. She said he had bad headaches, stomachaches, unusual twitching, and nosebleeds. He would not participate with the activities of the other kids very much, and would often wake up in the middle of the night crying. Feeling that something was very wrong, Lily had taken him to a doctor, "he didn't think anything of it, just growing pains." But Lily knew something was wrong with her boy.

I told Lily "God brought you in here for a reason, either for me to encourage you to get an MRI, or for the problem to be fixed, or both – maybe it is fixed even now. But, you need to know of the possibility of what I found. I am not telling you for sure, this is just what it feels like to me. You know I am not a medical doctor. I just feel strongly that you need to get this checked."

Two days passed, and I was working on Jason again. He felt he was coming to see me because of his stomachaches. In talking to the mother, I found out that Jason had felt very sick after the first treatment, even vomiting that evening. He had also been sleepy all day long. I knew that sometimes these were indications of a very strong healing. Often I have seen that when the Holy Spirit stimulates rapid cell regeneration and cleansing, toxins are released into the blood stream, and the body needs plenty of rest to recuperate. Drinking a lot of fresh water helps, and if the belly is nauseated, steamed vegetables (alkaline based – not acidic like fruits) help also. He had also told his mother that during the treatment, "I had a bee buzzing around in my head." He also said, "I like her, but her hands are so hot!"

This time Jason's head felt different under my hands – the vibration was different, and the heat was not like a laser. I grew very excited, but did not say a word. I felt there was still a bit of work needing to be done, and I would let the Lord tell Lily what was going on.

Two more days went by, and I came out into the waiting room to greet Jason and his mother. Her face was glowing! I didn't ask why, but I knew within five minutes of touching Jason that the tumor was gone. The joy inside overwhelmed me, and I excitedly ushered Lily out of the room. "I don't feel anything wrong!" I said. "I knew it!" Lily answered. She went on to relate that yesterday Jason was playing baseball, and running the bases, and not getting tired. There were no nosebleeds, no stomachaches, and no headaches! She then said the words that touched my heart so deeply, and which I will never forget – "this is the little boy I remember!" we both cried and held each other, so grateful to God for putting us together and bringing his grace into our lives.

The next day, Lily's husband flew in and I saw him for a healing treatment. With each hand placement where I would find something on him, he would smile and then validate it. During his treatment, Lily told me of something extraordinary that had happened with Jason the night before. They had been in a store, and Jason and his brother were up ahead of Lily in the aisle. When all of a sudden a "black thing flew out of his ear - it shot straight out sideways and disappeared." Lily couldn't believe her eyes! Jason didn't seem to know that anything had happened. She wanted to know why this had happened, and what it was.

I didn't know why either, it was a mystery to me. So, I listened for the Words to be said, and told Lily that she had been shown this as a validation that the problem was gone, and not to worry about it anymore. She was thrilled. So many blessings for this family! As I saw the father carefully gathering up several business cards off the counter, I called to him and offered several brochures too, so that the work could be explained to others. He came back down the aisle and took them from my hand.

"Thank you," he said with tears in his eyes, "for my boy."

"Thank Him," I said, pointing up. "He is the one who heals, I am nothing."

"Well, just the same, he used you to do it," he nodded and left.

I love my job – I've got the best Boss in the world! And so many perks besides! Glory be to God in the highest!

No Withdrawal Symptoms from Heroin

A young woman in her 30's was introduced to me at a Christian Bible study; I thought to myself, "How beautiful she would be without the terrible sores on her face – Lord, may I have a chance to help her?" She had such a sweet and child-like personality, her blonde hair swaying this way and that. As we hugged, I was given a *knowing*. "Oh, drugs. They do such a terrible thing to the body."

Through the next couple of weeks, I was able to get to know "Christy" better. She had been on heroin for over four years. She had tried to quit before and it was painful and ultimately unsuccessful. The custody of her young son had been taken from her. Former addicts have told me that heroin is the hardest drug to get off – worse than cocaine. Every cell feels like it is on fire, and there is vomiting, sweating, and unbearable sensitivity when the skin is touched.

Now, Christy was staying with a friend who had successfully made the choice to be drug-free, and who consistently and freely opens his house to friends desiring to quit the habit and detoxify. There are rules - they have to be working with the process, for them to be able to stay there. He also conducts a weekly Bible study at his home and is actively participating with his church. He now knows where the true "High" is - the Most High! So, his heart goes out to others who are now where he has been, and *he is making use of the Godly Gift of compassion* to help them. Christy had the heart-felt desire to quit, but lacked the fortitude to do so. She was given the choice to have a person come to the house and administer a medical injection once a day for four or five days (which would put her in a coma-like condition while her body detoxified), or to go on a Christian retreat. She chose the retreat.

As I have stated before, group prayer is a beautiful bubble bath inviting the Holy Spirit in for a dip! Such prayer Christy was immersed in at the retreat. Friday night she received a healing treatment - her liver felt on fire, there were so many toxins in her system, great repair of the organ was being done. In the wee hours of the morning, Christy opened up the door to the blazing wood stove and threw in all the drugs and paraphernalia she had. *She took physical action to show her faith and dependency on God.* The possibility of terrible reactions while undergoing detoxification in the middle of the woods without a doctor or hospital around was very real, but she was willing to risk it. She would rely directly on God to save her. She was at her point of brokenness. So, what could he do, being the Good Guy that he is? *He reached down to save her, of course!*

Saturday she received two more healing treatments (one in which her enlarged and thin-walled heart could be felt to actually shrink back to regular size and beat!). On Sunday she received one more. The weekend had been a wonderful time of openness and confession, of Divine study, supplication and praise! And, it also proved to be a time of miracles for Christy.

Christy returned Sunday night to her home, and waited with anxiety for the "delayed" symptoms of detoxification. The morning after she arrived back, she felt nauseated, but nothing she couldn't handle. She braced herself for the next day. The third day is usually the worst. The day ticked by. Then the next day, and the next. Two weeks went by. "The worst" never came. No cells on fire, no convulsions, no unbearable pain! She had been Divinely healed by the Greatest Pharmacist of all! Those who knew her called it a miracle. God knows no bounds!

Miracle Healing from Pneumonia, Acute Pancreatitis

(As received by letter from Mrs. G., RN - Reprinted by Permission)

On Easter Sunday, my daughter was hospitalized at Alvarado Hospital, San Diego, in the surgical intensive care unit with acute pancreatitis leading to pneumonia, followed by a second pneumonia from aspiration. She was on morphine for pain, a respirator, TPN, N/G tube (to keep the stomach empty to prevent further vomiting), and much more. Her doctors had prepared us for the worst, saying her condition was serious and could be fatal. If she recovered, she was expected to be in the hospital for at least another week to 10 days followed by weeks of recovery at home.

I had asked Tiffany Snow to do a Reiki treatment (an alternative therapy recognized by the AMA) on my daughter but was told by hospital staff I needed to get a doctor's order. The doctor had heard of Reiki and graciously agreed. On the third day in ICU, Tiffany did the Reiki treatment with hands-on-healing and healing prayer. The nurses showed respect and worked around her schedule to avoid any interruption. Tiffany asked me to stay and pray. In the middle of the treatment, which took less than an hour, my daughter felt hot, and asked for a fan. The treatment was paused, as my daughter ate two bowls of broth and some Jello, which she was able to keep down (her first day on liquids). After another 10 minutes of treatment, Tiffany said a final silent prayer, and gave us both words of encouragement, "To watch for big changes about to occur," and left.

That evening, my daughter was tolerating liquids so well, that they took her N/G tube out (2 days earlier than expected). The following day she was transferred out of ICU and discharged home on Sunday after being in the hospital only 8 days (4 days after the treatment). The doctors were astounded with her speedy recovery and attributed it to her youth. I was told that other patients with the same problem are hospitalized much longer as pancreatitis takes a long time to heal.

I felt it was a miracle that my daughter not only survived, but recovered so quickly. Three days after hospital discharge, she went back to school part-time. I am extremely grateful for the powerful healing that was given my daughter, the many prayers from family and friends, and the excellent care she received at the hospital. It was a perfect example of Alternative and Western medicine coming together. I will never know exactly how much of the miraculous healing and speedy recovery was from Tiffany and the prayers, my daughter's young age (18), or exceptional hospital care, but I have no doubt that the healing that came through Tiffany (and as she says, "from the Big Guy" – from God) was powerful and made a difference.

CHAPTER 8

Archeology Comes to Life - Old Souls Go to Heaven
Civil War in Tennessee; 1100 AD in Hawaii; Indians in N.M.

Part of my morning routine is to awaken as gently as possible, with the conscious intention to linger at the "in-between area" of asleep and awake. This is a great place to remember your dreams, do affirmations, and to reinforce a positive schedule of achievement for the day. It is a lovely place to meditate and pray, actively seek Divine Guidance, and work on openness and ability to hear, see and feel the "other sphere." It also helps keep you in a state of constant receptivity, with the additional perks of having adventure appear consistently in your everyday life.

TWILIGHT God-Spot: The Place Between Asleep & Awake. *Do not wake up with an alarm clock, this has to be a natural awakening, as gently as possible. When you do realize you have awakened, Do Not Stretch. This would clear your mind too much by circulating blood and energy. If possible, and with as little movement as you can, turn on a near-by lamp that you have set there for that purpose, already focused on shining on your face. Recognize the feeling in your bladder, but do not get up to relieve yourself. You are creating the optimum environment for slight stress. You do not want to fall back to sleep, so an irritant that will not wake you up completely, but through which you can still relax, is the key. Use this TWILIGHT tool every morning to prepare your mind, body and spirit to be mentally conscious yet physically calm. Know that you are now actively ready to embrace the opportunities presented to you to share your gifts.*

Columbia, Tennessee

In middle Tennessee, the early morning hours often bring a misty fog that lifts up from the ground as the day's deep humidity builds. It gives the open fields and meadows a soft, eerie look. I am sure an active imagination could lead to many things. But, what if you weren't imagining, and history opened up before your very eyes? Would it lead you to fear, or to a greater understanding of life? A person doesn't really know how he will handle things until it actually happens to him. But, you must be *open to the interaction.* One day while bicycling down a country road south of Columbia, I found out how I would react.

It was during the misty hours – not too hot yet, and still morning enough to have some work traffic. I was bicycling up the left-hand side of the road, wanting to leave enough distance between me, the edge of the pavement, and the oncoming trucks as they drove by. Beside me was an open field, fenced at the front and edged on three sides by trees. I smiled as I rode by, looking forward to my destination, a small corner gas station where I bought my morning java. I was endeavoring to do my exercise, but still needed a proper incentive to do it!

All of a sudden, out of the corner of my eye, *a man jumps up from the fog, runs about 15 feet and falls back to the ground!* He had a gray scrunched hat clinging to his head and his right hand grasped a long rifle. I stopped my bicycle and watched in stunned disbelief. *Where is this guy from?* Or, more properly perhaps, *when* is this guy from? After a moment the man jumped back up, lunged forward, and dropped again, as did the other six or seven fellahs in the group with him! They were scattered like rabbits across the field. They would run and drop under the mist, only to jump back up again. I realized I was glimpsing into the Civil War – a moment had come to life from long ago, and I was seeing it *today* with my very own eyes!

I made a subconscious note to be sure to ride on the *other* side of the road on my way home that day, and to have *two* cups of coffee! But I found *I was not afraid* of what I had seen, but I was troubled as to *why* I had seen it. I felt that if I *had* been afraid, the connection would have clogged up, and these types of visions would not have continued to be seen. Looking back, I believe it had been a precursor to test if I could be available to be used for special assignments in the near future, to help correct unresolved issues from the past.

The Sacred Circle

A few weeks later my daughter, Sierra, and I were bicycling down another country road, and she pointed to a small turn-off to the left. We hid our bikes in the bushes. We determined to follow what was left of an old animal trail. It soon stopped at an old dry creek bed. We liked our country excursions together!

"Keep to the left and follow the creek," I said, while holding my hands out in front of me, "there was, or is, a structure in that direction, it feels like an old house."

We went further and came across an old rusty and partially burned-out school bus. It was overgrown by bushes and old blackberry vines.

Sierra looked back at me quizzically, "Is this it?" she asked.

"No, go on, to the left more and we should find it on the side of a ridge," I answered.

I scanned my hands over the bus, and touched a piece of metal black with soot. I asked in my mind for the information, and a connection was made to the One Who Knows All. "Hmm," I said to myself, "man in his late 60's, gray hair, homeless, heart condition - just wanting to be alone...who would burn him out? Oh...two boys, early teens, live in the neighborhood, father approved and gave them the stuff to do it. Wanted the old guy out. Too bad." I saw a vision of the faces of the boys in my mind, and the outside of the house where the father lived, and an electrical shot of anger sparked in my head and the vision "popped." Big emotions always clog the channel! Then I felt anger toward myself and shrugged my shoulders about my own stupidity to let emotions rule.

METAL AND JEWERLY God-Spot: The Details of Emotion. *Different metals provide different resistances to energy, and some scatter out the energy, like some rocks do. But, overall, metals are one of the easiest connections to understand. Gold conducts energy very well, and is the only metal I do not ask my clients to remove during a healing treatment, as it does not affect the flow of energy. When holding someone's car keys, a necklace or ring, and you go to validate the information, first ask in your mind if there has been more than one original owner. Metals hold information over a very long period of time, maybe forever. You might get many stories. What do you sense? Try to find the best part of your body to understand and access the information. Try holding it in your right hand, then your left. Place it up to your forehead, which has sometimes been called the "third eye." Hold it against your solar plexus (your belly). What place seems to make information clearer to you? Metals hold a lot of emotions and many things in sharp detail. Be prepared for many things to show up in your mind's eye all at once. Heirlooms and antique jewelry hold many stories of love, life and loss. Experiment by going to garage sales. First form an opinion, bring the item with you and ask the history of it from the sellers. You will be surprised by how accurate you will be! This is all about your learning to listen. Metal also applies to cars, and car accidents. Place your hands on the dent and form conclusions; then ask the owner how it happened. With practice, perhaps you will be able to give police and family members missing information. Metal handrails are like phone lines of information, all talking at once. If you are very sensitive, try not holding onto one while you walk; it can be very distracting and is often like holding an electric cable of confusion in your hands - thousands of emotions.*

"Here is something!" Sierra called out from a distance away. I caught up to her and saw the remains of an old building, and some outlying animal sheds tucked up on the hill behind.

"Yes, that's it. But I'm getting something *really neat* over in this direction," I said. We followed the slope of the ridge a few hundred feet, and pushed the undergrowth aside, while Sierra swung a stick in front of her to help ward off the spider webs crossing her path, gluing her in the face.

"Stop!" I cried out. "Look at them all!" Rocks, pile of them, brown, speckled and gray, mounded a few feet high, were scattered across the ridge. In many places large trees were now growing out from the piles, as if it had been a safe place to germinate, sheltered from heat and wind. I watched intently and waited. I studied one pile after another, while my mind automatically shut out any outer distractions. I held my head at an angle, while I focused on *listening…nothing.*

I remembered a trail ride I had gone on through piles like this. The trail boss said the horses would often get jumpy, and that these were mounds the soldiers had built and hid behind during Civil War times. He joked that the horses probably saw ghosts. I remembered stifling a chuckle, knowing that animals are very sensitive to such things.

I focused my mind on *seeing…got it!*

One of the gray rocks at the top of a pile began to rise up - and I saw that it was not a stone at all, but a partly-squashed cap, and the face rising up underneath it had sunken eyes and weathered, drawn skin. "Sierra, can you see all of them?" I excitedly asked. "It's the South, and they are laying in wait for something on the other side of this ridge!"

"I see all the rocks, mom, are these from the Civil War? Cool!" she said, looking around. We counted 20 mounds that we could see.

I continued further up the ridge, and on top walked out from the undergrowth and cedar trees to a circle of sun. Here, on the top of this hill that was dense with thistle, vines, brush and trees, was a perfect circle about 50 or 60 feet across – with not a thing growing on it except grass. Not a tree, not a single bush. No thistles. Just a bed of lovely grasses in a perfect circle, with nothing else there. I walked to the middle of the circle, and took my foot and toed through the surface, and picked up some of the dry, crumbly earth. Immediately a cool chill shimmered at the base of my spine. I held the dirt up to my cheek, felt the essence, and desired to *know.*

"What did you find?" Sierra shouted across the clearing

"Shhh," I answered, and motioned her to come toward me, "this is Sacred Ground."

I have always found it interesting how people respect and honor the places where lives are lost - battlegrounds, certain buildings, even places alongside the road are sometimes marked with memorials or crosses. Nature does the same thing, if left undisturbed. Blood, the connection of the spirit, and the high emotion of transitioning is a sacred thing on many levels.

I was standing right in the midst of where a lot of lives had been lost. Two tents were also pitched here, and one was for a doctor to do cutting and mending away from the eyes of the other men. I saw that there were men lying on the grass all around. Some were already dead, their eyes glossed, blankly staring.

Others were still being maintained, strips of cloth wrapped here and there soaked with blood, and men were being held sitting up, and water was being lifted up to their lips. The caps were gray, but there were a variety of styles of clothes all around. These soldiers seemed like a mixture of ordinary men and boys.

I stretched my hands toward the back tent - a tent for intelligence, men making decisions, pointing and talking, pointing past me over the ridge. Before my eyes, everything continued on like a movie. There was no indication that anyone knew I was there, no interaction or acknowledgment toward me.

Death permeated the area - and out of the tent a small woman in her mid-40's to 50's, wearing a gray ankle-length wool skirt, came out and moved through the men and back again into the doctor's tent. Her features were well-defined and easy to see - she came out once more and stopped...she looked straight at me, straight into my eyes, then turned and continued on her way. The hair stood up on my arms and I broke out in goose bumps, and my heart raced. She seemed so sad! I could feel her sadness heavy upon my heart. Who was she? Why was she here? One thing I did know about her; she was a ghost. A ghost moving in a re-created "energy-tracing" world of the Civil War.

I said a prayer of thanks to God for letting me see, and added my blessing and comfort to this ground. Now that I had seen the woman, I knew why God had allowed this occurrence and what my responsibility was. She had not been able to let go and move on. I was there to help her choose, again, to go to His Presence. There had been something holding her back when she was first given the opportunity. What could it be? How would I be led to help?

I reminded myself of some of the procedures and prayers in the Scriptures and in my Minister's Handbook, and the pile of various notes I had scribbled over the years for helping those in this situation. I wanted to review the procedures I had learned and return later to help release her. My heart went out to this woman - I turned and walked away from the horrid destruction, and reminded myself that this was the past, not the present. I must honor it as part of our history and heritage, and remember the sacredness of life, but I must not be overly saddened. Also, I knew that if I wanted to know more, I must not clog the channel by extreme emotions again, or I would not be able to learn the rest of the story...

I walked out of the Scared Circle over the top of the ridge, with Sierra at my side. I instantly felt myself wanting to drop down to the ground or duck behind a tree. There in front of me, down in the ravine was a leader on a horse, and perhaps 30 smartly-dressed-in-blue soldiers with him, staring up in my direction. I felt that they had not yet engaged the men at the top of the ridge. No bodies were beside them on the ground. All men were standing and had rifles at the ready. I felt that if I had a pencil and paper with me, I could have drawn in very good detail the stylish uniforms. I even thought I saw a quick glint of a sword. Had the bloodshed really happened yet? Or was I seeing a segment of time immediately before? I decided I didn't really need to know – and moving back off down the ridge, I avoided the sacred meadow, and found an old animal trail to take us down toward the bikes.

"Boy, mom, I like history lessons with you, I can remember these!" Sierra piped in.

"Yes, nothing like going out into the field and getting it narrated for you, right?" I answered as my eyes twinkled. We made our way to the edge of the woods and found ourselves looking across a dry meadow. I started across it, my hands open like a radar dish looking for signal, my mind receptive to input – *something* was afoot!

Civil War Mary

About fifty feet from the woods, I stopped abruptly. I felt a strong impulse to look up to the sky. "Sierra! Here she is!" I shouted and pointed.

I looked up to see a small, very bright outline of a woman, escalating down to me, with the sun at her back, almost like an eclipse getting larger and larger as she advanced. Like a moth gliding down a flashlight's beam of light, she stood in front of me, in her woolen long skirt, and sad, sullen eyes. "She's so beautiful! Oh, she's so sad!" I said.

She was thin-boned, had a pale complexion, and she stood no more than five feet tall. Her name, as I heard it in my head, was "Mary...Mary S..." She was the same woman who had been in the Sacred Circle on the hill.

Now *seeing,* for me, is much easier than *hearing,* depending on the strength of the "spiritual essence." Remember, there is no interaction with energy tracings, they are simply a vibrational image of past memories and events. And, often hearing is like seeing lips move behind hazy Plexiglas - and sometimes you feel like tapping your arm and asking (as in charades), "Is it one syllable or two?"

But, the slower the spirit energy, the easier the communication. And, as experience has shown me, the stronger communicators and the easiest spirits to see are those who are still not letting go of their previous physical, emotional, or spiritual trauma in this life. These are the ones who need to, as we say, "Go to the Light of the Lord." These are the ones who have unfinished business and fall into the category of "ghosts." They are the ones who haunt. They are the ones where God uses those who are sensitive and willing to the Holy Spirit for this kind of gift, to call back Home.

In this case, most of the information Mary gave me was like seeing her life in my own head, through her eyes. Her husband had moved her here, away from her relatives. She had had seven children, two lost as babies. Of the five, two of those died from a contagious disease. The three who were left seemed to be boys, and one was much younger than the other two. Her husband had brought her here to start all over, to get away from all the sickness and bad luck that had plagued them.

Mary had me walk a few feet forward. "You are now at the front door of our house, look around you." she motioned.

I turned around and saw in front of me a small one-room cabin, with a ladder alongside the left wall, which angled up to the boys' bedroom loft. There was a pale wooden table, which I thought to be made of pine, on the left side of the room. On the right were Mary and her husband's bed, and I could see a quilt hanging across a beam on one side for privacy. There were metal cups hanging on the wooden wall, and also a faded black-and-white photo of a busy street with two-story brick buildings with people standing in front of them. While living in this house, one of her boys had died in the winter (an accident), and another by poison (it felt like snakebite, or perhaps tainted food).

No wonder Mary was so sad. Overall, she had experienced the death of six children, and had seen the ravages of Civil War, and those were just the things I knew about.

There was another photo, what we would now consider "wallet size," of a woman's large pale face. It looked like it was made on metal, it seemed to be shimmering. She was not smiling, and she wore a button-up white collar with black buttons. Her bangs were curled, and the rest of her hair seemed to be up in a bun. She looked about 35 or 40 years old to me, although I know that people in previous times often looked older than their true age, because of the ruggedness of their lives.

"Is she your mother?" I asked.

She nodded, poor Mary, always sad to the point of tears. I related to Sierra all these things, then I ran out into the field and pointed.

"Look! She had a milk cow! And a garden! And her husband diverted the water up here and made a little pond, but it kept going dry! She grew corn and beans too!"

Mary kept following me and answering in my mind any questions I might have. She was unmoved by my excitement. The "gray leader" at the top of the hill (I don't know what the correct military term would be for his rank) had asked her to

147

assist the surgeon. She refused to address him as 'doctor' (Mary said he didn't deserve that honor), and many men had died. During the war, Mary's cow was killed and the vegetables were always stolen. Not long after the war ended, the house had burned. But, although her life had been hard, it was the loss of her children that made her so extremely sad.

When I asked her about her husband, there was no emotion, and no answer. But her youngest son had lived and there was a connection with Kentucky. I didn't know if the son had moved there, taken a wife from there or what.

The connection was weakening. Although *her* energy still seemed to be strong, I felt like *my* head was going to burst! It had been several hours of being "on" and I had stretched my envelope as far as I could go, and for as long as I could, at this period of time in my spiritual growth.

I thanked her for the information, asked her not to be sad anymore, and to move on to The Light of God's Love (she truly fit the category of "ghost"). I encouraged her to come close to the Almighty, who is the Source of All Comfort, and that her loved ones were sure to be there and ready to welcome her. She did not seem to hear what I was saying. Then she left the way she came, floating up toward the sky with the sun behind her, smaller, and smaller, until I couldn't see her anymore.

Sierra and I got on our bikes and headed home, my glorifying God for the glimpses, wondering what it was all about, and if I had actually done any good for Mary, and thinking of all the other questions I should have asked but didn't think of. For example, "Where are you buried (if she realized she was dead)? What was your son's name? What was your husband's name? Do you have descendants now living?" Little did I know that I would receive the answers to several of my questions within the next couple of weeks.

The next day I ended up spending a good part of the day resting, and just doing idle activities. My God-Spot continued to be strengthened with each new experience, but it didn't expand all at once! I needed to reflect on the experience and give myself time to balance and adjust to the new level of Energy the "larger conduit" had produced in my soul. God was training me on his own timetable: I wasn't on my schedule.

Cemetery Communion, Mary's Last Farewell

In Tennessee, people have cemeteries everywhere. Sometimes you will see a tombstone or two in the corner of the yard, or sometimes you will see a 30x30 family plot in the middle of a pasture, with barbed-wire strung all around it to keep the cows out. And, there are church cemeteries, town cemeteries, and city cemeteries too. I started to look for Mary and her family. One by one I would stop

148

and inspect all the cemeteries I could get to, and actually found several 'Marys' from the same time period. But none of them was my 'Mary S...' I was thinking I wouldn't ever find her, when I absolutely did.

There is a cemetery near the freeway and across the road where I lived, and still being an active cemetery, a man had been buried there shortly after my meeting with Mary. I try to avoid new burials, since the mourners bring such a high energy of remorse and grief to the place, and it bothers me. Also, the newly deceased still have high energy tracings from their transition, and often I see them in their grave, sense what they died of, and what condition their bodies are in presently. This is not a pretty sight (one of the gifts I have been allowed to develop is Medical Intuitiveness, and it doesn't stop when people die)! But, the tracing fades to a tolerable low hum after a few weeks, and even faster if it has been raining. But it never, ever, goes away altogether.

Mary was in this cemetery. I had driven or ridden by it almost every day, without even giving it a second thought. Now, two weeks later, fresh after my morning of "Twilight God-Spot," I felt an irresistible urge to pull over the car and stop. I have found, if you truly wish to be "Led by the Spirit," you will find yourself breaking many schedules! I pulled in, got out of the car, and walked straight to the middle of the cemetery, being pulled right up to a tall marker under a large maple tree. And there she was *(last name, birth and death dates withheld for privacy of the family):*

"In Loving Memory of
Mary S...
Born... Died..."

Two other tombstones lay beside her, her husband and her son. She had been in her forties when she helped the surgeon in the Civil War. Mary had lived a very long life and was brought back here from Kentucky (had she lived with her son?) to be laid to rest with her husband and son, both of whom had died earlier than she. More pain and family loss. I felt Mary's presence and looked over to my left...there she was, her ghostly presence about six feet from me, looking down at the graves – and it was the first time I had seen her smile.

"I'm glad you were with your son for a while, Mary." I said, noting that he lived to be in his 30's.

She just kept smiling. Not long after, I came back to Mary's grave, with Sierra at my side, and broke bread, read scripture and shared communion wine, including her presence in our annual remembrance of Passover, as part of our extended family. I too am a mother, and have experienced loss. I could easily identify with her grief. The wound of a lost child is a very deep wound indeed.

How nice to understand that the destruction of the physical body is not "the end of it all." But rather, as Einstein said, and scientists since have eagerly proven, 'energy cannot be destroyed, but simply changes from one vibrational quality to another.' Everything is done or allowed for the Highest Good of the spirit and those around him/her. Lessons are learned, we make the transition and move on. And sometimes, if we need help moving on, we might even get a nudge, like Mary was getting, again.

By my offering of communion at Mary's grave site, I wanted to honor not only the traditional remembrance of God's Angel sparing the ancient Israelite children and leading God's people out of Egypt (Passover), but also how the sacrifice of Jesus opened eternal life for us all. Religious customs *can be* another successful tool for opening the God-Spot, as thousands of churches will tell you. But if the custom doesn't *resonate down into your soul and sing songs of love to your intuition,* throw it out - it may just clog you up instead.

I once again invited Mary to join herself to The Almighty One and leave her sadness here, telling her that she was sure to *reunite again* with her loved ones if she *just lets go!* I projected toward her my glimpse of heaven and the love I had felt before the Presence. *"Mary, please! Unconditional love and joyous reunion are waiting for you!"* And "poof" she disappeared. No light show or gliding, just "poof"…and she was absolutely gone! It happened so quickly. What made a difference this time over the previous time? The communion, or maybe something I had said? I still don't know, and it really doesn't matter. The work was accomplished, and my responsibility was fulfilled. I was glad that I could help.

I visited her gravesite a few more times after that, just to make sure, but she never reappeared. When I closed my eyes and placed my hands on the tombstone, the energy felt different, and I had a sense of peace. In a way, it seemed that this was the place where her transition had occurred, and not at her death. It always amazes me how many similarities death has to the feeling of birth. Mary's war was over now, and sorrow would not camp at her door anymore. She was connected in love and peace with everything around her for the first time in her life, and in her death. I had been able to tag along in the Great Adventure to help her finish The Connection. After nearly 200 years of being away, I'll bet she was glad to be home! Many Blessings, Mary.

***

Kauai, Hawaii

Sometimes just when you think you know what you are doing, the universe throws a curve ball. How wonderful when we can catch it! I have found that to work consistently with "The Big Guy" I must be willing to change my plans of what *I think* I'm doing, at a moment's notice. Once again, this scripture sums it up beautifully: "The wind blows wherever it pleases. You hear its sounds, but you cannot tell where it comes from or where it is going. So it is with everyone born of the Spirit…" (John 3:8)

I had visited Hawaii as a kid, and had always dreamed of returning to its blue waters and lush scenery again. Without my pursuing anything, an opportunity fell in my lap and the deal was closed in less than a week. An opportunity was presented to help establish a new clinic on the island of Kauai, one of the most beautiful islands in Hawaii. My parents were also vacationing there and I would have a place to stay at no cost. I was excited as I boarded the plane, eager to meet in person the new friends at the clinic I had been conversing over the phone with, and start the work.

I was to take a few days to visit with my family and see the island, and then arrange a work schedule. But, unknown to me, during this short period of time one of the main practitioners accepted a job offer on the mainland, and his partner decided to move back also. The clinic was closed; and I had to wonder why I was truly there. But, as always, God knew what he was doing, and I didn't have to wonder about anything. It ended up being a time of immense growth for me. I produced over 30 pages of "ancient Hawaiian experiences" from numerous locations on the island – and ended up shocking and encouraging a respected and well-known archeologist with the accuracy. Here are a few examples:

The Cave of the Outcasts

There is a sunken cave not far from Poipu, on the island of Kauai. My father, Fred, had discovered it one day while bicycling down a little-used road. Later, he brought my mother, Trisha, and they spoke to an archeologist working in it. The woman was somehow related to the local college, and she said raptor bones had been found in it. This is all I knew when the day came to travel down the twisty road. I prayed and meditated in the car ride there, and opened up all my sensors. I was anxious to begin!

When the car was parked, I got out and heard a high-pitched wail. It seemed not to be from this earth, and indeed, no one else had heard it. I felt it was somehow related to the cave. My auditory perception had been the weakest of my senses, so I was excited to begin with such a strong confirmation of another adventure on the horizon! I could feel a tingling in the air, an expectation. I took my time and walked and breathed slowly, opening myself up to what might be waiting. There was dense shrubbery, and branches with thorns on them, with a narrow sandy trial bending in between. I imagined a jungle movie scene from "Indiana Jones."

Up on a rise, we came around a bend and looked over. Before us was a huge sinkhole. Inside there was a short cave and overhang off the right side and a much longer cave and overhang coming out from the left side. It looked to be a large tunnel that the roof had caved in on thousands of years ago. It was perhaps 145 feet long and 80 feet wide from my position, where I was perched up on the side looking down to the floor perhaps 40 feet down. The sides were very steep. There was a modern grated steel door to keep people out along the right hand side. A small cave opening came out by a streambed where people could crawl through when the door was unlocked.

I stood at the precipice and opened my hands, scanning this way and that. There was *the detailed figure of a woman squatting down* along the right side of the cave with her back towards me. She had long dark hair and was either grinding or taking care of someone. She did not turn to notice me, and at this point I did not know if she was a ghost or an energy tracing. I wondered if she knew I was there. She was probably in her 30s at the time. I left and continued down to the right side tunnel, hoping to get a better view of her through the locked entrance.

As I came to the stream and saw the rock face wrap all the way around the stream, I looked out over the meadow across from me and saw a vision of a garden area with people digging. They held long-handled tools, and were swinging them up and down. There were a few buildings there also, with palm fronds hanging over the tops. They were well-made structures, their openings facing back at me and behind the workers. There were some children working, and people of other ages, about a dozen in the field. They each had different facial structures and physical builds, and did not look related as a family might look.

Looking at the rock wall where the small tunnel entrance was, my eyes were drawn to a natural rock ledge a few feet above the entrance. In my mind's eye I could see where there had once been a round-topped stone with a symbol carved on it. It had been placed there with clay and rocks underneath it to cement it in, as if placed on a small pedestal. I knelt down to the ground and wiped the leaf debris away with my hand, and drew the symbol I had just seen in the dirt. I had a strong sense that the symbol meant "The Exiled," or to that same effect, "The Outcasts."

EARTH God-Spot: The Time of Past & Present. *Center yourself, find that quiet place in your soul. With the intent of Love and Understanding, dig through the top layer of leaves and debris with your heel. Scoop up a handful of dirt. Does it feel hot, warm or cold? Play with the coarseness or smoothness, rolling it between your fingers. What colors do you see – what colors do you sense? Are they different? Bring the earth to your face and breathe in the aroma. Is it new earth or old? What do your five senses tell you? What about your other senses? Now, ask the questions you want to know. The soil helps as a connection. You may ask about any time period, and the dirt does not have to be the precise age you are asking about. What were the biggest energy experiences that happened here? Who were the people, what did they look like? What happened here in*

152

1200 A.D., how about in 1950? Remember, the more specific you are, the clearer the answers. (Side-Note to Gardeners: Most soil is alive and has microorganisms in it. You will often feel the warm vibration of life in your hands. I have found a medium-high vibratory rate makes an excellent soil for germination and plant growth. Too fast a rate seems to indicate high acidity in the soil or contamination, including some kinds of chemical pollution). Remember to start all 'asking' with prayer. This is the Godly Connection from which you are getting the information.

I went in and sat in the small entrance of the cave, up against the locked gate and looked through to the large open area. I made sure not to touch the heavy steel grating – I did not want to know about the archeologists. What I wanted was much older. The light was muted, and I felt it necessary to slightly cross my eyes to bring in the 3-D effect of the visions, making them easier to see.

There, about ten feet in front of me, the visions became clear. There were old people and sick people lying down on woven mats. Some were propped up and were looking *past* me with casual indifference. They had on very few clothes, just the bare necessities to cover their bodies. On many, there was a paste on their skins, a sticky dark green substance, which seemed to be used as a salve for them. In places, the salve had dried and cracked, the fresh dressings seemed to be the wet, lighter colored ones. There was a small amount of food near each of them, within arms length. There were many bugs flying about them. There was a very large container, man-made and brown, barely inside the overhang, with water in it. I got the feeling of skin problems, and disease. The word "leprosy" flashed in my mind. Most of the people seemed old, in that they looked like skeletons with the flesh hanging from their bones. There were also deformities, and several had thinned or gray hair. But, there were children here also.

In front of my eyes, the essence of a young boy, with a big smile on his face, raced by me. He must have been 6 or 7 years old. He had no arm below his right elbow. A younger girl, about 5, with a mongoloid look to her face, chased after him. I got a strong message that they were each considered a "bad omen" and had been left here to be taken care of. I felt the pain of the mothers' crying, leaving their babies by "big rocks." If the families had kept them, they would have been brought out and killed by "the men." I could not tell who these 'men' were, I thought at first it was a religious connection, but I also felt political/leadership ties too. This was indeed the "Cave of the Outcasts." It was also their sanctuary.

I saw again the woman who had been sitting, and a metamorphosis occurred before my very eyes - she changed into a young girl - and the movie of her life began. She came here very young, before the marrying age, and brought her mother who had a disease. She ended by staying to take care of her mother, grew up here, and even stayed on after her mother's death. Even though I felt she herself had never gotten sick, I got the feeling that she would *not* have been welcomed if she had returned to the outside world. The girl grew up to be the

153

most important person here in this very special group, who never numbered more than 40 persons at any given time.

This woman (I was not able to get a name) never married, but she enjoyed the children here immensely. She was the coordinator of everything, she was like a matriarch, and highly respected. She nursed the older ones, feeding them, changed their salves, and cooked and worked in the garden. She had helpers - any who could work and had strength, would do whatever they could to help. There were two or three cooking fire areas in the open space, and food gathering and processing took a large part of the day, especially the pounding and grinding of food.

This woman was the one who appeared to me the most, with clearly defined facial features. It was almost like she was sharing her "home movies" with me. She wore a knot in her hair, on the front side, her hair wound up in a wood bristle-like thing that she considered flattering. It looked like a teased knot that would be impossible to comb out. It had carved fingers of shell or bone sticking out of it. There was a darker lobby to this side of the cave, where the sicker ones would be separated from the others, before they died. Looking in from the grate, this would be on the right-hand side, in semi-darkness. This is also where her mother was in the days before she died.

I climbed back up to the edge of the cave, to look back across the open expanse. Along the back of the wall there were poles standing up and mats laid over the top, no sides, just simply for shade, all along the back wall. Straight down from where I was were more of these sun shelters, with people sitting on mats there. Some were busy. There was one where women were grinding together, four of them at a time, moving forward at the waist and pulling back. It seemed very slow but steady. I do not know what food they were making. The roof mats seemed to be coarser mats than the ones on which the people were lying, some of these were very finely made, and I got the feeling they came as gifts from the families outside.

My father, the agile adventurer that he is (even in his 60s') decided to climb down the twenty-foot drop to the floor of the cave, and I requested he take my camera. I also asked that he first ask permission of Our Almighty Father, and to enter with respect and humbleness. I was hoping that images would show up on the camera for others to see, just as I see them myself. He took several pictures, including some in the dark tunnel and various spots to which I had pointed. Amazingly, out of the eight photos, two have transparent images, presented as wispy whiteness. One is in the *darkness* of the left Death Cave, and one in the *open daylight,* facing the communal area.

When we developed the photos, I saw that they were not as detailed as my "spirit vision," as I had been hoping for, but it was nice to have something that other people could see, if they wanted. I would have loved to have gone deeper into the "Death Cave" and taken the pictures myself, and photographed the other side of the cave, at the exact places that the woman and the children were, in my visions.

What I am calling the Death Cave is actually the left side entrance going back into the hill. This is where the people who died were placed, far back in the void. They were laid out flat, and covered with large leaves over and below their bodies. Sometimes I got the feeling of small sacrifices left with the body, the bodies of fish and birds, and all kinds of necklaces. There was a large surfboard-shaped piece of wood leaning against the rocks by the entrance. It must have been eight feet high. It had a carving at the top of it, and I believed it to be the face of a god. There was an inscription on it, and I called it the "Blessing Board." It basically gave a blessing, "for all who enter the darkness of this life in death."

Also, on the rock beside the Blessing Board were small gifts placed outside on the rocks, left for those who died or to the gods, I do not know. But, I knew that after a death, there were many more of them placed there. Some were wrapped in leaves, some were food, and some were carved items. It reminded me of the same custom of people bringing vases of flowers to a cemetery. I shouted down to my father where the board was, and to go see if he could feel the energy of it, since I had been training him and others to be sensitive to such things. He stretched his hands out and felt the parameters of the energy - and he felt that the energy stopped approximately two feet from the bottom. I said yes, that made sense, because that is where the writing stops. Of course, this dirt was not the same dirt now as it was then, I felt the original dirt was deep below, but the images of what I was seeing were through ancient eyes, and how things looked as they had existed before.

I gave a blessing to the cave and thanked the Lord for sight. I waved to the woman and the others, who were still going through their daily routines. I said a releasing prayer for the ghostly woman (even though it was a brief releasing prayer, when I returned the next year, her presence was not to be found). The others couldn't see me - there had been no interaction, they were only energy tracings of a time gone by. But I felt friendly towards them and felt honored to see this interesting place.

Upon leaving the cave and going up the trail, there was a place where the trail divided and a person could turn left and go to the sea. I saw a big rock, and turned and hurried down to it, excitedly exclaiming for the others to follow. *Etched upon the face of this lava boulder was the exact symbol* I had scratched into the dirt by the front cave entrance - "The Outcasts." *And here it was in real life!* I felt certain that there had been at least four (and probably 6-8) more boulders just like this, used as a boundary system around the parameters of this area. The idea that they were trying to get across was this: "No One Allowed to Come Any Closer - Keep Out - Unclean Land of The Outcasts."

And, I also knew that folk on the inside and on the outside felt that the natural rock setting of the cave would "keep the badness from contaminating others." These symbol boulders were also set in places where relatives could put food, clothing and other items, which would later be brought into the cave. Sometimes even babies would be left there. It would be their only chance for survival.

In a natural sinkhole, surrounded by rocks and tunnels extending this way and that, this cave of deformed, diseased and unwanted people made a life for themselves. Though they were a people cut-off from all others, and would surely be killed if they wandered outside of their parameters, they had found unity in their despondency. They took care of each other's needs as best they could, no matter what they looked like or what their problem was. They had become a family, coming together to face the hardships their lives threw at them. An excellent lesson for us all, from this most ancient of peoples.

Birth Stone Heiau and the Chief Priest

There is a sacred place on Kauai where the beautiful Wailua River comes through the island down to the sea. It flows gently by the boarded up "Coco Palms Resort" made famous by Elvis Presley in the movie "Blue Hawaii." The Wailua is well traveled, both by paddle boats, taking tourists up to Fern Grotto, and kayakers doing the "one paddle, two paddle" up to Hidden Falls. There is a small paved road that follows the Wailua River up the valley and over the mountain. It is a truly enchanting place!

Going into this adventure, all I knew was that Heiaus were ancient holy places, and at some, kings were supposed to be born there on special birthing stones. As always, to strengthen my sensitivities, and to not be distracted by anything that else that might influence me, I did not read any information, nor any posted signs at the area. In fact, I recommend not reading anything until you are out of the entire country, state or province, until you are *completely done* with your "sensitive research." That way, there is no unconscious "fitting the pieces together" as you go.

Following along the highway, on the left hand side there was a structure of gray rocks, stacked like a low fence, circling around to make what looked like an old animal corral. It was at the foot of a rocky-outcropped hill that continued up the mountain as a slanted ridge. This was a very interesting place. I went over to one of the flat layers of rock and held onto it, bracing my body close to the natural outcropping.

ROCK God-Spot: Guardians of the Ages. *Rocks can carry the most ancient and most interesting stuff you will ever read - if you can. I have found rocks to be extremely difficult to understand, and often confusing. They have spent thousands of years being washed by all forms of energy, possibly including creation itself. They are almost like pearls, layer upon layer of information thinly applied onto the whole. But, the good thing is that the most recent dustings of energy are on the first few layers, and they hold this very well. Especially in high-energy situations, the energy clings itself onto rocks. Be sure to try the ROCK God-Spot at crime scenes. Also, there are many minerals and crystal arrangements that create different frequencies in the rocks, some of which can focus the energy, some of which can really scatter it out. It will take discernment. Learning rocks is like learning a million new colors and having to name them all! Meteorites are especially interesting. Be patient and keep trying. Bring home rocks that feel in some way feel familiar or resonate with your energy. Place them in places of honor in your home and garden path. They will add stability and dimension. And, perhaps, hundreds or thousands of years from now, someone will touch the rocks you chose for your life and get a wonderful reading of you!*

"The *stones* of the wall will cry out, and the beams of the *woodwork* will echo it." (Hab.2:4)

I let go and walked backwards into the corral. Facing the rocky hill, my eyes quickly adverted to the left, where I saw a very tall priest standing, looking directly back at me. He was very well built and brown-skinned, and his head was bald (it seemed like a natural baldness), and he had on a tall hat. He wore a white or light yellow robe off his shoulders. His features were very easy to see. Another ghost.

It is possible that this could be the oldest ghost I have yet encountered. I didn't know the date at the time, but I later found out that his life occurred about 1100 A.D. He definitely knew that *I* was there, and did not seemed pleased that I was aware of *him* being aware of *me*, although he seemed O.K. to let me observe for now. He gave me the clear impression of being in a "watcher/guardian" position, and one of spiritual authority and power. Not someone to be messed with!

This priest had an assistant, a shorter man, who was also bald - but with him it did not seem a natural baldness, but rather a shaved one. He was younger than the tall priest. There were large sexual overtones between them, and I am wondering if they were homosexual or if the younger man procured females for the other one. I came to the conclusion that the assistant was an energy tracing. The priest let me know that he was a very powerful and important person. The king himself had named this place for him. He was an advisor to the king, and watched over the women, one in particular. He also watched over the hill itself. Just below where the priest was standing was a small ledge where I saw a carved stone god, about a foot or foot and a half high, propped in a corner where two rocks met. Moving right, as I faced him, toward the middle of the rock outcropping, seemed to be a planting of yellow flowers, and there were herbs of various kinds in groupings. It was very pretty, and I believed they were planted by women. I felt nothing in the front area on the ground, in the corral area surrounded by the rocks. It just felt like animals and grass and time.

On the ground at the right side was a small outline of a shelter, and a flat rock lying in front of it. Standing on this stone, I felt very hot and strong female energy, and the high vibration of blood, fear and happiness I realized that I didn't want to touch it with my hand, it might be too hot (silly thought)! I knew this was the birthing stone, and I questioned my folks, who were familiar with the area, and they nodded that it was true. But, I also felt that it had been moved, and that this was not the original place it had been.

I felt that mother and child would stay for 5-7 days and that the mother had four other women with her for the birth and to take care of her. She was a large native woman, the women around her were much thinner. I got the feeling that she belonged to the king who owned the mountain, the same one for whom the priest worked. One of the priest's responsibilities was to watch her. This building used to have sides and a roof, and seemed pretty dark inside. There were no windows, and a very small opening for a door. But, this flat birthing stone had not been in the front of its doorway like it was now.

There was a trail winding up the hill above the birthing stone, and I found an old Oriental Cemetery there on the first small plateau. But I kept going up the ridge, past the cemetery and through the thick brush and undergrowth. I felt drawn to keep going, past the trails the tourists knew, past the signs. There was something up there compelling me. I came out of the trees on a small level area on top of the ridge. It had a beautiful view looking down on the Wailua. There were four very weathered rocks placed in a semicircle. The priest was here too, and so strong I could *audibly hear him calling out to me,* and I stood on the top of the hill and wept, being very moved. I listened to the priest and tried to sound out the syllables through the foggy Plexiglas that separates us from space and time.

"O-A-K-U-I," or maybe "O-A-H-I-U." I kept repeating it, not knowing how to spell it (I still don't think I have it right) with its Hawaiian sounds, just sounding it out, and repeating it, I actually cried the word out loud, there on the mountain. I struggled so hard. This thought was put into my head: "This was the name of the man who named the mountain for the priest." So, this was the name of the king who started this Heiau, and owned the woman at the bottom of the hill. That, I told myself, should be easy to confirm.

I soon found out the reason for all the high emotion and passion I was feeling here. The high priest, much more accepting of me now, told me that this was the place where he buried the babies who did not survive.

158

They were offered back to the gods, and buried with bright colorful birds, and with leaves. It was the hardest thing that this powerful priest had to do. No rocks were placed over them, no marker above the ground to show where they laid. There were many of them, and not just from this one woman. This place where I was standing on was sacred ground, used only by the royalty for this purpose.

I was now muddy from the tears, and praised God with thankfulness for the information. Now I had a talk, minister to minister, about God's will for this priest. I shared with him my near-death experience and the vision of the Glory of God. I explained who Jesus Christ is, and how important he is to mankind's history and future. I did all this with my mind, not saying a word with my lips at all. There was silence at the end of my talk with this earth-bound priest, who had known only the plethora of gods of his ancient people. Next, I prayed to the One and Only to let this lost son see the way to go to His Light.

Then, in my heart I felt a euphoric burst of energy and a sense of weightlessness. I felt slightly dizzy and very blissful, and in a state of gratitude.

The priest was gone.

My mother and father had long since finished looking around the area and had decided to wait in the car. Upon seeing the smeared tears, I was greeted with an arm around my shoulder and a hug. They had become accustomed to unusual things occurring when they were with me, and they knew they would hear the story soon. I asked if we could drive on. I wanted to go all the way to the top of the ridge, and look out over the river.

On the very pinnacle of this small mountain ridge was a wide flat place, and beautiful green mountains shot hundreds of feet into the air on both sides. I asked in my mind for the significance to the ancient peoples about these mountains. On the mountain on the right I saw a scene of young boys ascending as a ritual pilgrimage to find visions, to sleep on its ridge and dream.

Later, a map I looked at called that spot, "The Mountain That Sleeps." I wondered if this was a modern name derived from an ancient one that had been carried down through the years, referring back to this sleep/vision quest?

Along this same road is the beautiful Opaekaa Falls, fluffed sheets of tropical water cascading into a white puff below. Almost directly across from that is a very large Heiau. I went up to the lava rocks outlining the ancient place. I opened my hands and "scanned" slowly over the entire area. I did not enter into the enclosure. There were signs clearly posted to Keep Out. I bent down and cupped my hands over some rocks of the lava wall. I said a prayer, closed my eyes and felt for the ROCK God-Spot.

This was the Heiau of a king. I got the distinct feeling of respect and royalty, and a king's "palace," or home base, but with military always around him. I had such a strong feeling that he was a peaceful man. I wondered about the military connection. Also, this place definitely had a priestly/holy connection. It felt like the same energy as the priest down below, so I felt this must be the King about whom the priest was telling me.

I felt this was a good king, and that games happened here, but I did not feel like women could enter in here. I felt like this space had been used by *many* kings after the first, but my page was set on the first king who *built* the place. Perhaps if I had wandered in I would have felt many different and conflicting energies through and on the rocks of the place. But, I did not go in, and I must go with my immediate feelings. An interesting note to this Heiau is that I saw no energy tracings of the people who had once lived here. I was just being given the information to satisfy my questions, as far as I could tell.

Validation – The Rest of the Story

I knew that the main reason I had been given this historic information, as in Tennessee, was to help release an earth-bound spirit to the heavens. But, as I followed my curiosity around the island and explored many different things, I ended up accumulating over thirty pages of ancient drawings and information on how things used to be. I thought perhaps it might also encourage the local archeologists and fill in some blanks for them. There is a part of the brain that also feels strong about receiving validation. Besides, a good deep conversation about many of the things I saw, and their correct identification, would be a lot of fun. And, more importantly, *I felt compelled by Spirit to do it!*

I decided I would not do any research on my own to validate anything, until I gave the information, in its purest form, to the archeologists. I try very hard not to be influenced by spurious information. I called up the Kauai Museum and they gave me two names – one for the state archeologist for all the islands of Hawaii (they had no phone number available), and for "Dr. M," an archeologist and teacher at the local Community College. I called him directly.

Dr. M. listened intently to the information, and asked for a copy of the drawings and papers. He also ended up stating, "I can validate 60% of what you saw, the rest we just don't know." My heart jumped, as I repeated happily in my mind. *"Sixty percent! The rest we just don't know!"*

He also said, "Tiffany, all my life I have been using rocks, soil, and seeds to write history. It is amazing that you can just walk into a place and see all this. I would love to see the people in their daily lives as you do."

I let him know immediately from where the source of the Power came, and that it was *not* from me! All glory goes to God! But why had I been so compelled to share my information with him? Because he needed a "God-Boost" right then, as you will soon see. He not only received information about his passion, but could also see that The Lord can supernaturally work in *any way he chooses* in everyday, ordinary people.

He was especially excited about what I named the "Outcast Cave," a place he has been excavating since 1993. He said ancient Kauai didn't want to send their lepers to the island of Molokai, since they were a proud people and liked to keep separate from the other island groups, because of island politics and factions. He said it made perfect sense that they would use a cave. He said his team had to dig down through five feet of mud and clay to do their work; and at one time it had even been filled with water.

He was also able to verify that there had been houses out in the field, where I saw the gardens and the huts. Also, that it was correct that this community never supported more than 40 people at a time. I told him where the boulder was, with the large carving of the "Outcast" symbol, and he was excited to follow up on that.

Even though I had only two days left on the island, I offered to go back and show him where all these things were. But, unfortunately, he was in the process of battling cancer (hence the reason God let him have this information as *reassurance of Divine Power* working in our lives!) and not able to come onsite, having even a difficult time keeping his teaching schedule at the college. *He encouraged me to continue what I do, no matter what people's reactions might be to it.* He said that I had given him accurate information that had *not been published anywhere.* He was happy that I had found him and shared. I praised God in my heart!

Dr. M. suggested I purchase a video recorder and take it on my journeys. When I asked if he could perhaps forward the information on to the head state archeologist for all of Hawaii, he hesitated and said, "even though I have heard of people doing this before and I feel you have been very accurate, I don't think it would be accepted well here." So I left it at that. The Lord opens the doors that should be opened, and locks those that should be closed. He then listened with interest about hands-on-healing. I could tell that the accurate archeological information had helped open him up to God's Divine Power. Below is some more validating information from Dr. M. and also some things that I missed.

It was the king's wife who lived at the bottom of the mountain. It is said he would visit her there. This part of the island was sacred and the home of the kings. If any person, not of royal blood, happened across here, he would be killed. Dr. M. said that I was correct about the birthing stone, that it had been moved, and that this one had been desecrated by having a dog buried underneath it. They had even found the bones. This Heiau at the bottom of the mountain was the only one where royalty could be born. I had missed the large rock at the back of the birthing area – there was a crack in it where each babies' umbilical cord would be placed.

Dr. M. said having bald priests made sense. The ancient people felt someone who was bald or had no hair on his body was special. They chose psychics to be their priests. He said he didn't know about the shoulder cape the priest was wearing. He could not confirm anything about this location of the baby burial ground, except that I was correct that sacrifices of birds were used, and that bodies would be wrapped in leaves. He also said that after the missionaries came to the islands, the natives were instructed to run pigs in the sacred enclosure at the base of the hill, to desecrate it. He thought that was why I probably didn't pick up any information there.

Also, he said the biggest thing I missed was at the top Heiau. It had been heavily used for human sacrifices! This took me back a bit. I found myself questioning this, stating that perhaps it was the *other* kings who came after the first one who did these terrible things, but that the original builder/owner of this Heiau did not. Dr. M. said it was possible, but he had no reason to think so.

It conflicted so strongly with what I felt, that I decided to spend some time researching the first king; read what ever I could find about him, and see if there could be even any possibility that he could be "in the clear." I am not saying human sacrifices were not done there, but that they came later (this is the Heiau that had the warning signs not to enter, and I did not - perhaps I would have gotten a different idea if I had). But, I did have that lingering question in my mind about the military connection.

Throughout my research a recurring theme stood out, all records showed that I was definitely stuck on a particular time line – 1100 A.D!

I did some book-learning and museum research the day before I left the island. The book quoted below is said by the author to be "a collection of place-names and of the stories connected to them from storytellers past and present, from dusty files in libraries and archives, and from out-of-print books." So, we can take these stories as possibilities to shed more light on the information received, including what I called "the first king" and his priest. Let's start with his father-in-law.

"Punanuikaia'aina, leader of the settlers from the Marquesas, placed a *kapu* on the land on either side of the river from the sea to the top of the range which divides the shore from the uplands. This area was named Wailua-nui-a-ho'ano, "great sacred Wailua." It quickly became the seat of the royal family and center of

162

all religious life. Punanuikaia'aina's grandson Puna-'ai-koa-'i'i became the most famous chief of his time throughout all the Hawaiian group. His court was known for the chivalry of his chiefs and the splendor of his feasts, which included displays of dancing. He enforced his *kapu* but was known to be merciful with those who had thoughtlessly or ignorantly broken his laws. He held the ali'i to strict standards, which made him popular with the commoners. Since there was no warfare during his reign, he gathered all the potential warriors around him and kept them busy in sham fights and athletic games." – *Kauai Ancient Place-Names and Their Stories* by Frederick B. Wichman, 1998.

The story goes on to say that he had only one daughter, a beautiful woman who had rejected every male on the island. So the king announced a contest, the winner receiving his daughter's hand in marriage. A man named Mo'ikeha, of impeccable genealogy, born on O'ahu, won her hand. (Yes! That was the tie in! Instead of having the tougher name to sound out of the future king, I had been given the simpler name of the *island* where the man was born!)

"To celebrate his marriage, and to consecrate the place where his children would be born, Mo'ikeha ordered the building of a Heiau, nestled at the foot of a hill...he named it after his priest, Holoholo-ku...it is the oldest known place of worship on Kaua'i..." -*ibid*

So *that* was the name of the priest! How interesting! Sources say that this same king is the one who soon built the Poli-'ahu Heiau on top of the mountain, one of the largest on the island.

I feel there is reason to doubt that he started the human sacrifices that happened there. His peaceful father-in-law, mentioned earlier, was "the most important chief of his time" and "popular with the commoners." That was bound to have had a very large influence on him, the son-in-law. His wife, the daughter of the great chief, could possibly have a peaceful influence on him also. Their daughter, Ka-ili-lau-o-ke-koa, (the histories mention only two surviving children of theirs) later went on to become the first female ruler of Kauai.

More on the Poli-'ahu Heiau: it had an oracle tower, a four-sided structure of wood with three floors, and it was the sacred place where the ruling chief *(ali'i nui)* and the head priest *(kahuna nui)* sat waiting for the advice of the gods. The priest sat on the top floor, the chief directly under him. This agreed with the "holy" feeling connected with the king here.

There are those people who are going to say, "we probably will never know." Well, that depends on who your Source is, and also your own ability to accurately interpret what you are given. Yes, the sensitive information received through the gifts can be difficult for our imperfect minds to "get" at times. It may not be completely what we are looking for, or may not include all the details we would like. But one thing we *do* know for sure – the information we are given, that helps in the direct fulfillment of our responsibilities to help others, will be accurate enough, and detailed enough, to get the job done. *He often lets us explore beyond the basics,* which shows us his qualities of generosity, patience and adventure! Aren't we blessed to be "made in his image!" He made us with an adventurous spirit, just as he has!

***

Albuquerque, New Mexico

I have found that to be truly open to Spirit, I must be ready to accept changes in plans at any time. Accepting a gift from God and working with him means to always put him first, and have faith in knowing that whatever happens, happens for a reason. So it was, as my daughter and I moved across the country, from Tennessee to California.

We had decided to make it the dream vacation – we were both starting new lives, and knew and that we might never have this opportunity to travel together again. So, in the months and weeks before the journey, I laboriously researched and highlighted the best routes to take, trying to squeeze in every State and National Park and scenic route I could find. I didn't really expect the gifts to be used much until I reached my final destination. I was wrong! Everyday is a glorious opportunity after we have told our God, "Here I am, send me!" Many adventures occurred during the trip; let me tell you just one.

DEJAVU' God-Spot: Remembering the Unknown. *We are all connected in the web of life and creation. We are made from the dust of the ground, and our blood is close to the composition of seawater. We are also 70% water, as is the balance of the earth with the sea. We are made of the same elements that surround us. We all have the same Master Builder, and we share most of the same DNA strands. So why shouldn't we feel connected to the things around us, sometimes in a most unusual way? If you find yourself in a "familiar" situation, just pay attention to the information as it is received and make a note of it. There is a reason for everything, and it might become clearer later on. God himself made the space-time continuum. Do not be afraid of it or read too much into it; just accept what is going on. Let me say this again, make a note of it – or use a notebook - just be sure to write it down. If you are in a place where you can touch the items around you, perhaps you will find more information waiting there. Often, looking back on these experiences is where you will see the real meaning for their occurrences. Since this God-Spot comes at random, it is often a tool that God uses to reach us with information we need. As far as I know, it cannot be induced to occur, but we should make the most of it when it does happen.*

Looking back on my June journal entry, I see that I wrote: "I feel like I'm heading toward something, I don't know what, or who, it is. Here we are in Amarillo,

164

Texas and there are so many things to see and do. But I feel anxious and want to hurry on – what could be waiting?" I was being compelled onward, and in a hurry! What would I find?

Here's another: "Traveling I40 west, have put on 200 miles so far today. Had a strange dizziness overtake me, which has stayed with me through the second day now, and the anxiousness has increased. Am taking a break now, but have decided to drive on through, and finally see what this is all about. Am trying to be very open to any inclination to turn right or left, or to stop at any time."

I had always been "B-NDE" (Before Near-Death-Experience) the kind of person who likes to know the destination before setting my foot upon the path. That isn't how it works anymore! When you go in faith and let him guide your way, you don't even know where the path is - he places you upon the wings of angels! It is then that you find true freedom. Indeed, who needs a path when your focus is on the Guide?

"You have made known to me the path of life; you will fill me with joy in your presence, with eternal pleasures at your right hand." (Ps. 16:11)

Petroglyphs and Mountains

It was raining and dark when we drove down into Albuquerque, New Mexico. As we topped the pass we had a bird's eye view of the lightning flashes all across the valley. My daughter's voice trembled a question, "Mom, are you sure about going down there? This is worse then Tennessee!" She was always afraid for me around lightning now, although I kept assuring her that mine had been a "Divine strike." I had never been in New Mexico before, and there were petroglyphs to see if I could convince myself to stop. We drove down and parked the motor home at a parking lot for the night, and ran through the storm to a fast food place to eat.

All of a sudden, as I was sitting there, wiping my mouth from the last of my taco and looking out into the dark, *it hit me*. I knew this place! I knew all the mountains around us! I knew this valley! Dejavu' God-Spot!

"Sierra, get me a pen! I know this place!" I said. She got me a pen and I turned over the paper placemat on which the meal came.

I knew these mountains. Hurriedly I started drawing the mountain range surrounding us. I seemed to know every nuance of every angle and dip, every sharp climb and deep ascent. On the north side of one of the mountains I put a cave and a small lake, and a steep rock face. I circled it and marked it with the words *"sacred area."*

165

I knew this valley. There used to be great migrations of big black and white birds that came through each fall. They were a mainstay of food, besides the herds of large deer (elk?) that moved through the valley. There were two rivers that came together, then a smaller one came in later; and the river turned into a bean-shaped large lake at the south end of the valley, where the boundary for "my" territory was the red hill on the left and the hill-with-the-face on the right. What did this all mean? Why was I being shown this? Why did I keep seeing a drawing of a hand with a design drawn on its palm?

This was where I was supposed to be. Smack-dab in the middle of a mystery!

The next morning I grabbed the placemat off the motor home table and pulled aside the curtains to meet the new day. I couldn't believe my eyes. I pulled on my shoes and jumped outside, slowly turning around and around, my fingers running over the angles of the mountain range that encircled around us.

…The drawing was an exact match!

This was *definitely* where I was supposed to be! Next on my list, I wanted to find out what the drawing of the hand, and the symbol in it, meant. I had guessed it might be a petroglyph, so we headed across the valley to Petroglyphs National Park, driving over two main rivers (the ones I had drawn), as we went.

There is an information center in the middle of the park, and it is basically a self-guided tour to find the petroglyphs in the area. There are thousands of them here, scrawled everywhere, the symbols in good contrast to the black surface of the rocks. I would never find "my symbol" unless I asked. I showed the hand-image to the man at the desk. He didn't recognize it, and suggested I see "Diane" about it, an expert in these things who just happens to be on the next road over. I thanked him and left, thinking to myself, "this could take some time, I want to know *now*…(patience, a virtue I am *still* working on)!"

I met Diane and asked her about the history of the valley: did she have any old photos, what about aerial shots, was there a lake south of town? I asked about the migrations and what kind of animals and birds came here. I asked her about the petroglyph and showed her the drawing. I told her about the mountain range and the sacred place on the mountain. She seemed quite supportive of my quest and was very helpful in answering many of the questions.

Yes, she said, this valley is on a main migratory route for birds, she wondered if perhaps what I was seeing were the Canadian geese with their black and white markings. I answered that I didn't think so. These seemed smaller, like ducks, and their wings had the contrasting colors, not just their necks. She didn't know if the elk/large deer came this far north, but there were herds far to the south of here.

One thing that Diane was able to confirm was the lake I saw in my vision. Except one thing - it dried up hundreds of years ago! She said that when the Spanish came in 1692 there used to be a lake. They named the lake "Isleta" because there was a small island in the middle of it. Now it was the name of the Indian reservation there.

Diane wasn't able to confirm about the sacred place on the mountain, nor the petroglyph. She said the Indians rarely talk to each other (different tribes) and "a person has to be a member, and high up in the tribe to have access to certain information." So, she gave me another person to go to, "Mr. A." at the Pueblo Indian Cultural Center. She felt sure he would be able to help me. He had written many books on the Pueblo people, besides winning the New Mexico Endowment of the Humanities Lifetime Achievement Award and being the director for the Pueblo Archives and Institute.

I thanked her and drove down to where the lake used to be, the Islet and Los Lunas area, across the Rio Grande. The paved roads gave way to dirt ones, the stucco houses to adobes. Everywhere there were nooks and crannies filled with the old ways, and the old life. It seemed an entirely different *country* lay just outside Albuquerque. How I would love to explore this area. But being a tourist, and a white female one at that, I found myself hesitant. I headed back to Albuquerque to talk to Mr. A.

Unexpected Surprise

Mr. A. leaned back in his chair and kept an easy smile on me. I am sensing he feels; "Oh, not another one - I've seen this all before - some tourist comes to New Mexico looking for a spiritual awakening, and winds up in my office." He would be joking and carefree. He would be friendly, let them have their say, than send them on their way.

Today would prove to be different.

I looked at his walls. There was a letter from the governor of the state of New Mexico, giving Mr. A. authority as spokesman for all Pueblo peoples. I saw that he was also an elder and high chief for his tribe and on the council. If anyone could help solve the mystery, I thought, it would surely be him.

I went through my story. I told about the rivers and the lake, the migrations, the mysterious petroglyph, the accurate drawing of the mountain range in the dark...and the sacred area on the north of the mountain, where there is a steep rock face and a cave and a small lake.

167

Mr. A's jaw dropped and he frowned. "What, how do you know about this? Only Indians know about this place!" he questioned in amazement. Now, he was ready to *listen* to my story, not just *hear* it. I grinned widely!

I went back over the information, in more detail this time, especially when I got to the sacred place on the mountain. I told him about the high place above the north face, where the lake was, and the size and shape of the cave entrance door.

"Yes," Mr. A. said, "The north face is a sacred place, and the high place above it is where all pueblos gather for talks. But the rock face is special to the Islet people. The cave is from where all peoples are said to originate." He shook his head in disbelief, looking at me straight in the eyes. He wasn't in a joking mood anymore.

I went on with my story, about how I had been struck by lightning, had come before The Presence, and the gift of healing. He asked some questions about the lightning strike, and said he knew several who had become healers after being struck. He said he knew a healer at his church and, "perhaps in four days I will have some information for you."

He tapped at his knees. He said, "the top of my legs are not strong enough sometimes to get me out of my chair." He accepted my offer of a healing treatment, and we did it there in his office as he sat in his chair. He did not state how he felt afterward, although I knew by the warmth of my hands that the Holy Spirit connection had been good. God had a purpose in mind. Was it fulfilled now, had my purpose been to give a healing to Mr. A? I wondered if this was the end of the journey.

He asked us where we were staying, wished my daughter and I well, and left us with a free tour of the Indian Cultural Museum. I thought that was that. After all, I had confirmation on the sacred site, the rivers, the lake, and the great flocks of migratory birds. Mr. A. thought the elk were too far north and south of us, he didn't see them as ever coming here.

I cringed at the thought of staying in a parking lot for four days. But, I did have one piece that didn't fit anywhere (the petroglyph), and he did say he might have information (what kind, I didn't know) for me. We would just stay put and see what comes of it. After all, we had time, and what if God had something else planned for me to do here? I prayed to God that if he wanted me to stay he would give me a sign or a "heads-up." The phone rang.

It had been only three hours. "Maria," a healer from Isleta, had received my number from Mr. A. She asked, "would you and your daughter come to my pueblo tomorrow and meet me at my home?" "Yes!" I said. The adventure was still on! And my "heads-up" prayer had just been answered, and the training about continued patience was tested as well.

Adobe Walls, Open Hearts

I followed the directions and (what a coincidence?) ended up going the *same* way, crossing the *same* rail-road tracks and entering the *same* side road, that I had traveled in my meanderings the day before. Only this time we had an open invitation to stop and visit. Wow!

All the roads here are narrow and made of compacted dirt and dust. I parked in front of a well-kept yard fenced with a low adobe wall. A large domed "horno" was in the corner, waiting to be used for cooking fresh bread. All the dirt was swept clean and there were only a few plants around. A tall, slender woman in her 60's, with her gray/black hair up in a bun, came to meet us.

"You better put this sign in your window or you *will* get in trouble," she says, handing me a sheet of paper with 'Maria' written on it. "Stick it in your window." I do, and introduce myself.

This was Maria; Medicine Woman, responsible Catholic and respected member of the Isleta Pueblo people. She sat on the church council and the tribal council for Isleta pueblo. She had organized purchasing and bringing a statue of Blessed Kateri Tekakwitha (the first Indian woman to convert to Christianity) through the village and into a permanent place in the church. And yet, she was a guardian of the old ways. Also, when she didn't agree with something, she let people know it. In her younger days she had danced at the Pow-Wows *and* marched for women's rights. She had remained single all her life.

Her family-built adobe home is over 200 years old. When you enter, the first thing that you notice is that the walls are nearly two feet thick. Inside, the decor is a mixture of simple basics and spiritual ancestry. There are baskets, pottery and old family pictures on high hand-made shelves. There are finely woven colorful rugs hanging on the walls and draped over the couch. There are paintings on animal hides, pictures of the Pope, Jesus Christ, and a photograph of her being hugged by Mother Theresa. There were the Kuchinas, her father's ancient sacred tobacco, crucifixes and beadwork. There were things just *everywhere!* Many museums would have swooned to have even *some* of her collection!

My hands were hot the entire time I was in her home - proof that the wonderfully familiar God-Connection was there. This was a sacred place; not only filled with the energy tracings of many of her blessed healings, but also the energy of all the things that had occurred through the great number of years in this very old home.

Maria and I talked and talked, both of us telling healing stories and she telling stories of the ways of long ago. I could write pages and pages of her stories and experiences, but will leave that up to her. Gradually, she is putting it all down, before it disappears forever. She wags her head and states that very few of the new generation want to learn the old ways.

Maria asked for a healing for her leg. I said a prayer out loud and started the laying on of hands on her head; and in silent prayer continued to different places on her body, focusing a period of time on her knee. She was very quiet during the treatment.

Afterward, she said she would like to give me a "blessing." She calls a healing a blessing; I felt it was aptly named. As she began, she uncurled the hair from her bun, and it flung beautifully and wildly about her shoulders and face. With anointing oil she touched my forehead, chin, both shoulders and hands. She smudged me with incense, blowing on my face, shoulders, hands and feet. Then she held two eagle feathers, one in each hand, and danced around my chair. Every now and then she would slap the feathers together to get the "bad" off, whisking my head, shoulders, chest, back and legs.

She quietly chanted in her native tongue and put her thumbs in my eyes, rubbed to the side of my mouth, and stretched, rubbed, and shook my entire body – head, hands, and chest. Then, out loud she did a blessing of sacred words and said, "I pulled something out of your belly – I felt a 'pop.'" Then she went and spit up in the bathroom and recoiled her hair upon her head. She says she spits up at all her healings – and that she needs to bring it up to let it out and go back to mother earth.

There is so much showmanship in her healings! Mine seem so simple in comparison. I could see how the pageantry of the Catholic Church could be so easily accepted by the native peoples. Also, I don't normally call God the "Great Spirit," although he certainly is the Greatest Spirit of all.

I had to think a bit. How did I feel? Did I feel violated or that this was wrong in some way? No, I didn't. I knew the God she was calling on, that she honored Jesus, and the power of the Holy Spirit felt familiar to me. I came to the conclusion that looking at the methodology was an *interesting* part, but not the *important* part. *The underlying Great Healer was the same.* And, the "good fruits of the tree" were plentiful, as she busily took care of house calls to ailing clients among the Pueblo people.

Actually, it seemed no more different to me than various denominations of Christian churches incorporating different customs in their worship. Some may use very formal customs, some relaxed. Some have elaborate stages, full bands, and large sound systems for the worship presentation. Some churches have one piano player, simply accompanying the happy voices praising God. But, the underlying reasons for coming together are the same.

Across the table, Maria said abruptly, "I saw that petroglyph of yours on the North face. I even have a photograph of it around here somewhere, if I can find it. It is on a big rock next to the cave."

I sat there dumbfounded. "Can I go see it?" I asked.

"No, you can't do that. The whole area is protected, you can't even drive up to the mountain at the bottom of it…"

She went on to confirm the lake and more of the area. She and Mr. A. must have had a good conversation.

I took her out to dinner and we talked about distant healing, charging for treatments, and so forth. Even though our methods were different, our conversation flowed smoothly. It was now late in the evening, and she wanted a healing for her brother, too. She tried to call him but he was gone. Would we come back tomorrow and see the sacred tree and meet some other people? I eagerly agreed. Here I was, a white female tourist being welcomed into a very tightly woven, rarely experienced view of *real* Native America. Only by the grace of God!

Healing Under the Shroud of Turin

The next day found us looking at a tree that seemed to actually have a face in the bark – and there were also several numbers which could be distinctly seen. The face looked to me like the face of Jesus – it seemed similar to pictures I had seen of the Shroud of Turin. To Maria, it looked like Blessed Kateri. Although many plantings had been done under this tree, nothing would grow. It grew in the front yard of the daughter of one of the tribal elders who was also a medicine man.

The daughter wanted a healing, so I asked if we could do it here, under the tree. I took off my shoes and stood barefoot on the soil. At this point, I felt my feet tingling. I also felt the healing power of the Holy Spirit ascend strongly. At the end of the treatment, the daughter started crying, stood up and said, "I don't do this, I never cry!" And I held her, and she just wept and wept, being touched and released by the Spirit. I encouraged her with words of comfort, and so did Maria. I looked across at Maria and smiled. *This* is why I was here, to help heal the pain; in more ways than one, I was to find out.

From there we went to "Alice's" family and did a treatment for her, her mother, her mother's brother, and her father, who is next in line to be the lead elder/holy man. When I had first entered, he gave me a blessing for coming into his house. I thanked him and he shook my hand. I held onto it, and asked if he wanted me to make the arthritis in his hands and his back feel better. His eyes widened, and he grew quiet. I did the treatment, while all the rest of the family gathered around us in the living room. At one time during the treatment I felt an electrical surge go down my arm to my hand, which was then over his heart. I felt a release under my fingers, and knew his once-constricted arteries were now fine. God the Cardiac-Care-Physician!

Later that day I facilitated a healing for Maria's brother "Joshua," who had bad arthritis in his back. My experience with the Holy Spirit had been that bones often take a longer time to respond than other things, even longer than cancers or tumors, on the average. But, this is God's work, and he can go "zap" and fix it in one swoop, if that is the best plan. That "zap" didn't happen this time, and I remember wishing I could do more than one treatment on Joshua, as he was in such pain. The medical services available for the Pueblo people are terribly lacking - and the clinic is often out of even the most basic of medicines.

So much wounding has taken place in these people's lives for so long. There is an underlying and unspoken resentment toward the white people, who forced them off their lands; forced their children to stop speaking their Native language, and forced them into new ways of worship. Now, there is an uneasy mixture of Catholic and native ways often seen side-by-side. "Yes," Maria said, "We are Catholics. But we are Indian too."

I knew one of the reasons I was brought here, and given the Dejavu' information. It was to Supernaturally touch all these people as I was filtered through the proper channels. I was accepted because of his Divine Information - God had given me the "password of knowledge" to work in Isleta. All the different pieces of the mysterious puzzle were clues to where I would be led next. Each person being sent to decipher one, yet having to send me on for deciphering another. How incredibly ingenious! God wanted the Native Americans to see that we are *all* his children. Let the White Tourist Woman and the Native Medicine Woman work together. Again, he is making it clearly seen; *he* is not as prejudiced as most people are! Brown or white, male or female, different ways can still be *his* ways, and he truly *is* the Greatest Spirit of all. This was yet another way to *bring people to faith, and in working with one another.*

At the end of the day, my daughter and I came home with turquoise and red coral necklaces, a silver bracelet, a small amount of money, steak from a newly-butchered cow, and *a lot* of delicious fry bread! The next day we would be heading out. Maria had a schedule to keep and I thought we had fulfilled what we had come to do, as the news about the healings had jumped all over the Pueblo.

172

Maria and I hugged and said our good-byes, hoping to see each other again soon.

Back in the motor home, Sierra leaned over to me and said, "We got more than money today – we got family." What a deep comment from a teenager. She was absolutely right! We both felt so Blessed. Slowly we drove away from town, back on the "real" road of pavement and modern street signs.

Then it happened. Bang! Bang! Screech! Clink, clink clink...oh no! We were less than two miles away when something became seriously wrong with our vehicle. I crept back to a station we had just passed. The report came back much worse than we had expected. The differential was bad, and the axle was cracked. It would take approximately five to seven days to order and replace. We could not go anywhere. We could not stay in it at night either, for insurance reasons, since it would be inside their shop enclosure. Here we were, in the middle of our 4,100 mile journey. What would we have done if this had happened anywhere but here? What would we have done if we didn't know anybody to help us? But, because of God's big plan, we had friends, we had a new family, and evidently, we still had *a lot more work to do!*

The Medicine Bear

Maria was gracious and let us stay at her home. We ended up going to a wedding that afternoon, and I was given the honor of saying the blessing over the food. Yes, we were definitely not strangers anymore! The next day I helped Maria with a "Fry Bread" bake sale in front of the church – the ladies were raising money to attend a religious convention in San Diego, the same place I would soon be moving. In front of the "Blessed Fatima" shrine we rolled the dough out flat, into huge circles about 12-15 inches across, and threw them into the hot oil pot until puffed and golden brown. We had a line of people. Well, let me tell you, these ladies were quick with this, and they soon figured out that I wasn't!

What I ended up doing instead created a line also, healing in the shrine of the "Blessed Fatima," where there was shade, a few chairs and a reverence for prayer. I also did healings in the rectory. God did wondrous works that day! I was glad to be a part of it as stomach cancer, bad knees, bad backs, heart problems, headaches and a malady of other problems disappeared through my hands under the direction of the Holy Spirit! I heard a voice in the crowd say, "I hope she doesn't get too tired, I want my turn!" Another said, "Her hands are like hot irons!" I had never helped so many people at one time, but the energy is not mine, it is his, I am just "along for the ride!" Wow! What a ride!

That night I did another treatment on Joshua, the brother I had wished I could work on again (God had already a plan for that), and his wife, and another friend of Maria's. When it was time for bed, Sierra and I lay on Maria's couches, surrounded by all the beautiful things in her museum house, and thought over the blessings of the day. My heart felt that it would just explode with gladness! I fell asleep praising the God of all Love and Blessings…

In the middle of the night I awoke to a sound of "clack, clack" and felt a hand gently wiping my forehead. I looked up expecting to see Maria or Sierra, but no one was there. I smiled and was not afraid, knowing that only good would be allowed to come to me, that I am protected in Unconditional Love, so this must surely have been a good thing. I blessed God again and fell soundly asleep until morning.

The next day I recounted the experience of the night, and found out I had probably been visited by the loving spirit of Maria's mother, and that the sound of the cane she had once needed was her calling card to let us know it was her indeed. It seemed that her actions toward me were her way of showing that I was welcome in her home, and that she was happy for what I was doing! Again I felt blessed by the spirit connection that he sometimes allows for us.

I was facilitated for many other healings throughout the next few days. Often people would come to the house and I would work on them there. More of these are recounted in the chapter about Healing. Especially interesting was "David," (the Pueblo "War Chief" in charge of spiritually protecting the people), the brother of Joshua. Besides having a wonderful healing, we talked about my mission, his mission, our visions, good and evil spirits (how to recognize and fight them), and many other deep spiritual matters. It was wonderful and we were both surprised at the similarities in how we worshipped our Loving God.

On the day we left, we received more blessings, gifts and baked goods. Especially memorable was a small brown bear made of pottery from Joshua (a sign that I also was considered a "medicine woman"), and a white deer-skin beaded bag (to carry sacred objects) from Maria. We were also offered a brand-new room in the War Chief's home (it even included a rare air-conditioning unit) to live in, free of charge! "Please, won't you stay?" They asked. We felt so honored! But, we had to refuse and move on.

These people have such commitment to wanting the best for each other, and for the highest good; including family, the Great Spirit, and the Catholic Saints. Theirs is a combination of tradition and progress, with all the struggles that includes. It was a privilege to be able to see the Pueblo people as fellow travelers, each of us on our own unique spirit journey, yet the One God showering healing and blessings over us all. *We are all his kids! Love each other!*

CHAPTER 9

Love Never Dies –
Sometimes God Allows Communication
FBI on Sept.11th; Abducted Child; Parents Who Have Crossed

Since being struck by lightning, I have been opened up to the will of God, like a child opens a book. I do not know what page will be turned to next, and how I will be used. Sometimes it is hard to interpret the writing on the pages I see. But I let the Spirit of the Most High move freely in my life, knowing that everything that happens will be best for everyone concerned.

Sometimes I end up experiencing things that I did not know existed, or things that I did not know a Christian would be authorized to be part of. Yet, when I yield and the Holy Spirit establishes his work, then often I am allowed to see, *after the fact,* why he does what he does.

Such is the case of passing information from the spirits of those who have died, to the living. And such is the case of helping those who have died, to decide to go on to the Heavenly Presence.

We know from the scriptures that God had strictly forbidden the Israelites to have anything to do with divination, mediums or anyone who consulted the dead. (De. 18:9-14) Occult practices were carried on in the name of pagan gods, and people turned to them for answers, and the foretelling of events that God would not give. And once, in Endor, a woman was used by Saul to try to reach Samuel, a beloved dead prophet of God.

But in this instance, *God* used the opportunity to manifest the spirit of Samuel by *his power*, not by trickery or Satan's doings, to make a *prediction* regarding Saul's fate. (1 Sam. 28:7-21) So, here again we see God stepping in and turning something around from bad to good, to suit his higher purpose. Usually, the woman was overstepping the bounds of what God permitted. But this time, *he used her as a tool* to teach Saul.

Over and over again in the scriptures we find *we can't put God in a box;* he will break out every time. I have found this to be the case in several the situations where I've been facilitated by the Holy Spirit for unusual work.

Please note that I do not go looking for these situations - these are cases where I have been *contacted first* by His Holy Spirit, given an assignment, and then seen the will of God being fulfilled. Maybe that is the difference. I understand the hesitation and questions that may arise as you read this chapter. All I can say is, this is empirical knowledge - first hand experience. I probably wouldn't have believed it myself if I hadn't been the one experiencing it! I know nothing. I am only in a servant position with the Lord, and *I know* who He is.

There are those who may hold to theology or even point to quantum physics and time/space in referencing how this all works. Again, I know nothing. I am just presenting my experiences, as an encouragement for you *to have faith in following the One True God wherever he may take you.* To be used as a vessel available for his Divine purposes, we must know and trust that he has used unusual circumstances in the past to bring people to faith. He requests following without hesitation wherever he leads, and *without fear of what mankind might say.*

You may agree to disagree. That is totally up to you. I do know that if there is a gift or a way of being used by the Holy Spirit with which you may not feel comfortable, he will not pressure you to do it. Such is the power of Free Will. Such is how I feel about speaking in tongues, and he has not given me any responsibilities for it. That is my choice, and he continues to use me, but for other things. All the same, *I do not judge* those who speak in tongues – *I pray all gifts to be manifest for the glory of God!*

Having said all theses things, I pray for more workers to go into the field. There is much work that needs to be done, and so few who yield fully as his tool. It is all about bringing people to faith. *However he wants to do it!*

Inside Information for FBI about 9-11

I did not feel the tragedy before it came. I was completely surprised, and in shock when I heard the news and saw the footage of the planes flying into the twin towers on September 11th 2001. I spent the rest of the day organizing a worldwide prayer circle of my friends, situated for 7 P.M. California time. We estimate that there were about 400 of us; including groups in Sweden, India and Little Tibet. We had participants from the Isleta reservation in New Mexico; folk in Louisiana and Tennessee; a group of Carmelite nuns in Northern California; and various healers scattered to the four winds of the earth!

There is a bluff overlooking the ocean here. It is part of the city park system. It is one of my favorite places to go and listen for the whispers of God, and to feel the ocean waves softly caress my heart and mind. One can watch the surfers and beach-explorers from here, and see the children run excitedly to and fro in the salty froth. Many marriage vows are exchanged in this small park, and a memorial is dedicated to the accomplishments and life of John Denver. He was a lover of the earth and the sea; an accomplished singer and poet; and one whom I had the privilege of calling a friend. There is also a stone picnic table where I have often sat to read and meditate.

At 7 P.M. a few selected friends and I started our candlelight vigil and prayers. I did a Purification and Sanctification Ceremony, donning my priestly robes, stole and symbols, and lay down on top of the table, with my daughter at my head, and one of my best friends at my feet. I closed my eyes and asked the Lord to use me in any way he saw fit. Praying, I then reached out my mind...and disappeared. From above I saw my body on the table and my companions all around me. I knew my body would be safe. I saw the twilight of dusk glowing orange over the sea. Then I felt my consciousness go straight up into the sky; so high that I could not even see where the ocean met the shore. I was out of my body, but I was not afraid.

Since the lightning strike and near-death experience, I have found it fairly simple to "slip out" of my fleshly shell. It is almost like "the key has been left in the lock." I have been able to have many interesting experiences, and have learned many things. When you see as a spirit does, you do not just use the eyes in the front of your head, *but are able to see all around you at the same time;* just like what happened when I was in spirit form before the Presence of Jesus. It can be a dizzying experience. There is no perception of right and left, and although up and down is a little easier to grasp, it also takes some getting used to. I can see why spirits and ghosts are often seen to be "floating" or moving softly this way and that. Control is better over time and with practice. It is in this state of being that I was called out by God on 9-11.

From my consciousness in the sky, I saw rapid movement of clouds and light around me, although it was dark, and a blur of speed, and then felt a feather lightness of descending toward the ground. I had traveled a great distance in a very short period of time.

In front of me, hanging in the air at varying heights, were translucent white objects, thousands of them glowing, each one being six to seven feet high and about three feet wide. As I got closer, I saw definition in the midst of the radiant glowing. I saw faces. These objects were scores of ghostly white spirits – they were hanging in mid-sky above a destruction of debris. I had been brought to the twin towers, in New York City.

I saw immensely bright angels of God placed here and there; they seemed to be in deep conversation with the glowing spirits. They were very tall, up to 9 feet I would guess. There were other spirits with the angels, they were a bluish-white color. Since I have been present at death before, I guessed that they were family members there to help ease the fear of the ones making the transition. There was no hurry. Every now and then I would see an angel going upward, the new spirit in tow, with the bluish-white spirits behind, pulling up the rear in a semi-circle. There was a subtle white "funnel" over the top of this area, which I guessed would help transport them where they needed to go (is this the "tunnel" that so many people experience in their deaths?). It was lovely! But, there was so much work to be done, so many glowing spirits. And I knew this had to have been going on all day.

In out-of-body, there is not much difference between seeing good detail during the day or the night (almost like wearing night-vision glasses). There was a yellowish-orange tinge everywhere, with mild differences of light and shadow, but it was still easy to see everywhere. What was my purpose here? Only to observe? How would that help anyone? But, I would do what ever the Lord asked of me. To the side of me there floated an angel; there were two other bright spirits gathered near him; *he motioned me to come over!* In an instant I was there. A woman in a spirit body introduced herself to me as (sounds like) "Asa'rita." I had the feeling that she was a traveler who had been sent for, just like me. She glowed differently than the others. I remember wishing I had a mirror, what did I look like?

The next thing I knew, *I was in one of the planes!* I was beside a child of 4 or 5 years of age – her mother was on the other side, and didn't seem to know I was there. We could see the tower in front of us; the plane was heading straight into it. I felt terror in my heart – so much fear, and confusion! I was re-living and *relieving* the last few moments of this child's life! I was sharing her emotion; *it was if she and I were the same.* Her emotions clinging to me, our minds as one. *Her knowing she was not alone.* The fear escalated within us – I looked past the girl and saw her mother, round eyes in silent shock facing forward. I see other passengers, shrieking and screaming and climbing over the seats, falling over each other. I see the terrorists; two men with dark skin, one way up by the open cockpit door, the other to the left in front of the passengers. They are shouting loudly in a foreign tongue over the screams. It seemed by the faces and the shouts of the one beside the cockpit door, that he was shouting with joy. The other one was screaming in fear. I felt my stomach turn over.

We hit. I feel the release of letting go…*there is no pain!* The worst part is the fear beforehand. I have died with the girl. *There is no pain from death!* Now she has relived it, and I am standing there in front of her, her glow just one of the thousands around me. Evidently, this "re-living" had been going on all day. It was time for the cycle of fear to stop. It was time to go Home.

I look in her beautiful eyes, face to face. I tell her it is OK, and not to be afraid. I tell her that she is *Loved by God*, and that *her other family is waiting for her.* I think all these things in my mind, and know that she can hear me. I remember my own experience of going before the Presence - the feeling of all-encompassing love. *I project the experience to her in my mind.* She smiles. She understands. She is going home. *I feel the pang of wanting to go home too.* I look above and see the relatives - five or six bright faces, some with their arms open toward her. She turns back to me and I hear her question in my head, "where's mom?"

I am back in the airplane. I am sitting where the girl used to be, alongside the mother in shock. I see the passengers, I look around and notice even more than I did before. I see the terrorists. I hear their words again. One is younger than the other, and is in a brother-like relationship - submissive to the other. The dominant one has a symbol on his upper right shoulder - *somehow I can see it under his jacket.*

Again I feel the growing terror. The fear mounts. It is overwhelming, we feel that we will burst from fear. We hit...*again, there is no pain.* We are floating. We have been released. The woman's glow is before me, I tell her it is O.K., and not to be afraid. She looks me in the eyes. *I recall to her my experience of heaven.* I tell her that her child is safe and is among the relatives waiting to greet her. I tell her she can go to the Light of God, now, or stay until the funeral is over. I tell her she will be allowed to visit here on earth later, if she wishes (I don't know where I got the authority to say such things. I didn't even know these things myself).

An angel comes to our group, and descends gently amongst us. The brightness is beyond "white." *Angels have such a high vibration!* It is much easier to see the details of them with my existing in a spirit form, as compared to wearing my fleshly body. In my physical body, it is hard to make out facial features of angels, everything is bleached out with brightness. There is a whirring sound, like a vibration, that corresponds with the presence of these angels. I look intently, wanting to memorize every detail, this experience is so extraordinary. For the first time, here I see that *wings* are actually *shafts of energy* radiating out from their bodies! The angel starts to ascend, with his entourage. My body feels like lead weight. I want to go too! *Let me go too!* Their group glow gets absorbed by the funnel of light. I can't see them anymore. I feel sad for myself, but happy too. It is like the feeling of a mother at the graduation of her child, knowing the young adult needs to move on without her.

Next, I help a young blonde pregnant woman (she is only 2-3 months along); a woman in her 50's; and one of the pilots, who met with a violent death before crashing into the tower. *Five people. Five deaths.* Each time I had to relive (and relieve), the last few moments of their lives, when the fear was so great (especially for the 50's woman, who had not believed in God all her life and was really fearful of death), and then the *blissful release.*

I saw the final moments so clearly that I knew where people were sitting, and felt I could even draw a diagram and sketch their faces. I especially paid attention to the details of the terrorists. *It was like a movie repeating over and over again.*

The main terrorist, who killed the pilot, also was the leader of this group. He is the one with the symbol. This man used a thin (green?) instrument to cut marks into the front wall by the cockpit; and there seemed to be foam, or a white background, seen under the cuts. At first when I saw this, I thought he was just

179

being destructive. But, when I did a sketch of the angles of the lines, I saw what was probably the lettering of a word. He was taller than the other man by about two inches, though both were slender. I heard the sounds of the names, especially since the younger one was calling so much to the older one. The younger one was frightened. He wanted to live. He had not been shouting with joy. They were wearing headbands.

I saw many empty chairs in the front of the plane. I do not know if there were more people crowded in the back. I do not remember looking behind me, only to the front and sides. I will not relate to you the cutting of the pilot, but please know that there was not any feeling of pain with his release. I do know that his essence chose to stay for his funeral. I don't remember the choices of the others. I know the mom and daughter left together with the angel. I had encouraged the mother to go, now. I wanted the Unconditional Love of the Father to envelope the little girl as soon as possible.

I do not know what happened to the 50's woman. The last time I saw her, she had an angel in serious conversation with her, then I felt a draw (like a magnetic pull) and "pop!" I was back in my body. No feeling of travel this time, just "pop!" I remember lying on the cold picnic table, looking up at the stars. I saw I had been escorted back; just at the top of my vision I saw the familiar glow of an angel spirit, now ascending out of sight. I felt such a peacefulness as a child of God! I praised him for using me in such a special way. The clock said I had been gone about 40 minutes.

It was related to me that my body had tensed up and spasmed *five times* while I was gone. Then it would relax completely. My friends had become fearful and placed their hands on my head and feet. They had also felt and seen a definite jolt when I "popped" back in. Under the pin-lights of the stars, in the cool sea breezes blowing up the bluff, I related to them my experiences. We all cried. We prayed. And we praised The Great Comforter.

"Let Us Know…We Keep a File"

Two days later I jotted down the phone number that had been advertised on TV for contacting the FBI with any information on the terrorists. I had hoped for a fax machine number, since I had also made sketches of the tattoo, the slashes/word on the wall, and the face of the main terrorist. These could not be explained, but had to be shown. I called the number and asked the man I was talking to if they had a fax machine. He said "No. We don't have one." He asked what I had, and how I got it. After skirting around about "how I got it," I went on to tell him what I had. Half way through he stopped me and said: "Here's our fax number." I asked him, "Whom do I direct it to?" He said "No one; I am going to go stand by it and wait." I smiled to myself. *Evidently God had given me some information that they already knew* - enough that this fellow knew that this was not rubbish, and to question if it might contain other accurate information too. Maybe something there helped on the investigation. At this early time the press had released very little to the public. The FBI was keeping information close to them, guarding things well.

He continued, "Let us know whenever you work with the police departments...we keep a small file on hand. There is a small group we run things by at times. The FBI is not closed to unusual methods of retrieval (of information). There is also some money involved." I swallowed hard. I couldn't believe this guy was being so open with me. Here was proof that the FBI does use "sensitives" in their work!

Evidently I had some information that corresponded accurately with something they knew, that had not been released yet. It seemed he was convinced that I could "qualify" for this group at some time. In my mind's eye, I imagined myself being a "007 for God," being flown under cover of darkness to meet with other "sensitives and prayer warriors" to "help the world." I quickly told the fellow that this was all of *God's doings,* nothing special about me. The "real 007" had saved the world 2,000 years ago!

As the days went on, I watched the news more and more. Terrorist names and faces appeared, including the two I knew. They announced headbands - red ones, and other points of validation through time.

I wondered if I should try to contact any of the families, and decided it might be too strange for them. They didn't know me from Adam (or Eve), why would they trust me to have important details about the last moments of their loved ones lives?

Shortly after this, a movie came out called "Hearts in Atlantis." It is about a sensitive guy (Anthony Hopkins) who has escaped from working for the central intelligence agency (CIA) and just wants to have a normal life. They keep coming after him until they get him, taking him away from the ones he loved. He has become too important for them to let go. After seeing this movie together, my daughter turned to me and said: "You are not going to tell the FBI anything anymore!" I agreed - although later, with the War, I tried to give information anonymously, and they would not accept it. *The Spirit of the Lord will not be contained.* It will burst out anywhere and everywhere. From then on, if I worked with a police department, I kept it to myself. I did not let "my right hand know what my left was doing." I felt safer that way. I still do.

***

Little Girl Lost

The day after I had returned home to California from my adventure in Hawaii (see the "Archeology" chapter), I saw a poster of a lovely blonde girl with a big toothy grin. She was missing, and a reward was offered for her return. We will call her "April" (all names changed to protect the privacy of the family). I looked at the poster and remembered feeling sadness. I whispered a prayer for God to give her his mighty arm and guide her home (whichever one that may be). I asked a friend about her, and I was told she had already been missing two weeks. That is all I knew.

That night, *I was gently awakened by a little girl peering down upon my bed.* It was the same sweet girl from the poster. She smiled and was silent, levitating there not more than three feet from me. She gave me information, and I saw that she had been murdered. I saw the man who did it. I saw it all from her perspective. Had the prayer I said in her behalf connected her with me? I knew that God was allowing me to have another adventure. I let her know I would do whatever would be allowed. After a little more time with her, I then asked her to leave, and not to contact me again unless I called for her (I always ask ghosts to leave after their presentation is made). I needed time in prayer to God about it, and it gave me a needed sense of control in the situation. I cannot allow ghosts to follow me all the time, they are so focused on only their immediate needs, it can drive a person nuts!

The next day, I called the police number listed on the poster, to offer my services. I said, "I was struck by lightning several years ago, and with it God has given me a special sensitivity to find things." I never quite know what to say in these situations! They took my name and phone number, and said they would present the information and call me back. Well, throughout the next day, no one called. I hadn't really expected them to. I remember how I used to feel about all this too! That's why the Lord allows some of us to be slapped 'upside the head' (i.e. lightning strike), just to wake us up! Just plain stubborn I guess!

The next day, I drove down to the town where the "April Recovery Center" had been set up. I was going to present myself to the 'earthly powers that be' and see where the Lord leads. I did not know what else to do. Outside the building, there were TV crews set up, vans with big antennas on hydraulic towers, and lots of people. There was supposed to be a big press release at 10:00, and I had gotten there at 9:30. I gently made my way through to the door and inside to the people at the counter. I told them what I do (I said the same thing as I did on the phone), and they escorted me to the volunteer room, where I talked to two coordinators. They listened and went to talk to the head volunteer director for the center. "Pam" heard my story, and said, "we are not closed to this sort of thing" and brought me upstairs to the main room where food preparation was occurring for the searchers. I also met a woman named "Debbie," who helped coordinate the food. She offered me coffee, and Pam disappeared.

A man came into the room and said, "Did you want to see me?" I asked if he was the father, and "Todd" said "Yes." Up to now, I had not looked at anything on TV about it, although I knew there was a huge campaign nationwide about it. I was glad that I had been out of the country for two weeks; I did not want to have any preconceived ideas in my head that might alter God's guidance in this. I had come into this clean and uninfluenced. Todd then brought me into a small upstairs room with a table in it, where Pam already was, and a woman named "Susan." I asked the woman if she was the child's natural mother, and she said, "Yes." I asked if Todd was the natural father, and he said "yes." They were hopeful, of course, but openly skeptical. Could I prove myself first?

I asked if there was anything that they had from April for me to hold, and asked for a very large map. Susan said the police had closed off her room (in fact, that day they had even taken the closet doors down, to get fingerprints), and there was nothing they could get for me. Except, that April had made a gift for her, so she took it off and I held it – I then gave it back, and asked to hold her hand instead. I explained that the natural DNA would help connect me to make an energy search, to help the connection to April. I told them this would all be by prayer and the Holy Spirit, and that he is perfect in his work, but that I am not, and may make many mistakes in the interpretation of what I'm shown.

Susan said, "First, can you tell us something about our house?"

She needed some proof that the information I would be giving had a basis in fact, which is a very good thing to do if you are ever in doubt about something. I closed my eyes and opened my heart to God, knowing I could now be made a complete fool of, and thrown out on my nose, if he chose not to answer the request. It always amazes me that I have initial fear, no matter how much he has worked with me and produced miracles in the past! I overlooked my fleshly and sinful tendency to doubt, and undoing the 'block' it created in my head, I am immediately given the information. I felt a descending glow upon my head - just like I do at a healing - and I knew the Holy Spirit was working. I lift my eyes and see April smiling at me from behind her mom's shoulder.

"You have a staircase up the right hand side of your house, the room at the top of the stairs is not hers – there is a 2nd door, down a hallway, and a 3rd door – let me see – this one's a bathroom. Am I right?" I went on to describe the color scheme in her home, and also the layout of the bottom floor, kitchen and living room.

"Yes," Susan says, her mouth slightly opened, she turns to look at Todd, and she fearfully withdraws her hand from mine. Now the Lord has proven to her that he has given me insight, to help them. Then I started telling much information. I described a man with white skin, older, with short brown hair and bald on top. I saw a deformed foot. I believed it to be the man's foot, the toes seemed strange. I saw April being pulled along by the arm, in sand. I saw that she was not far from fresh water, and that the rocks are gray. I saw a motor home related to the man, it was light colored, with a brown stripe along the side, and it was an older model.

Then Susan said, "but how did he get her out of the house?"

I explained, "She came downstairs to meet him, that she was all excited - this man was someone that she knew and he said it was a surprise they were planning - that her folks would meet them later at the lake for a picnic and a party the next day."

Pam turned to Todd and quietly said, "That is why the dog didn't bark."

Susan then said, "Wait, I think I know how I can get April's shoes - would that help?"

I said "Yes...especially if they were used a lot – the older the better."

"I'll go to the house and bring them back," she said excitedly. She and Todd left, leaving me with Pam. She had a notepad, and was taking notes of everything I said. Meanwhile, my hand got very hot over a lake and a reservoir. The map was not very detailed. But, there was no "heat" anywhere else. I drew a picture. I was told the search teams had been looking by the ocean, and in the desert. This place under my hands was nowhere near either of those.

Todd came back in the room, said Susan had just called him and that she couldn't get away from the house because of the media. He was going to go to the house and get the things she found that were April's. April had a really good connection with me, and the Holy Spirit allowed the communication to be strong. Todd left.

I took a piece of paper for Pam to give to Susan when she was ready (Susan was not ready to know April was not coming home; the latest "sighting" had been only two days ago in Mexico). But, April had been trying to tell her folks that *she was still here,* and *three times she thought her mom had seen her.*

I wrote to the mother:

(1). "I have something of mommy's that I took from her room and have in the top drawer of my dresser. When she finds it, she will know that I am still here, because I am telling you about it!"

(2). "Yes, that was really me in your dreams!"

184

(3). "I thought you saw me when you were looking in the mirror in your bedroom, I ran by!"

(4). "I love you, I'm O.K., Grandpa is here taking care of me."

I wrote to the father:

(1). "I'm sorry. Please forgive me. I love you."

(2). "Take care of mommy and (some kind of nickname – "spiffy," "denny" ?) for me."

I later asked Todd about the "I'm sorry" part. He looked at me with sad eyes and said that he and April had had a big fight a couple of days before she disappeared, but that they had worked it all out.

So I gave the letters to Pam, she disappeared again, and I worked on the map. She reappeared with the items of April in a bag. A silver tennis shoe that had been worn once or twice to a costume party; a black slip-on that felt like school and lockers and giggling with girls (later, Todd said those were her school shoes); and a cowry shell that Pam had thrown in that April had given her (Pam herself had only touched it twice now). And, lo and behold! A sweater! A light blue sweater, with buttons up the front, unwashed, and here and there pieces of her hair still on it! This was the item that connected me the most, and I would end up carrying it with me all day.

Pam wanted to know exactly what had happened to April, and I told her. She said, "You can't tell Susan that!"

"I know. I won't, I really wouldn't do that." I said.

But, I hoped the letter would find itself into her hands at the correct time.

Todd came back into the room, and asked how we were doing. I showed him the drawing I had made, with the rocks and a man-made cut of ground, and how what I was feeling seemed west of a lake. He said, "Are you sure that is not salt?" And I said I was *sure* it was not salt. She was not by the ocean. I showed him on the map the area where I felt she was. There was a lake in that area, I thought he should search there.

I asked Todd if he wanted all the information. I asked him if he wanted to know if she was alive or not. He said he had just recently come to the conclusion, in the last few days, that she was not. I related to him the whole story, which was one of the hardest things I have ever had to do. We both had tears in our eyes, and at the end we hugged.

I will not relate here all the details, due to the perversion of the assault. But, please note that she had no reason to fear until near the end, and it was relatively quick. I will tell you that during the episode she passed out, and transitioned *without pain*.

April had sneaked down the stairs between 10 and 11 P.M, all excited, and went to the corner of the sidewalk where the murderer met her. Todd said that made sense, since he was awake and had heard no screams. I saw a *motor home* again, and it seemed about 28 feet long. I got a word sound in my head: *"frees"* or *"ees." I said that was the name of a road that she was on or near.* Pam asked if we could try to follow the trail they took – I said yes; I was here to help all day. So, she made the arrangements for us to go. The food was put in a big bag – sub sandwiches had been donated that day, and a variety of granola bars and brownies. Todd handed me a silver-foiled "Ding-Dong." "These are my favorite things," he said. "They go way back."

We got in Todd's van and Pam drove. Todd got in the back seat behind me, with his GPS system – it had a phone-type plug that I kept on having to put in the dashboard – and the system kept crashing. We stopped by the house first, so I could see the "lay of the land." The mass of reporters had moved there, and were anxiously eyeing us and moving forward as we slowed down. I shrunk down in my seat and moved my head down. I did not want any of this. They were everywhere. I apologized to Todd for him and his wife to have to go through all this. How could they even breathe? He answered that they were happy for the coverage, if it would help bring back their little girl. I realized he was right. I thought of the media in a different light.

I went back into prayer, and saw April going to the edge of the sidewalk. We went down the road and turned left, out towards the open country. He had a blanket for her, she wrapped herself up in it, while still sitting in the passenger chair. She was in the motor home. He had a bag of junk food for her, and while they were traveling she got thirsty. He told her to get up and get a soda from the fridge. Then she needed to use the restroom, and I saw a red-roofed building on the opposite side of the street, with bathrooms outside. I got the feeling "gas station, but we didn't get gas." All these things I was feeling and *seeing through the eyes of April.* I could even feel the fullness in my bladder. All the while, in real life Pam and Todd and I were in the blue van, about to drive through a small mountain town. We passed by a couple of gas stations that could have been used, but none fit the description.

Suddenly I yelled, "Stop! There it is!" On the opposite side of the road, in the front of a large K-mart parking lot, was a fast-food restaurant with a red roof, and driving behind it we saw an outside bathroom with a separate entrance. It was an odd looking drive-in, and I wondered if it had been a gas station at one time. Todd went to find out who was working during that time, and also found that if a person needed to use the restroom, they had to ask for the key. *That means the perpetrator would have been seen by one of the employees.* Perhaps even with April by his side (at this point she still had no fear).

Todd also went into K-Mart and asked about the security cameras, but was told they didn't extend to the end of the parking lot (this is where I also walked out the footage of where he had parked the motor home, and its interior layout). Also, the tapes are reused and re-taped every week. A lost opportunity! Todd used the restroom, and coming back out the door he remarked, "I had to go in there, that might have been the last place my daughter had been alive."

In the parking lot I drew the layout of the motor home; placing the bathroom, closet, exit door, bed and refrigerator in their respective places. I suggested that her hair should certainly be found on the front passenger curtains, and reminded them that she had also opened the refrigerator. They told me that their neighbor had a motor home. I asked if he fit the description I had given them earlier. They said yes. I felt the warmth of the acknowledgement of the Holy Spirit. *This neighbor was the one who had hurt her.*

We got back in the van and headed up the highway. I could feel April waning, and I guessed she was falling asleep. Everything in the "vision" had the orange/night look, and I had guessed that all this had happened at night, right after she met him at the corner. Now they were together, going up this road and she had fallen asleep in her pajamas, wrapped in a blanket, in the front seat of his motor home. Every now and then this man would poke her shoulder with his finger and grin. She thought it was funny but irritating, because it would wake her back up. But, she was still not afraid.

After a while he leaves her be, and drives past another mountain town (which seemed to be very familiar to him) and pulled off the road and went and laid down on the back bed – he left April up in the front seat where she was, asleep. He "relieves" himself and went to sleep. At this point, April was still safe.

Later on (I am thinking the next morning, if all this happened the night she left the house) he gave April one of his t-shirts to wear over her night clothes because she had awakened cold, and she used the motor home restroom. Then, they went for a walk. He started poking and teasing with her again, and she thought he was playing, but then he did something that scared her, and she screamed, and tried to run back toward the motor home. She was going to lock the door and wait for her parents (still thinking they were coming to the lake). He grabbed her by the arm and swung her around. Things happened very fast after that.

187

He was surprised she had died so quickly, he was not expecting that. He acted almost like it was an accident. He seemed to be in shock, and staggered around. During the attack, my perception (through April's eyes) moved from a position where I am looking up, to a perception of floating above and looking down. She was now out of her body, seeing the final acts of violence without being a part of it. I felt relieved for her. God is a glorious one, who has mercy and brings peace to all his children, *especially the young ones*. She was hovering over her body.

I now pay strict attention; I see him pulling her along by the arm; he is wearing a watch, it has a big silver face on it with a black or dark brown circle around it, the same color as the band. It seems very large on his wrist. He is wearing pleated shorts, light tan ones. He has dark curly hair on his legs. He is not wearing glasses. The bald spot is very visible on top of his head. Very short, brown hair. I guess him to be a couple inches taller than I; it is hard at this perspective, but perhaps 5'9 or 5'10. He has on a jacket and a tee-shirt and is wearing socks with his shoes. I get more information. It seems the left foot is not right somehow, like an injury to a couple of toes or a deformity.

He does not know exactly what to do with April's body. She is by big gray rocks and he pushes her between the rocks, and puts more rocks over her. It looks like she is by a waterway or reservoir. She hovers above and watches him walk back to the motor home and drive off. He will be back. She waits for her parents. I see her (dead) grandfather get closer (there were several bluish spirits massed in the background, as if waiting) and he and she merge as if in a celestial hug. I know I am seeing what has already occurred, and just what I am required to see. For example, I do not see the angel, and I do not have to be told what her choice was. She knows that she is dead, but is not ready to go home until things are O.K. here with her parents. At this point, April was a ghost with unfinished business.

The next thing I see is April out of this situation, back in her own house, and trying to get her mother's attention, but she can't see her. I see a small dog wagging her tail and looking in her direction, it knows she is there.

In real life, Todd, Pam and I are now beside the lake I saw on the map. My head feels like it is going to burst. All of this area felt full of her, him, and the violence. I had been "on" for 12 hours now. It was getting late in the day. Todd talked to a policeman directing some workers on repairing a fence. I asked about the "Frees" or "Ees" road. The policeman gave us a few that had that as a major sound, and Todd entered them into his laptop, which then promptly broke down again. One of these sounds I was very interested in, it sounded like "ees, sha" and I kept asking about it, how far it was, where it was, were there gray rocks there. Most of the area, until you get almost right to the lake, had pale and brown rocks, not gray. I should have pursued my interest, but it was not meant to be.

We got out and searched around the lake. A man came out and yelled at us when we were on the dam. Nothing. At one place, on the lower side and out of sight of the road, I felt for sure this is where it had occurred. There were also big places where the gray rocks in the dam leaned against each other, but there was no body. Everything else matched, and it looked exactly like the vision area. We were all disappointed. Everything had been so extremely detailed up to now. Now there was no new information, and I didn't know what had happened to her. Why was I not being led to her body? Was it still here? I suggested to Todd that he bring out the dogs to search here tomorrow. We got in the van and turned around. What had I done wrong? I felt like I had failed. *Why had the Holy Spirit closed down the connection?*

We traveled back many miles in silence. I could feel them doubting everything now, from the very beginning. I prayed, and asked for the pain in my head to be gone – I had definitely stretched the envelope today. Being in connection for so long, listening so intently to the whispers of the Holy Spirit and what he allows to show me, and my ability to try to interpret them (good thing a lot of it is in pictures – less problem to mess it up).

Todd wanted to stop and look at another dam; it didn't fit the profile at all. It was a concrete dam and the rocks were all wrong. Driving out of there and back onto the road, part of the mystery became solved as to why we weren't allowed to find her tonight.

"You know," Todd started, *"the police told me I shouldn't be out in the field looking for her.* Because they told me the first thing I would do if I found her was to hold her. And they're right, that's what I would do. That would put my fingerprints on her, and they said that wouldn't be good."

Ah ha! That right there would be a good enough reason to not have her be found today. Perhaps it wasn't my fault; maybe I hadn't "messed up." But yes, I had gotten too involved with my own ego, wanting a specific outcome, instead of wanting what was "for the Highest Good." Also, I knew that the crush of media attention would not be good for me. I wouldn't be able to slide out from under it then. I would be smack dab in the middle of it, and pegged for only these assignments, from a worldly point of view, from then on. And this was harder than anything I had ever done! I work on the Lord's time. I refuse to be forced to do otherwise.

Also, after I had gotten home and slept for many hours, I awoke in the middle of the night and felt I needed to pray: then I asked April to visit. She did. She showed me a view of her body, naked now, sprawled out flat on the ground and with a leg turned wrong. Her foot was difficult to see in the vision, but looked deformed. The tee-shirt was gone. *The man had returned and taken her body to another place.* He had come under darkness and taken her and the pajama bottoms that he had thrown in the rocks with her. He had returned because he was afraid that the tee-shirt she was wearing, which had been his, might be traced back to him somehow. Fear had made the murderer return to the scene of the crime!

April said only one sentence, "I didn't want Daddy to see me, because I was naked."

I smiled at the shyness of a little girl, her darling personality intact after all these changes. I called both Pam and Todd the next day, keeping in mind what Todd had said when he gave me his numbers, "Remember to be careful what you say, the phone lines are being tapped by the police." So the police knew that I was working directly with the family, and that I was bypassing *them* completely.

Todd and I discussed new places to look around the lake, and I encouraged him to stay around this National Forest area; I knew the man didn't take her too far. We wondered outloud (by way of suggestion, since we knew they were listening) if the police could find DNA evidence in the motor home sewer system, which had now been taken into custody.

It was released in the newspapers that the motor home of this fellow had been heavily washed by him, with bleach inside. It was also reported that police dogs sent to sniff for clues in it were made sick from the fumes, because it was so strong with chlorine smell.

The perpetrator was arrested a couple of days after my time with Todd in the field. I saw the image of the fellow on the news (I decided it was O.K. to watch now) and he was the *exact same guy I saw with April.* The hair stood up on the back of my neck the first time I saw him, and a chill made goose bumps go down my arms. *They definitely had the right man.* In searching his house, they also found child pornography on his computer, and many other deviances were brought out in time, including testimonies from other people. They also found DNA evidence in the motor home, and two spots of April's blood – one on his jacket, and one on a bed linen, both retrieved from the drycleaners. But nothing can be hidden from The One Who Knows. The Psalmist said of God:

"If I say, "Surely the darkness will hide me and the light become night around me," even the darkness will not be dark to you; the night will shine like the day, for darkness is as light to you." (Ps. 139:11,12)

"There is nothing concealed that will not be disclosed, or hidden that will not be made known." (Lk. 12:2)

What they don't know, is that this same man, before moving to the state of California, had *sexually abused and killed a young black boy also.* Of course, I can offer no hard evidence of this. None except faith in the discerning Spirit of righteousness, the One who knows all of what has been done, and every drop of blood that has ever been spilled upon this earth. He is the one who knows, and will exact vengeance.

"Vengeance is mine, I will repay," says the Lord." (Ro. 12:19)

A few days later, not many miles from the lake, "as the crow flies," a team of searchers found the naked body of a little girl sprawled upon the earth. *Her leg was twisted and partially gone* (I wondered if the deformity of the foot/toes that I felt and attributed to the perpetrator was actually April's?). She was found on a road called that had the *"ees, sha"* sound in it, in the same *National Forest area*. I was glad that it was over, and a closing and letting go could begin for the family, and those around the nation who had tuned in so tightly to the plight of this wonderful little girl.

I watched the public memorial on TV that was held for April. I didn't want to go in person. I felt like I needed to keep any connection between the family and me a personal one, not in the public eye. About a thousand people showed up to pay their respect. The parents released white doves, and balloons of her favorite colors. Music played, the sweet words of "In the Arms of the Angel," lilted through. Many friends, children, and family members spoke in her behalf.

I knew in my heart that her death had helped many other children to live. The media attention about April had placed fear in the hearts of mothers and fathers around the nation. *There were thousands of children who were now fingerprinted and photographed. Seminars* and *public talks* were held around the country to educate the public about predators and *how to protect their children*. Numerous other things were done. There was such a spirit of community. April was everyone's little girl. They had adopted her with her innocent smile, and they wondered how they would cope, identifying with the despair of her parents. *April's death* had accomplished what many people could not have done with their *entire lives*. She had been given a special assignment, indeed.

Toward the end of the service, I felt the presence of April beside me, and I welcomed her, I hadn't expected her to visit again, especially coming to see me during her own funeral. I thought my purpose had been fulfilled toward the family. But, there was one more item left undone.

One more time, April wanted me to relate a message to her mother.

When Todd and Susan and their other children got home that day, they heard on their answering machine one last note of love from their little girl, who still felt the need to convince them in any way they could, that she was O.K.

"Hi, this is Tiffany." I said. "April wants her mom to know that the item that she took from her mom's room and hid in her dresser drawer was this – a pink swirled plastic box, about five inches long, and two inches wide, with a rounded top. In case the police moved it, that is what it was. It was in her top dresser drawer on the right side. She is not telling me what was in it, but this is what April wanted you to know – that she exists, and is indeed "flying with the angels." She is going home now. She will visit you and her brothers now and then. I hope you know what I am talking about, I am just here to relate the information. From me personally, I would like to offer Many Blessings to you and your family."

The perpetrator was later found guilty of murder; and is now facing the death penalty, which his attorneys are appealing. The open-to-the-public trial and courtroom drama was broadcast minute-by-minute across the country. It had a permanent spot on the front of newspapers for several months.

My wish for you is to keep a watch on your children; keep communication going; have a "code word" so the child knows to *only* go with adults who have that word; and continue to have current photographs and fingerprint your children in case the unthinkable happens.

***

A Father's Apology from the Grave

I was doing a healing treatment on my father. So many injuries had occurred over the years; scars here, broken bones there. Yet, often the most tremendous and consistent pain is that which is invisible to the eyes or to the touch. Such can be the emotional pain of childhood. Again, a healing would go much deeper than flesh and bone.

Often I see those loved ones who have crossed over still residing by the ones they love, hovering there, smiling and guiding. Relatives and friends often choose to stay in touch with us after they have left their bodies. It seems that God allows them to come and go as they please, and they also have instant access to heaven, where they spend a good part of their time. They do have better things to do than to 'hang out' with us. Their spirits are bright and vibrating loudly, a good healthy and happy bluish-white-yellow glow. I suppose it wouldn't be true happiness in heaven for those who have crossed if they weren't allowed access to their loved ones back here on earth.

As I continued in silent prayer with my hands upon my father's back, I felt a familiarity, and looked up. A tall, skinny, spirit was before me, and his energy felt related to my father and to me. He pulled together his shoulders, and was almost slumping. His lips were straight and he had piercing eyes. I knew he was my grandfather, Lawrence Wallace. Not one time in my vision did I see him smiling.

192

As I watched, I saw him riding a large brown horse, with brown mane and tail. Riding high and proud, with tall black boots almost up to his knee, he rode straight up in the saddle. He wore a cowboy hat.

The vibration of the man changed then, and I saw him once more standing on the ground, and felt a slow buzzing feeling from drinking beer. He pointed to a lower rib cage injury, with a cloth square over it, and bandages going across. His chin was more pointed than my father's. Also, there was a reference about frogs and fishing. I saw a long water ditch with a wide brown dirt path beside it on which to walk.

Next, I saw an outside building, like a wood planked garage, where dad wasn't allowed to go. His father worked on cars here, and dad in his youth would get yelled at if he entered. I got the vision of a house, a gray weathered wood clapboard style, and being barefoot, and big climbing trees, with outspread branches. Safety. Back East. Small outbuildings and chicken wire were all around, in the tall grass.

Now, I see him in a uniform - a brown shirt with a hat on, and a small red rectangle on his chest pocket. I see this face framed in a picture. Still no smile, his shirt neatly pressed. There were other colors besides red on his patch. Did he go to war? I see another photo - one with a young (grandmother) Helen in a bathing suit, turned sideways kissing his cheek with her toe kicked up; him standing looking straight ahead, feet shoulder-width, hands on hips.

I see him dying - he is in a chair by a desk, falling off and onto the floor, and one side of his eye glasses crack (I do remember being told he died at work in an auto sales store, that he was young and that he had a stroke).

There was a message he wanted me to tell my father. "I'm sorry that I let you down. Wish we could've gotten along better, Bunky." I was told to remind him about "trains," and that "he will know what it is." He says he was too strict, "Didn't want no mama's boy," and that he used to use a switch from outside – dad would have to go get a fresh one himself – and that he especially used his belt. At times he had a real explosive temper and would throw things, or at least slam them down. He was sorry about all that. I needed to tell dad that.

I completed the healing treatment, and thanked the Holy Spirit for allowing this special healing to occur. As father hurried to meet some friends for lunch, I struggled to write down the information I had received. It vanishes so quickly when it is information being given *through* me instead of being *developed* by me, and it does not stay long in my memory! I felt I would have to approach giving dad this information at a later time, and I needed time to think about how, since I didn't quite know how to go about it.

193

Later on that evening, I found dad reading the newspaper, and I started to present the information. "His nickname for me was Buddy, not Bunky," he said, and dropped the paper on the floor. I apologized, saying, "I'm still not really good with name sounds." He listened carefully, and I suggested that he should talk to his dad tonight, through prayer, since he had been hanging out with us all afternoon, ever since the healing. "I'll try," he said.

The next morning found father validating the details of the information I had given him. Some he had to get from his mother. Yes, the house had been back east, and had been wood, not white. Yes, he was a drinker, of beer. Rarely was he found with a flask of hard liquor. He had had an injury on his ribs from a machine. The bandages had been wrapped the way I described them. The house they had when my dad was young was by a water canal. The house I described (wooden with clapboard walls, etc) was actually where Lawrence had grown up. My dad remembered plainly how he was not allowed into the garage, because "yes, he was working on cars, and yes, I would get yelled at!"

I had to laugh when I heard the explanation about the train, and that dad "would know what it is." It rose quickly in his memory, although it had been over 50 years ago. Dad had received a lovely train for Christmas one year, complete with track. But he didn't get to play with it much, because Lawrence was "hogging it!" He was down on his knees playing with it, and didn't let his son get much time to have his turn. So many things we carry with us from years gone by! On both sides!

I asked about the war picture. Dad said his father had never gone to war – and this was a stumper for us for a while. Then dad asked his mom if Lawrence wore a uniform to work. Before he had started to sell cars, he had been a mechanic. Grandmother she said yes, he did, a brown one! With the company patch on the pocket, in red! Thus, the mystery was solved. He also loved to ride horses, and considered himself a cowboy; and wore tall boots up to his knees, and his horse had not a speck of white on him, being totally brown. When Helen was asked if she remembered the picture where she is kissing him on the cheek, she replied that she posed that way, with her toe up, in lots of pictures. That was her style.

Father and son reunion, from beyond the grave! Blessed be the Lord thy Almighty Father, who brings comfort to those living and dead, and heals all wounds. Glory Be!

CHAPTER 10

Letting God Be God, Out of the Box
Why Bad Things Really Happen; The Power of Brokenness

"...It's only in the darkness that we dream –
Search out His Guiding Light,
believe in things unseen.
It's only when we're broken that we yield-
then he reaches down to save us,
and be healed..."

(song excerpt from: *Be Healed* © 2003 *SnowCat Music*/Tiffany Snow)

What is your purpose in life? Have you ever asked someone else, or even paid someone, to tell you what it is? Did you actually believe it, or did you still have your doubts? Many people will go to extremes to know this most spirit-wrenching question. But, many will only believe the answer if it comes verified supernaturally, *which is how it should be, Divinely Supernatural!* People want to know why they are here, what happens when they die, and the reasons behind the trauma they are experiencing. All these answers come through the many tools that fill the God-Spot. Now you have the tools. *Use them! Answer your Questions!*

Often people will say, "If it's not broken – don't fix it." If we continue in our mediocre ways and thoughts, we will never attain anything else – we will never go to the next level, a higher plateau to see the view around us, and over us. The problem is, we are a people *who can't do this on our own.* We can't fix ourselves, so how can we move forward?

We must be *broken* before we can be *fixed.* We must come to that point in our lives where we are empty and know there is nothing in our own power that we can do. We feel weak, in pain, afraid, crushed and forgotten. At the bottom of the hole, our struggle to climb out only makes more dirt fall down in our face. We might try to devise a scheme on our own, putting stock in our own ingenuity and reasoning – we try everything. But it all fails. What do we do now? This is when we look for answers outside of ourselves. *This is when we find God.*

Gina's Brokenness: *Brightly dressed with well-worn tennis shoes and a pink floppy hat, Gina skipped along the well-worn forest path towards town. Off the trail a short distance she saw an interesting glint of light dancing carelessly over some fallen leaves. Choosing to leave the safety of the path and ignoring the cautionary pangs of her built-in intuition, Gina went toward the frolicking reflections of light.*

Poof – Gina found her footing weak and fell through the roof of an old dry well. Down past layers of rock and moist earth, she landed with a "thud" some thirty feet below. In pain, Gina slowly sat up among the rocks, leaves and dirt, and tried to focus. The only light was straight above her head – pitch blackness saturated the area around her, and try as she might, she could see only as much as a blind man. She felt the walls – stones stacked upon stones. She agonized when she moved her left arm – it must be broken – and when she tried to stand up, she couldn't put her weight on her right ankle.

What was she going to do? She felt around, hoping to find something that would aid her in getting to the top again - her hand found an old rope - probably from the bucket it once hoisted years ago. She curled it up and held on to one end, steadied herself against the wall and flung it with all her strength towards the light. It fell back down, bringing a cascade of pebbles and sand along with it. She tried again and again - each time with the same result. Time went by. If only she was smarter, she thought, she could figure a way out of this hole. She tried piling up all the dirt and rocks to one side. She took the longer sticks and bound them together with the rope to make a ladder - not strong or long enough. There was still no way out. She got angry with herself for going off the trail and getting into this mess. She blamed the people who made the well so long ago. She screamed and yelled and pounded her fist into the dirt where she collapsed, and blamed God for allowing this to happen to her. She was in terrible pain, cold to the bone, and completely worn out. She didn't know how she could go on.

She leaned against the wall and started to think about her family and friends. If only she could talk to them one more time! There was so much that she would say and do differently. She remembered the good times and smiled. She felt the hopelessness of her situation and cried. She couldn't do anything more on her own. She knew her power was useless, and that, if she was to survive, it would not be by her own devices.

She wept in the darkness; tears cleansed white streaks down her cheeks. Silently she prayed, mumbling through her tears. As her prayers increased in intensity, she found herself beseeching God to forgive her, and promised to do everything right if he would just get her out of this hole in the ground. After a while of this, and seeing no sign of God's presence with her, nor any answer to her prayers, she screamed resentment toward God; was convinced that he didn't exist, and bitterly fell forward with her face to the ground and wept until there was no more weeping left.

She was broken…a calm and quietness came over her and she wondered if she were dying – the 'peace of God that excels all thought' encompassed her very being. She talked now, to God, as a child does to her father, and only asked to *be with him, and begged for nothing more than his forgiveness and love and to be in his arms.*

And at that point, the Lord could not resist showing his tender mercies towards her vulnerability, and reached down to save her.

As Gina slipped into unconsciousness she dreamily heard a voice beckon to her, "Do not fear, you are my child." Gina smiled and felt a warm glow around her. "God?!" She said and blinked at the illumination of the stones in front of her...

"Hey, anybody down there?" a voice boomed down as a flashlight shined into the well. "Anybody down there?"

"Yes, yes!" Gina softly whispered, as she realized this was a different voice, one from above the hole. "Yes, yes!" she shouted more strongly as she awoke to the moment. "I'm down here! Help me!" Soon a looped rope was lowered down and Gina was able to put it under both arms and slowly crawl herself up the side of the well. She was saved!

At the top, Gina sat exhausted on the ground, squinted at the brightness of the afternoon sun and rotated her ankle with no pain. She knew her arm must also have been sprained or broken, but she could move it freely without any problems.

"How did you find me?" she asked the unshaven man with the tattered shirt, now standing before her.

"Just luck I guess, ma'am. I was walking along the trail and saw this bright pink hat and went over to get it - it was just lying on the leaves. When I got there, I saw the cave-in and sort of put two-and-two together. You were really lucky you weren't hurt, or killed," he winked.

"Yes," Gina replied, "really lucky. Thank you for saving me."

And the man helped her up and back onto the trail, where he continued on his way with a wave of his hand, disappearing through the pine boughs and around the corner. As Gina watched him go, she wondered if he were an angel or a man.

And as Gina slowly wandered back up the trail toward her home, she wondered if the voice that she heard in the ground had been only in her mind. And the bright light could have been the flashlight reaching all the way down. And it was true that her pink hat had fallen off and lain beside the hole – that would attract anyone's attention. And her arm and foot had probably just been badly bruised and felt better because she had rested. She was probably just lucky after all.

197

And as Gina was sorting out these things, those pangs happened again inside her - that silent voice that we often ignore, the angelic whisperings of right and wrong. And Gina stopped. And Gina listened. And Gina dropped to her knees and wept, thanking the Lord for saving her, and vowed never to excuse away His Love again.

From that point on, no matter what Gina had to deal with in the rest of her life, she moved through it with grace. Thankful for the lesson of the well, she looked at trials in a new way, never getting overly worried or fearful about the darkness that would try to trap and surround her. She knew she could always crawl up the rope and onto the lap of her father and be safe there. And any struggles put before her, gave her more opportunity to do just that.

How many times do we find ourselves ignoring God's voice and going off the path towards something that glitters? That "glint of reflected light" that frolics carelessly amidst danger can be a strong attraction. Ask any fisherman - it's not the deadly hook that attracts the fish, it's the flashy lure. God's people today have to ask themselves the same question - "is that a reflection or true light?" One of the ways to know the answer is this - do you have to go off the path onto dangerous ground in order to get to it? Another is - what is my "gut-feeling" about it; what does that still, small whispering voice inside of me say? *Am I open to God giving me direction about this?*

When we do get in a mess - do we blame God for it, and say, "why me?" or do we see it as a golden opportunity to draw even closer to the Divine? Do we only turn to God when we have run out of ideas and devices of our own? And when we do approach him, do we only ask for the blessings, his gifts, or do we ask only for The Giver? And when the Supernatural reaches for us and we find ourselves experiencing "Something" beyond our concept of reason and reality - are we quick to excuse it away? How many times will we chalk up to "luck" or circumstance that which is God's Doings and Divine Interventions?

Do we minimize his healings and tell ourselves, "Well, maybe I wasn't as sick as I thought I was." And, when we vow in our hearts to "do better," do we forget our vows once we are out of the danger zone? Are we able to forgive injustices in the past, and all the times we have fallen in the well ourselves or been thrown in by others, and see it through the wisdom of thankfulness of lessons learned? And, most importantly of all - do we shed ourselves of adult presumptuousness and layers of veneer and come to our Father as an unassuming child, just wanting the closeness of being held? Abba, Father! *God is Unconditional Love.* He wants all people to come to him, *for all the right reasons.*

Nature's Brokenness: *Look at the puppy cower down as the adult dog runs up to it; growling and snarling and showing its teeth. It's ready to rip and kill at a second's notice if need be. Any wrong move could be the puppy's last. The pup* *knows it can't fight, and it can't run – what does it do? It rolls over on its back and exposes the white of his neck, whimpering. It is Broken. In total submission it tells the adult "kill me if you must, I am no match for you. But if you let me live, I will humbly submit to your authority."*

The stronger dog immediately stops the aggression and takes on a dominant but protective role; often allowing the puppy to lick his face and wiggle all around, biting playfully at his legs and tail. A relationship is born that allows the younger dog to survive and prosper while the older dog enjoys the companionship. A similar scenario occurs between almost all animal families: when submission is relayed, mercy is shown and survival is assured. Nature knows Brokenness.

When we look back at God's love letters to his people of ancient times, we see numerous incredible things. Where did this concept of "I'm a good person, nothing bad will happen to me" come from? *All the early Christians were persecuted and put through numerous trials and tribulations.* Those traumas expanded the power of God's word throughout the world and throughout the centuries. It strengthened his people.

Even before Christ redeemed us, the before-Christianity God-seekers, prophets, visionaries, etc...were all put through extreme tests "as if thru fire." Imperfect, cracked vessels tested as to their worthiness. All these God-praising men and women were *all first Broken.* Then, *God would fix them and use them as he saw fit.* He used them for healings and resurrections; for penmanship of his word; for prophecies, signs and miracles. He used them for his Divine Will in all cases – to show his love and protection to his people. *He does the same thing today.*

We have to die to ourselves to come before God. Pour ourselves out. Not care about our flesh. Not care about our past or our future. Only care about him and his will. All else is refuse, just useless garbage. Then, God can resurrect us again to himself, for us to be a useful vessel. And, since the out-pouring of Christ's blood as a balancing point for Adam, we now have opportunity to come before the face of God when we give up our flesh in death. "You cannot see my face, for no one may see me and live." (Ex. 33:20) But when we are flesh no more, the opportunity is there! "Blessed are the pure in heart, for they will see God." (Mt. 5:8)

Often, we may not be aware that there is anything to "fix." We go about our lives taking care of things the best we can - providing shelter, food, clothing and a measure of time and love to those around us. Perhaps we have our "dream" job, a large house or the sleek car we have always wanted. We are the concerned wife and mother; the protective and sheltering husband and father. But, are we happy? No, I mean REALLY HAPPY! The kind of happiness that feels like your heart has a sunburst in it; like your blood stream has seven cups of caffeine in it; like you've just told your family you're all going on an eight-week cruise to

Hawaii; like you've just won 10 million dollars! *That kind of happy!* If you come broken before the Lord - *he will make you that happy!*

That happiness may first come as uncontrollable weeping and tossing yourself upon the ground. That glory may make you "act as crazy" before the eyes of "regular " Christians. Perhaps you will find yourself in a self-imposed fast, or hiding yourself away for a few weeks in the desert. But it will *always* change your life, and move you to *own* less and *do* more. It will re-arrange your priorities; often change your job; the people with whom you surround yourself; and sometimes the area in which you live. Are you ready for that? Are you ready to submit your Free Will to ask for only His Will*? Are you truly ready to receive the gifts he will give you freely, and take up the responsibilities that those gifts bring?*

If you are ready for the "Peace of God that excels all thought," every day will be an adventure in how he will use you, and every night you will sleep in the grand peace that only a covenant with him can bring. Are you ready? *Are you really ready!* God Himself is hoping you will say "Yes!" *He yearns to draw near to each of us* – but we must acknowledge our weakness (sin) and allow ourselves to be "fixed." Not only allow it, but *have a passion* for it! Go to the *brink of death* for it! And, if we *are* asked to give our life for him, what a *grand way* to get so much nearer!

Abraham's Brokenness: *"Why God? Why do you ask this of me?" Abraham the prophet cried out as he clutched the knife over his young son's head. "You promised me a great nation through my loins – now you ask me to kill my only son – oh Lord! I love him so much…but Your Will be done, not mine!"*

Through a miracle, Isaac had been born when Abraham was 100 years old and his wife Sarah was 90. A promise had been made to him by God that a great nation and a great blessing would come through his family lineage. Abraham had left a prosperous land, undergone a multitude of hardships, famine, family conflicts, etc, and had relied upon God's promises through it all. He had survived and prospered. But now this! He was asked to throw all the promises away. Abraham was broken. He was asked to do something unthinkable and without reason. Why? It was in Abraham's power, and also in the power of the young teenage boy, to stop it; but they didn't…God did.

"Abraham!" God's angel shouted, "Abraham, do not hurt the boy! Now I know that you truly love me, because you have not withheld your most precious possession from me; your only son. And all nations on earth will be blessed because you have obeyed me." (Ge. 22:1-18)

Abraham was saved from his trauma, and received abundant blessings because he did not hold back. We received those blessings also, as God's promise was

200

fulfilled in the grandest of ways when Jesus Christ came to earth, born through Abraham's descendants, and gave his life in balance for all.

God had allowed Abraham to be tested to see if he was *only after the gifts, or after the Giver.* The testing deepened his capacity to obey and rely on God. Difficult circumstances stretch us out. They prove who *we* really are. And they prove to us *who God really is!*

"Consider it pure joy, my brothers, whenever you face trials of many kinds, because you know that the testing of your faith develops perseverance. Perseverance must finish its work so that you may be mature and complete, not lacking anything." (Jas.1:2-4)

"Before I was afflicted I went astray, but now I obey your word. You are good, and what you do is good; teach me your decrees. Though the arrogant have smeared me with lies, I keep your precepts with all my heart. Their hearts are callous and unfeeling, but I delight in your law. It was good for me to be afflicted so that I might learn your decrees. The law from your mouth is more precious to me than thousands of pieces of silver and gold." (Ps. 119:67-72)

"Blessed is the man who perseveres under trial, because when he has stood the test, he will receive the crown of life that God has promised to those who love him. When tempted, no one should say, "God is tempting me." For God cannot be tempted by evil, nor does he tempt anyone; but each one is drawn out by his own desires. Then, after desire has conceived, it gives birth to sin; and sin, when it is mature, gives birth to death. Do not be deceived, my dear brother. Every good and perfect gift is from above, coming down from the Father of the heavenly lights, who does not change like shifting shadows." (Jas. 1:13-17)

"And the God of all grace, who called you to his eternal glory in Christ, after you have suffered a little while, will himself restore you and make you strong, firm and steadfast." (1 Pe. 5:10)

Free-Will and God's Rightfulness to Rule

There is another reason why we undergo trauma in our life. There is the *enemy* of God. We see him bringing problems to mankind all the way from Genesis to Revelation, where we see a war break out in heaven between good and evil. Here in these key verses, we see a great drama unfolding that involves each and every one of us in our daily lives.

(1). "Did God really say, 'You must not eat from any tree in the garden'?" The woman said to the serpent, "We may eat fruit from the trees in the garden, but God did say, 'You must not eat fruit from the tree that is in the middle of the garden, and you must not touch it, or you will die.'" "You will not surely die," the serpent said to the woman. "For God knows that when you eat of it your eyes will be opened, and you will be like God, knowing good and evil." (Ge. 3:1-5)

(2). "On another day the angels came to present themselves before the Lord, and Satan also came with them to present himself before him. And the Lord said to Satan, "Where have you come from?" Satan answered the Lord, "From roaming through the earth and going back and forth in it." Then the Lord said to Satan, "Have you considered my servant Job? There is no one on earth like him; he is blameless and upright, a man who fears God and shuns evil. And he still maintains his integrity…" "Skin for skin!" Satan replied. "A man will give all he has for his own life…" (Job 2:1-10)

(3). "And there was war in heaven. Michael and his angels fought against the dragon, and the dragon and his angels fought back. But he was not strong enough, and they lost their place in heaven. The great dragon was hurled down – that ancient serpent called the devil, or Satan, who leads the whole world astray. He was hurled to the earth, and his angels with him…Therefore rejoice, you heavens and you who reside in them! But woe to the earth and the sea, because the devil has gone down to you! He is filled with fury, because he knows his time is short." (Rev. 12:7-9, 12)

Lets take these events one by one: *(1). The Fall of Mankind.* The question: *"Man can choose for himself what is good and what is bad, and do it successfully without God."* Why didn't God choose to destroy Adam and Eve after they rebelled, and start all over again with different children? Because God had not created humans as mindless robots, these humans were perfect creations who had made a God-given *Free Will* choice. Now, *a question was also raised before the angel sons of God* that needed to be answered, no matter what the final outcome was for Adam and Eve.

This question would take thousands of years and many generations of mankind "doing his own thing" to answer. Now, the evidence speaks for itself. We are peering into a celestial courtroom, where the attorney is compiling the mound of evidence. The final conclusion will stand forever and never be changed through out all time. What about your free will? Have you been choosing your own path over God's way? *Has it been successful for you?*

(2). The Question of Integrity. "Mankind only loves God for what man can get out of God," and, "When tested as to his flesh, mankind will turn away from God." This is similar to what Jesus stated at my NDE when I was commissioned for healing – "The Flesh is the Test of the Spirit." But, as always, Satan has contorted it, saying that mankind will turn from God in time of bodily peril. Most of the time, we see just the opposite occur. We also see that at one time, Satan and his demons still had access to the Presence of God. We also see that God knew beforehand whom Satan was tormenting, and that *God is proud of us when we*

show integrity. We also see God *allowing* the test to be performed, as undeniable proof that *those who really love God don't do it for selfish gain.*

What side of this issue are we on? When we are sick or have disease, do we cry out in bitterness against God, saying "Why me?" When presented with the temptation of drugs, illicit sex or abuse of alcohol, do we allow the selfish stimulus of temporary gratification turn us away from God? Or do we only "love" God when we are on a "sinking ship" or when we are not presented with *something else that we would rather be doing?*

(3). Satan Permitted to Tempt the World. "Through time and pressure, mankind will see that God doesn't exist, or if he does, he doesn't care enough about the world to be personally involved. Evil Rules. Salvation is a lie." Here we see that a mighty war took place between Michael the Archangel and Satan, and Satan and his demons lost their place in heaven and were banished to the earth. On earth, they have escalated the world's problems, especially in maneuvering the governments of mankind, in response to Issue # 1.

Knowing that the time of being allowed to do so is short, the marketing and advertising program of brainwashing people against the belief that the God of Love exists is fully underway. This lie is one of the reasons that God allows Supernatural events and communication to occur as a direct life-line to his people, and why we must persevere in prayer. *Even though God permits the devil to do his work in this world, God is still in control!* Are you overly concerned about the affairs of the world, thinking that God is looking the other way? Do you realize that no matter what occurs, Satan has still lost because the ransom was paid for us long ago? *Who controls your life?*

We Were Created with a "God-Spot"

Hundreds of religions in the world...thousands of ways and rules of worship...millions of different points of view. Everywhere, in all parts of the earth and in all periods of time we find people expressing a need to worship, whether it has been the sun, idols of stone or TV personalities. As a person searching for the face of God, it may easily seem like an insurmountable and impossible task. But, yet, a gnawing feeling inside of us keeps driving us – we need to have the validation of God. We need the personal realization in our lives, the manifestation of "*I AM."* Why is that? Why can't people feel complete happiness in just meeting the needs and wants of life? *Because we were made that way! We were meant to be empty without God.*

"God did this so that men would seek him and perhaps reach out for him and find him, though he is not far from each one of us. 'For in him we live and move and have our being.' As some of your own poets have said, 'We are his offspring.'" (Acts 17:27,28)

We were created with a God-Spot. Nothing else can fill that need but spiritual union with him. It is similar to having an automobile, and trying to put water in the gas tank. Whether it be a state-of-the-art Lexus or an old Chevy, it still needs petrol to operate. Nothing else will do! And just as a car is created with all of its parts on the drawing board for a *specific purpose* and the design sent to the factory, so God created us with a need to have a *"God-Consciousness"* and use it.

This is the reason why money does not give true satisfaction, nor does fame, nor the dreams coming true from our childhood. How many *wealthy* people do you know who are *truly happy?* On the contrary, doesn't the happiness of the rich and famous seem extremely short-lived? On top of the world one moment - then recovering from drugs, alcohol or other forms of addictive behavior the next. Very often rich people will spend all their lifetime searching out various combinations of pleasures that promise to bring true and lasting happiness, but to no avail.

When a *famous* person commits suicide, what is one of the first things people say? Isn't it something like this: "but they had everything in the world that they could ever want!" Famous people often have the ultimate ability to create happiness for themselves, with all the best resources and personal attention available to them. People clamor to meet them; take their pictures; buy magazines with their images on them, and the products they endorse. But, instead of making the God-Spot content and peaceful, the hole seems to get even bigger and the emptiness inside more hollow. They try to fill their hunger with the wrong things - big houses, fast cars, designer clothes, trips to Spain - *but money and fame can't buy what God gives for free.*

"When Simon saw that the Spirit was given at the laying on of the apostle's hands, he offered them money and said, "Give me also this ability so that everyone on whom I lay my hands may receive the Holy Spirit." Peter answered: "May your money perish with you, because you thought you could buy the gift of God with money!" (Ac. 8:18-20)

Money is not the problem. *Money is just a tool,* and a necessary one, to exchange for goods and services that we all need. A person does not have to be poor to have a relationship with God, and being rich will not necessarily stop one, either. "The *love* of money is the root of all evil..." (1 Ti. 6:10) *It is how you view money that matters!*

Very impoverished people think about their situation all the time - it is right before them in the eyes of their family and children - they need the basics of life, which money can give them. So, they spend most of their waking hours thinking of money, lack of it and possible ways to get it. They feel if even their basic needs are met, they will be happy. Yet, millions of immigrants come to wealthier countries, fill their baskets with the goods that the different economies may offer; *and yet feel empty*. Many decide after a while to go home. Why? They were happier at home. They needed the goods, but *it didn't fill all their needs*. They wanted to go home to be with family and the culture they grew up in, and where their customs were familiar tools to seek God. Material possessions never fill up the God-Spot.

A wise man once said *"Give me neither poverty nor riches*, but give me only my daily bread. Otherwise, I may have too much and disown you and say, 'Who is the Lord?' Or I may become poor and steal, and so dishonor the name of my God." (Pr. 30:8,9)

So, as in all things, a balance is needed with money. But, it doesn't drop a feather amount in the God-Spot! The *time and diligence* you use in expanding your Divine Connection is worth far more than money.

How much the God-Spot is filled up is also in direct relation to how much we can withstand, and how well, in times of *trauma*. It is the reason that people who have that connection can successfully overcome extreme obstacles, and often, even smile while doing it!

"But we have this treasure in jars of clay to show that this all-surpassing power is from God and not from us. We are hard pressed on every side, but not crushed; perplexed, but not in despair; persecuted, but not abandoned; struck down, but not destroyed." (2 Co. 4:7-9)

Now You Have the Gifts – Use Them!

Remember the boy in the introduction, who received a big box from his dad? Well, together we have opened it and read several of the "instruction manuals" that came for using the gifts. Some you may have already known how to use; some may not "fit;" and some you may just love and want to use as much as possible! Even *one* new gift or the *confidence to use it* will be worth the effort. A strengthened connection with God and the satisfaction of the God-Spot being filled is a feeling that can't compare to *anything else!*

We have looked and listened to the child inside of us who lived for so many years with a hollow feeling...we screamed for roots and reasons, a future and a past. One morning, we awoke with a single-minded purpose - to search out our roots, find out where we came from, and who our Dad is. The reason? We were born into a family. We craved a soul-connection that nothing else could replace, and it lingered tantalizingly just beyond the veil. *Now, the veil is lifted!*

Most of us have instinctively known for a long time that we are sons and daughters, and that there are siblings *just like us*. They have the same questions, the same need for identity, and the same emptiness that only a God-Spot connection can fill. Now, you have some questions answered, and many tools to use to attain more. Share the information with your siblings – it will change lives and help heal scars. *Touch the world for Healing!* You have Keys to Connection that nobody can take away from you! Never!

As Jesus reminded me as I stood before him in my near-death experience; *"Love Each Other!"* You will see how well (or not) you did this in your "life review" movie after you transition this world. Strive for an "Emmy" or a real "Angel" award! Share the Gifts!

"Let the Little Children Come to Me"

"Then little children were brought to Jesus for him to place his hands on them and pray for them. But the disciples rebuked those who brought them. Jesus said, "Let the little children come to me, and do not hinder them for the kingdom of heaven belongs to such as these." (Mt. 19:13,14)

He took them into his arms whether their parent's theology was right or wrong. He blessed them, and told us we should imitate their qualities. Even today, what are young children known for? Their lack of prejudice. To them, it doesn't matter what color skin a person has or what social standing or side of town they came from. *They play and interact together - until they are taught otherwise.*

We are *all* Children of the Divine. All of us, regardless of skin color, where we live in the earth, or what our custom of worship is - *all of us* - have *equal opportunity* in his eyes. Do we really want to know our Father better? If so, are we truly prepared to know and accept all these other siblings, the other kids that he loves? *He offers love to all of us!*

"From one man he made every nation of men, that they should inhabit the whole earth; and he determined the times set for them and the exact places they should live. God did this so that men would seek him and perhaps reach out for him and find him, although he is not far off from each one of us." (Acts. 17:26-27)

Kathryn Kulhman, a leading healer and evangelist of our time, once stated: "I have decided that God doesn't have preferences in theology. We are the ones who try to put a fence around God."

Many people at this point may be shuddering and find themselves bristling against the notion that other kids are climbing up onto Daddy's lap. Many come from other "schools of thought" out of our known community or "school district." Many use different tools to access and climb up - these may be different customs than we are familiar with. *But what they are using is working!* Often things that are unfamiliar, scare us. Especially when we see our Father welcoming others with open arms and blessing them too. Do we have the love to accept the will of God in these matters? Or do we feel we have a "corner" on God and react only with disdain and prejudice?

The ancient Jews felt this way back in Jesus' day. He had come to free Gentiles as well as Jews, and to open salvation up for all the world. But, The Jews wanted the corner on God's blessings for their own group. Jesus refused and told them:

"I am the good shepherd; I know my sheep and my sheep know me...I have other sheep that are not of this fold. I must bring them in also. They too will listen to my voice, and there shall be one flock and one shepherd." (Jn. 10:14-16)

In evaluating others, do you consider God's impact upon their lives? Are you aware of similarities between yourself and others who worship God, *even if their form of worship is quite different from your own?*

"A new command I give you: Love one another. As I have loved you, so you must love one another. By this all men will know that you are my disciples, if you love one another." (Jn. 13:34,35)

"Love Thy Neighbor?" Who is That?

Here in the United States, our motto, as seen on the dollar bill, is "E pluribus unum," which means "out of many, one." God's money would be a little different (an example of mankind getting things backwards as usual)! His money would say "Out of One, Many." The interconnectedness and oneness of humanity is a scientific fact. It is also a spiritual one. We must acknowledge that those who we should consider our brothers and sisters can be found not only in our Bible studies and churches, but on the street corner; in hospitals for the mentally disabled; in hospice and rehabilitation centers and care groups; in darkened alleyways; in lands of poverty, and in all parts of the world. *We are all neighbors!*

And just because some of these people cannot, for a variety of reasons, make a "brain" decision for God does not "disqualify" them. *Jesus made the way open for all.* Whether there is accurate "head-knowledge" or not, he knows whose *hearts* are his. The inner striving toward *Abba* is there. In respect for the Father, respect the Oneness of humanity. Be tolerant and appreciate the wide diversity. The Almighty created around you - in the animal kingdom, in the plant kingdom, and in God's Kingdom.

Jesus said, "...Love the Lord your God with all your heart and with all your soul and with all your mind. This is the first and greatest commandment. And the second is like it: 'Love your neighbor as yourself.' All the Law and the Prophets hang on these two commandments." (Mt. 22:37,38)

What Happens When God Goes to Church?

People throughout time have put imaginary boundaries on God - they talk about restrictions on what he is, what he can do, or not do. *They put God in a box that they have built with their own hands!* They have gilded it with prejudices, reinforced the steel bars with misconceptions, hammered the nails in with fear, and painted it with self-ego and intentional naivety. But, what have they trapped? It is not God, for he does not live within man-made boxes or imposed rules. What they have trapped is only air, and not Spirit!

The word "church" in Hebrew means "people," not a place or building. So, you can find "church" wherever there is a gathering of people. Often we don't need to travel very far from our neighborhoods to find a sacred place to go gather with others to worship, experience and learn about God. The scriptures encourage us to go and support each other in faith. (He. 10:24,25) But what happens when God is "unorthodox" and breaks out? *What do we do if God doesn't act the way we think he should?*

There are those who won't agree that God actively takes an interest in our lives today, let alone allow his Holy Spirit to work through humans. *God is simply a mystery to those who shut their hearts down.* Aren't we asking at every gathering for the Spirit of God to be in our very midst, and for his power and glory to work upon us and in our lives? Yet, when he does, why do we hide, tremble and fear? Are we still of the same mind of the timid and unresponsive people of Moses' day, who begged, "let not God speak to us, for fear we may die!" They did die! But *not* because of God! But because of their own stubbornness in wanting to keep God *away from them* in a 'safe and containable way.' *They wanted to keep God in a box!*

"When the people saw the thunder and lightning and heard the trumpet and saw the mountain in smoke, they trembled with fear. They stayed at a distance and said to Moses, "Speak to us yourself and we will listen. But do not have God speak to us or we will die." (Ex. 20:18,19)

These "Children of the Living God" had hardened their hearts against him and decided *not to let any of his unique and powerful wonders influence them.* They had been delivered from impoverished slavery in Egypt, with multiple God-given plagues, disasters and miracles made in their defense. They were also given a promise by the Living God, the Keeper of Promises. But they were scared of faith in him, wanted a human intercessor (Moses) to come between them; and then actually doubted that God cared for them *individually* at all!

They were given 40 years of wandering through the wilderness to "get their act together," see more miracles of God, and atone for their attitude. This was also precious time they could use to teach the upcoming generation to do better and to share the stories of their miraculous deliverance from Egypt. And as always, the Lord kept his part of the bargain. He gave their kids a land "flowing with milk and honey." Now, *today* as Children of the Living God, do we teach our children to be *fearful*, or *faithful*, when they see Unique and Powerful Works? What about ourselves? *Are we afraid of the power of God?* And, most unfortunately, do we *stay unbelieving* when we see or are involved in these prophesied Signs and Wonders?

Many people today feel that anything more than polite conversation and small talk can have serious consequences, especially in church. They feel conversing about the deeper things of God always leads to problems. Do you feel this way? Are you just timid, or do you feel so threatened by the possibility of God working in yielded humans today that you are angry, fearful or resentful of even the thought of it? At the very least, you can just agree to disagree. You have Free Will, and the gateway to God or to evil is the gateway of choice. But know this: when you are ready to *drop your pride and bend your knees* and know there is a bigger picture – the invisible workings of the Holy Spirit – God will use you, too, as a useful tool to bring others to faith. If you are truly a seeker of God's will, then it is only a matter of time!

"The Spirit searches all things, even the deep things of God...We have not received the spirit of the world but the Spirit who is from God, that we may understand what God has freely given us. This is what we speak, not in words taught us by human wisdom but in words taught by the Spirit, expressing spiritual truths in spiritual words. The man without the Spirit does not accept the things that come from the Spirit of God, for they are foolishness to him, and he cannot understand them, because they are spiritually discerned." (1 Co. 2:10-14)

"But God chose the foolish things of the world to shame the wise; God chose the weak things of the world to shame the strong. He chose the lowly things of this world and the despised things – and the things that are not – to nullify the things that are, so that no one may boast before him." (1 Co. 1:27-29)

Let's tell each other what is going on with us, what personal experiences we have had of God in our lives, and how it has affected us. Let's talk about "Divine Coincidences," the healing of our bodies and minds, the God of Love, and miracles. Let's talk about real things, Supernatural Gifts, Signs and Wonders, and not be afraid to go deep!

Concentrate Upon the Reality of God

"Blessed are the poor in spirit, for theirs is the kingdom of heaven." (Mt. 5:3)

209

This scripture is basically saying: *Truly happy people are those conscious of their spiritual need.* Happy, that is, because they know they have a God-Spot, that their religious customs are imperfect and that their instruction concerning God and man is incomplete. Blessed are those *who know* that they *don't know* everything, because that is the first step in being willing to learn. You are learning!

Your ways are not the same now as others. For you listen to Spirit. You have learned to yield your will to His Will, and be different, and unique for him. If your intention is for the right reasons, he will *sanctify* you for the work. This means "to set apart," "to make holy." He will walk with you, protect you, converse with you, and let you be there and be involved when he does Big Things. It is a great honor, and you should show thankfulness for it everyday and gladly do the work when presented with it!

Constantly strive toward the "Perfection-of-Connection!" Know that His Will includes Unlimited Miracles! Share your words and gifts with others! Show respect for all people! Pray your prayers, be a healing to those who are brought to you, and *listen* to God. *Feel* and *see* his Spirit move within you. Let him share himself through you with all those whose hearts are yearning for him. Know that you are part of the bigger picture, and recognize the angelic forces maneuvering around you for the best possible outcome of all involved. You are stronger now! You are never alone! Be receptive and available to be a yielded vessel for good, for God.

As we continue to follow him, giving of ourselves completely, we need to remember that to keep his current flowing through us, *we must use it.* Continuing with the symbol of lovers of God being the "light(bulb) of the world," we must give the Holy Spirit an outlet so that it can complete its "circuit" and come to "ground." If we don't do this, our channel of flow can become clogged and will run less and less current through, until finally it doesn't function at all. When presented with opportunities, do them without hesitation!

"Love Each Other"

In many ways this has been a self-help book, because its theme is that we ourselves can learn to construct a wider door to our Lord so that His Spirit can come in and re-model, re-shape, and re-make our lives and the lives of others. Now, due to this new "construction project" and "expansive add-on" (that we approve and sign off on by Free Will), we can find much more freedom and spaciousness in God's house than ever before. And, a lot of our neighbors are "coincidently" showing up at our front door, and it is our job and delight to graciously invite them in and introduce them to Our Master Builder. They just might want a "re-model" too!

...IN CONCLUSION...

Just as salt does not insist on its own flavor, but brings out the natural best in everything it touches, I encourage you to be the "salt of the earth." Reach out to people, share the joy in your heart, and have no fear; fear is the opposite of love. Practice using the gifts; You are worshipping the God of Love, who gives to us love unconditionally, so love him and others the same way. *Your gifts help you to do that even better.*

"Which of you, if his son asks for bread, will give him a stone? Or if he asks for a fish, will give him a snake? If you, then, though you are evil, know how to give good gifts to your children, how much more will your Father in heaven give good gifts to those who ask him!" (Mt. 7:9-11)

What an honor it has been to spread before you a buffet of additional ways to widen the depth of your spirituality! My prayer is for more people to have their feet on the ground (body on earth), head in the clouds (mind on heaven), and arms outstretched (love of mankind), giving and receiving the love of God! There is so much healing to be done, in so many ways. "Ask and it will be given you..." (Mt. 7:7)

"Love is patient, love is kind. It does not envy, it does not boast, it is not proud. It is not rude, it is not self-seeking, it is not easily angered, it keeps no record of wrongs. Love does not delight in evil but rejoices with the truth. It always protects, always trusts, always hopes, always perseveres. Love never fails...And now these three remain: faith, hope and love. But the greatest of these is love." (1 Co. 13:1-13)

"We love because he first loved us...this is the message you heard from the beginning. We should love one another." (1 Jn. 3:11,4:19)

So Be It!

CONNECTION GLOSSARY

THE GOD-SPOTS, DELIVERANCE AND EXORCISM

Remain neutral – don't over analyze what you initially feel. Just observe and accept the impressions that these different tools bring to you. Later, try to validate it – get feedback – you will learn better and faster this way – don't be afraid to make mistakes!

- **PRAYER God-Spot: The Grace of Direct Access.** *Know that everything that you ask, if it be according to God's Will (for the Highest Good) will be answered. All of these other God-Spot suggestions are just a tool to help us ask what we need to know and be sensitive to the answers.* **Prayer is one of the greatest gifts we have been given – without using this gift, we will not have access to any of the others!** *If we are in a state of "non-ego" before God, and are humbly submitting ourselves to him to accomplish His Will as his vessel, he will shower us with answers, ability, and added responsibility. Utilize your prayers for praise everyday; and do not push in your prayers for a very specific result with your gift – have faith that he knows the timing and best outcome for all those involved. We are just instruments in his symphony orchestra, hoping to stay in tune and interpret the musical arrangements placed in front of us to the best of our ability. He knows that we are imperfect and will make many mistakes; God forgives us much easier than we forgive ourselves. If we use our gifts for the intended betterment of His Kids (humankind) and His Creation (the earth), then he will keep training us with patience and new opportunities. We can have faith that even in our imperfection our efforts become a beautiful melody of love, floating gently upward to God, through the power of the Holy Spirit and the grace of our Redeemer Christ Jesus.*

- **TWILIGHT God-Spot: The Place Between Asleep & Awake.** *Do not wake up with an alarm clock, this has to be a natural awakening, as gently as possible. When you do realize you have awakened, Do Not Stretch. This would clear your mind too much by circulating blood and energy. If possible, and with as little movement as you can, turn on a near-by lamp that you have set there for that purpose, already focused on shining on your face. Recognize the feeling in your bladder, but do not get up to relieve yourself. You are creating the optimum environment for slight stress. You do not want to fall back to sleep, so an irritant that will not wake you up completely, but through which you can still relax, is the key. Use this TWILIGHT tool every morning to prepare your mind,*

213

body and spirit to be mentally conscious yet physically calm. Know that you are now actively ready to embrace the opportunities presented to you to share your gifts.

- **EARTH God-Spot: The Time of Past & Present.** *Center yourself, find that quiet place in your soul. With the intent of Love and Understanding, dig through the top layer of leaves and debris with your heel. Scoop up a handful of dirt. Does it feel hot, warm or cold? Play with the coarseness or smoothness, rolling it between your fingers. What colors do you see – what colors do you sense? Are they different? Bring the earth to your face and breathe in the aroma. Is it new earth or old? What do your five senses tell you? What about your other senses? Now, ask the questions you want to know. The soil helps as a connection. You may ask about any time period, and the dirt does not have to be the precise age you are asking about. What were the biggest energy experiences that happened here? Who were the people, what did they look like? What happened here in 1200 A.D., how about in 1950? Remember, the more specific you are, the clearer the answers. (Side-Note to Gardeners: Most soil is alive and has microorganisms in it. You will often feel the warm vibration of life in your hands. I have found a medium-high vibratory rate makes an excellent soil for germination and plant growth. Too fast a rate seems to indicate high acidity in the soil or contamination of some kind, including some kinds of chemical pollution). Remember to start all 'asking' with prayer. This is the Connection from which you are getting the information.*

- **WOOD God-Spot: Life Absorbed by Life.** *Trees connect heaven and earth – their crowns lift up to absorb life-giving sun; their embracing roots absorb the life-giving water from the earth below. With their heads in the clouds and their feet in the ground, they take the energy around them and pull it into themselves. They are a storehouse of life-force and information. Have you wondered why people often get so emotional when a tree in their yard must be removed, or why we often spend our vacations camping in the woods? Trees feel like old friends - they store the energy experiences they are exposed to, mix it with heaven and earth, and release it as a low vibrational hum of calm and quietness in our lives. Even wood that is dead contains this peacefulness. Hug a tree when you feel overwhelmed or feel you are out-of-balance in some way; it will help you ground yourself. Trees can only tell of what has happened in their own life-spans; do not ask for anything older than their estimated age. Look for any signs of fresh sap – the energy will be highest where it is fixing an injury. Reflect love back to the tree, placing both hands in front of you, shoulder length, on the trunk. Be ready to listen.*

214

- **ROCK God-Spot: Guardians of the Ages.** *Rocks can carry the most ancient and most interesting stuff you will ever read - if you can. I have found rocks to be extremely difficult to understand, and often confusing. They have spent thousands of years being washed by all forms of energy, possibly including creation itself. They are almost like pearls, layer upon layer of information thinly applied onto the whole. But, the good thing is that the most recent dustings of energy are on the first few layers, and they hold this very well. Especially in high energy situations, the energy clings itself onto rocks. Be sure to try the ROCK God-Spot at crime scenes. Also, there are many minerals and crystal arrangements that create different frequencies in the rocks, some of which can focus the energy, some of which can really scatter it out. It will take discernment. Learning rocks is like learning a million new colors and having to name them all! Meteorites are especially interesting. Be patient and keep trying. Bring home rocks that feel in some way feel familiar or resonate with your own energy. Place them in places of honor in your home and garden path. They will add stability and dimension. And, perhaps, hundreds or thousands of years from now, a sensitive will touch the rocks you chose for your life and get a wonderful reading of you, from them.*

- **METAL AND JEWERLY God-Spot: The Details of Emotion.** *Different metals provide different resistances to energy, and some scatter out the energy, like some rocks do. But, overall, metals are one of the easiest connections to understand. Gold conducts energy very well, and is the only metal I do not ask my clients to remove during a healing treatment, as it does not affect the flow of energy. When holding someone's car keys, a necklace or ring, and you go to validate the information, first ask in your mind if there has been more than one original owner. Metals hold information over a very long period of time, maybe forever. You might get many stories. What do you sense? Try to find the best part of your body to understand and access the information. Try holding it in your right hand, then your left. Place it up to your forehead, which is sometimes called the "third eye." Hold it against your solar plexus (your belly). What place seems to make information clearer to you? Metals hold a lot of emotions and many things in sharp detail. Be prepared for many things to show up in your mind's eye all at once. Heirlooms and antique jewelry hold many stories of love, life and loss. Experiment by going to garage sales. First form an opinion, bring the item with you and ask the history of it from the sellers. You will be surprised by how accurate you will be! This is all about your learning to listen. Metal also applies to cars, and car accidents. Place your hands on the dent and form conclusions; then ask the owner how it happened. With practice, perhaps you will be able to give police and family members missing information. Metal handrails are like phone lines of information, all talking at once. If you are very*

215

sensitive, try not holding onto one while you walk; it can be very distracting and is often like holding an electric cable of confusion in your hands - thousands of emotions.

- **CLOTH God-Spot: Delicate Impressions.** *If you are holding cloth, try to make sure it is unwashed. Washing the clothes will take the impressions down to minimal, and the high energy fades away quickly enough to begin with. Often, cloth will also give you an added benefit of "scent" for the senses to connect with, even if it is imperceptible to you. Hold it to the most receptive part of your body, the place that "sees" or "feels" it the most. An item of clothing is often one of the few links to a missing person. If you can get a piece of cloth that was there from the crime scene (or, unfortunately, off the body) you may be able to help solve the crime by "knowing" what happened. The details are often very vivid. Be open and brace yourself, knowing that you must tell the information just as you see it Anything you say could be a clue, or could lead in the wrong direction. Combine, as always, with prayer. You must allow any strong emotions to simply wash over you at this time. Wait until you are done with your responsibility and away with yourself and God. Then, allow yourself the sorrow and tears, but know that Our Father knows even when the tiny sparrow falls. He is the Source of All Comfort. Remember; you have a gift placed here by God to help his children (of all races, religion and ages). When people want to make you a hero for your contribution, say "thank you," but immediately let them know you are only a beacon pointing heaven-ward, and they should "Thank God!"*

- **DEJAVU' God-Spot: Remembering the Unknown.** *We are all connected in the web of life and creation. We are made from the dust of the ground, and our blood is close to the composition of seawater. We are also 70% water, as is the balance of the earth with the sea. We are made of the same elements that surround us. We all have the same Master Builder, and we share most of the same DNA strands. So why shouldn't we feel connected to the things around us, sometimes in a most unusual way? If you find yourself in a "familiar" situation, just pay attention to the information as it is received and make a note of it. There is a reason for everything, and it might become clearer later on. God himself made the space-time continuum. Do not be afraid of it or read too much into it; just accept what is going on. Let me say this again, make a note of it – or use a notebook- just be sure to write it down. If you are in a place where you can touch the items around you, perhaps you will find more information waiting there. Often, looking back on these experiences is where you will see the real meaning for their occurrences. Since this God-Spot comes at random, it is often a tool that God uses to reach us with information we need. As far as I know, it cannot be induced to occur, but we should make the most of it when it does happen.*

216

<u>DELIVERANCE - The Power of Jesus Name</u>

Sanctification, Purification & Exorcism.

This is now often ignored in the churches, or kept as a sacred secret, known to only a few. I have given much prayer over this, and have continually been given this same answer by the Lord: <u>all Christians must know how to fight against the devil.</u> Jesus taught his disciples about expelling demons right alongside teaching them about healing the sick and proclaiming the kingdom of God.

"Heal the sick…drive out demons. (Mat. 10:5-8)

The authority and power of the Holy Spirit helps you and others resist the attacks of evil and those spirits who chose to rebel against God (Satan -"rebeller," "slanderer"). We have the weapons of warfare listed in Eph. 6:10-18, and the authority to bind and loose because of the blood of Christ. It is rare that a person is actually possessed (thus requiring a solemn exorcism). More often it is just an evil attachment/affliction that is occurring (simple deliverance).

Please note that alcohol and drug abuse opens the doors to evil entities to come to us because our normal Free Will is altered at that time. It is rare that people actually <u>choose</u> to let themselves be controlled by another spirit rather than their own (i.e. devil worship).

Jesus spent much time expelling demons, and taught his disciples how to do the same. Although there are many variables to the following ceremony, I have found that total reliance on God and absolute faith in his power is the <u>main intention</u> behind the protocol.

It does not take an ordained minister or priest to see the will of God in these matters. *It simply takes a faithful and prayerful child of God in Connection with the Holy Spirit.*

(A).

Create a Sacred Space: Smudge with sage or burn incense. Anoint your hands and forehead with oil (frankincense and myrrh is suggested). If possible, also anoint the forehead of the afflicted soul. It is best that he is sitting in a chair. Try to have a place where you will not be disturbed by phones, noise, pets or unwanted people entering the area. It is important to have two or more ministering to the afflicted one; do not be tempted to do it by yourself ("…where two or three are gathered in my name").

Say: **"The power of the blood of Christ surround and protect every living person in this room."**

Say: **"Thank you Lord, that when "the righteous cry out, you hear them and deliver them from all their trouble."** (Ps. 34:17)

Say: **"Thank you Lord, that when the 72 disciples returned back to you they said with joy, "Lord, even the demons submit to us in your name."** (Lk. 10:17-24)

Say: **"We thank you Lord that you have given us "the keys of the kingdom of heaven, and that whatever we bind on earth will be bound in heaven, and whatever we loose on earth will be loosed in heaven."** (Mt. 19, 20)

(B).

<u>Listen to the reason for the affliction, discern what the truth is and also what is not being said.</u> **With laying on of hands** (usually on the head, from standing behind the chair) **say a prayer, out loud for all to hear.** Ask if the afflicted soul is ready to **repent** and turn around from his sin, with a renewed **commitment to follow Jesus Christ**, and **be washed** in the redeeming blood of his sacrifice. (If the afflicted one is truly possessed, there may be fits of anger at this point, thus the reason to stand behind the chair).

Say: **"We come in the Blessed name of Jesus Christ and by the authority of his shed blood, we come in the power of the Holy Spirit, and with the Unsurpassed Holy love of our Father God the Almighty, to grant** (person's name) **the freedom of <u>Free Will without constraint.</u>**

Say: **"Do you** (person's name) **choose to have back the control of your own Free Will from whomever and whatever place of sin it may be in bondage now?** (wait for answer)

Say, **"Do you** (person's name) **freely choose God's will as your own will, for his word and Holy Spirit to guide you through all occurrences in this life and beyond?** (wait for answer)

If the afflicted one has answered in the affirmative, probably a simple deliverance is all that is called for. Come in front of the person and have him stand up. Sprinkle with Holy Water. Have him sit back down again with hands in prayer position. Continue.

218

(C).

Say: **"In the name of Jesus Christ, and by the power of the Blood and the Holy Spirit, and the authority given the rank of our adoption as Children of God committed to Almighty God, we command you, spirit of...** (pride, unforgiveness, sexual perversion, drug addiction, greed, etc) **to leave** (person's name) **and, without manifesting yourself in any way, and without entering into or otherwise bringing harm to anyone or anything else in this room, property or building, we send you straight to the light of the Lord Jehovah** (Yahweh - the personal name of God as first used in the Old Testament) **to be dealt with as He Sees Fit."**

(If the afflicted one has not answered in the affirmative, <u>you must intercede for the person's Free Will and state</u>: **"We intercede for (person's name) in the name of Jesus Christ and by the power of the Holy Spirit and the love of God Jehovah, to grant freedom from oppression by binding and casting out the evil spirits tormenting and controlling** (person)." Then continue with recitation of paragraph (C) above.

Do not allow vomiting or cursing or throwing of objects – many things the possessed soul may be forced to do in rebelling and trying to create fear in your heart (fear is the opposite of love – creates lack of faith in God). Stand strong and be prepared to see God fight for you and the afflicted one! Nothing solidifies faith as fast as observing the Lord battle for one of his own lost sheep – the invisible war of the spirit realm where the Good Guy always wins; our God of the Mighty Sword, the originator of "tough love!"

(D).

End with prayer: say a personal prayer out loud to God, ask the attending helper with you to say one also. Or you may use a traditional prayer, such as the Catholic end of mass prayer: "St. Michael the Archangel, defend us in battle, be our protection against the wiles and wickedness of the devil. We humbly beseech thee, O God, to restrain him..."

Communion: pray over the wine and the bread, stating that they represent the blood and body of the Christ, offered up in our behalf. **Include the "Lord's Prayer."** Conclude with each person attending saying consecutively, **<u>"In Jesus name/deliver us from evil/and in communion with you/we start anew/in body, mind and spirit."</u>** The last person to repeat this is the *formerly afflicted one.* All of God's children together say **"Amen!"** Sing a song of praise, or the Halleluiah song. Rejoice that another sheep is brought back to the fold, out of the mouths of wolves, then welcome him with Unconditional and Never-Ending Love, just as your Father has welcomed and loved you!

219

QUICK ORDER FORM
Psychic Gifts in the Christian Life – Tools to Connect

For orders via mail, please send this form along with check or money order
written out to: _Rev. Tiffany Snow_

Tiffany Snow @ Spirit Journey Books
P.O. Box 61
San Marcos, CA 92079
1-800-535-5474

For expedited orders, please order via credit card through our websites at:
www.SpiritJourneyBooks.com
www.TiffanySnow.com

Name:_____

Address:_____

City:_____State:_____Zip:_____

Email or phone number:_____

Amount for Book is: $24.95

CA. Sales Tax: (7.75% If applicable)

Book	**$24.95**
(Quantity) x	( )
+_CA. Tax_	( )
+**Shipping**	( )
TOTAL=	_____

Shipping: Please add $3.00 for first book, and $1.00 each additional book.

Tax: Please add 7.75% for books shipped to California addresses.

For wholesale or library discounts, please call 1(800) 535-5474

I would like Free Information Regarding Workshops, Seminars and Book
Signings: (circle one)   YES   /   NO

I would like to receive Tiffany Snow's monthly email newsletter:
(circle one)   YES   /   NO   Email address:_____

221

Lightning Source UK Ltd.
Milton Keynes UK
29 December 2009

147979UK00002B/6/A